After Daley

THIS BOOK IS JOINTLY SPONSORED BY

 Center for Urban Affairs and Policy Research
Northwestern University

 Institute of Government and Public Affairs
University of Illinois

After Daley

Chicago Politics in Transition

Edited by

Samuel K. Gove *and* Louis H. Masotti

University of Illinois Press   *Urbana Chicago London*

©1982 by the Board of Trustees of the University of Illinois
Manufactured in the United States of America
C 5 4 3 2 1   P 5 4 3 2

"The Urban Bureaucracy and the Chicago Political Machine:
Who Gets What and the Limits to Political Control" by Ken-
neth R. Mladenka was previously published in *The American
Political Science Review,* 74 (Dec. 1980): 991-98.

LIBRARY OF CONGRESS CATALOGING IN PUBLICATION DATA

Main entry under title:

After Daley.

    Includes index.
    1. Chicago (Ill.)—Politics and government—
1951–   . 2. Daley, Richard J., 1902–1976.
3. Byrne, Jane, 1934–   . I. Gove, Samuel
Kimball, II. Masotti, Louis H.
F548.52.C45   320.8'09773'11   81-10302
ISBN 0-252-00902-9 (cloth)   AACR2
ISBN 0-252-00936-3 (paper)

Contents

Introduction   ix
LOUIS H. MASOTTI and SAMUEL K. GOVE

The Last of the Great Urban Machines and the Last
of the Great Urban Mayors? Chicago Politics, 1955–77   1
KATHLEEN A. KEMP and ROBERT L. LINEBERRY

Mayoral Voting and Ethnic Politics in the Daley-Bilandic-Byrne Era   27
JOSEPH ZIKMUND II

The Daley Legacy: A Declining Politics of Party, Race, and
Public Unions   57
WILLIAM J. GRIMSHAW

Black Politics in the Post-Daley Era   88
MICHAEL B. PRESTON

Latinos and Chicago Politics   118
JOANNE BELENCHIA

The Urban Bureaucracy and the Chicago Political Machine: Who Gets
What and the Limits to Political Control   146
KENNETH R. MLADENKA

Capital Budgeting and Planning in the Post-Daley Era   159
DONALD H. HAIDER

Suburban Politics and the Decline of the One-City Party   175
LAWRENCE N. HANSEN

State Impact: The Daley Legacy   203
SAMUEL K. GOVE

Jane Byrne and the New Chicago Politics   217
MILTON RAKOVE

Notes on Contributors   237

Index   239

Acknowledgments

The authors acknowledge the help of many people on this project. Primarily we want to thank Anna Merritt of the Institute of Government and Public Affairs and Audrey Chambers of the Center for Urban Affairs and Policy Research for their valuable editorial assistance and other contributions. Ms. Merritt also prepared the index. Georgette Carlson of the Center and Jean Baker of the Institute provided important coordination for the project. The secretarial staffs of both the Institute and the Center did yeoman work on the typing of the manuscript.

Samuel K. Gove
Louis H. Masotti

LOUIS H. MASOTTI and SAMUEL K. GOVE

Introduction

> The Machine preceded [Richard J.] Daley,
> and, while it has prospered under Daley,
> it will certainly survive Daley.
>
> Milton Rakove

This book was conceived as an effort to evaluate the impact of Mayor Richard J. Daley's death, on December 20, 1976, on Chicago politics and on the viability of the political machine that has dominated it since 1931. Shortly after the brief struggle for control of the mayor's office, from which Daley protégé Michael Bilandic emerged the nominal victor in 1977, a small group of Chicago area political scientists began meeting to discuss ways in which the transition of Chicago politics from the "Daley era" (1955–76) could be monitored and evaluated. Although no consensus was reached, it was agreed that some members of the group and selected others would write perspective essays to be published jointly as the "Chicago Politics Papers" by the Center for Urban Affairs and Policy Research at Northwestern University and the Institute of Government and Public Affairs at the University of Illinois. Nine of the essays were published between 1978 and 1980 and, along with the article on the budget by Donald Haider, they comprise the chapters of this volume.

As indicated by the title of this book, the intent is to gain insight into the emergence of Chicago's new political era by examining the later years of the Daley regime, the Bilandic interregnum, and the dramatic, volatile initial period of the Jane Byrne administration.

In Chicago, perhaps more than in any other city in the nation, local politics has long been the dominant pastime—some arguing that it fills the gap created by the sorry performances of Chicago's professional sport franchises. For whatever reason, the personalities of the political players and the latent and blatant political strategies and tactics they employ are taken seriously in the Second City. At least since the days of "Big Bill" Thompson, journalists, both local and national, have capitalized on the significant events, the bizarre activities, and the colorful personalities that have characterized Chicago politics for more than half a century.

Republican William Thompson, the last of his party's mayors (1915-23, 1927-31) and a national figure because of his outspoken anti-British, "America First" campaign and his dramatic oratory, was succeeded in 1931 by Democrat Anton Cermak. Cermak's tenure was short-lived, but he became famous in 1933 as the mistaken victim of an assassin's bullet intended for newly elected President Franklin D. Roosevelt. The Democratic machine emerged and became established between 1933 and 1947 during the regime of Mayor Ed Kelly, who succeeded Cermak, and party boss Pat Nash.

By the time World War II ended, Chicago, under Kelly's administration, had become grossly mismanaged, and corruption was manifest. The Democratic machine was also beset with internecine warfare, which resulted in the slating of a "reform" candidate in 1947. Businessman Martin Kennelly served two terms as an interim mayor while two major machine factions sorted things out. Richard J. Daley emerged from the intraparty strife as both Cook County party chairman in 1953 and as mayor in 1955. Having combined the two most powerful offices in the city, Daley spent the next twenty-two years presiding over the strongest urban political organization in America. The Daley machine not only dominated Chicago and Cook County government, but it also had considerable influence in Springfield and a major voice in presidential politics.

Because the machine can only thrive when there is relative stability, factions are accommodated for the sake of the party organization. Thus it was the party leaders who chose Alderman Michael Bilandic to become mayor following Daley's death in 1976. Bilandic, an "honorary Irishman," was the fourth consecutive mayor from the Bridgeport area of the Eleventh Ward. When he received 78 percent of the vote in the special 1977 election, there was every indication that the city's politics would stabilize with Bilandic as mayor, Cook County Board President George Dunne as party chairman, and Thirty-fourth Ward Alderman Wilson Frost, a black, as chairman of the powerful city council Finance Committee.

And it did—for two years. But what a 1933 assassin's bullet, blatant corruption in the 1940s, or party conflict in the 1950s could not do, Jane Byrne did in 1979. The machine was defeated in the February 1979 primary by the persistent campaign of feisty Jane Byrne, aided and abetted by a record snowfall, the insensitivity and arrogance of city hall politicians, and an aroused, angry public. The voters were "mad as hell and wouldn't take it any more."

There has been considerable speculation about the implications of the

Byrne victory, the viability of the Democratic party organization, the dynamics of the political process, and, indeed, the future of Byrne herself. Byrne's stunning primary victory over the machine and the remarkable size of her general election vote suggested several political options for the newly elected mayor.

Since Byrne had been elected with popular support but without a political organization of any kind, she could attempt to govern as a reformer and a populist by using the considerable power of the mayor's office to pursue policies good for the city and good for the groups of voters who had been excluded by the organization for so long. A second option was to build her own political organization around independents, dissident regulars, and ethnic groups—especially the blacks—who had coalesced to nominate and elect her. A third possibility was for the victorious Jane Byrne to be magnanimous and seek a rapprochement with the Democratic machine leadership.

Early indications suggested that Byrne would follow the path of reform-populism. In one of her first moves, she appointed a Transition Committee headed by a university political science professor and studded with leading independents (former aldermen William Singer, Richard Simpson, and Leon M. Despres), neighborhood and ethnic leaders, and corporate and labor representatives. A few names familiar to the machine were to be found on the Transition Committee (e.g., Ray Simon, former corporation counsel under Daley), but the names of the powerful machine aldermen, committeemen, and officeholders were conspicuous by their absence.

At the same time, however, she moved unambiguously toward the organization. While a few machine names, notably state Senator Richard M. Daley, son of the late mayor, approached the mayor-designate following the primary, most were cautious and waited for Byrne to make the first move. This she did. She made it clear that she was a product of the Democratic party, had been a member of Mayor Daley's cabinet (as commissioner of Consumer Sales, a relatively minor post), and had run specifically against Bilandic and a "cabal of evil men" in the city council who, she felt, were bent on undoing the party and the policies of her mentor, Daley.

By these two actions in the first weeks after her impressive primary election, Byrne demonstrated her capacity to confuse and confound. Those who had worked so hard to defeat Bilandic, and with him the machine they thought he represented, began to feel betrayed when it became clear that she intended to make peace with the party regulars whom she had just defeated.

As this is being written, the Byrne administration has been in office less than two years. During that time, the mayor has taken a number of

initiatives that have won the applause of the community. Notable among
them has been the effort to correct the budget abuses she inherited from
Bilandic and to reestablish the city's financial stability. Moreover, she
has shown occasional evidence of compromise or accommodation, notably in the case of the ChicagoFest and the North Loop redevelopment
project, both of which Mayor Byrne has "adopted," although candidate
Byrne had opposed them vociferously.

But understanding the modus operandi of the Byrne administration is
not simple. From the moment it became apparent that Byrne would be
Chicago's next mayor, it was clear that her personality and her political
style would be a critical factor in her administration. Byrne had run a
tough, angry campaign, and it was soon evident that this approach to
politics would carry over to the mayor's office. In her first months in office, the mayor proceeded to reorganize large segments of the city's
unwieldy bureaucracy, to fire summarily some of the most professional
administrators who had been recruited by Daley to run the complex administrative machinery, and to replace them with persons of dubious
competence and limited experience. The new appointees, only some of
whom had machine sponsorship, appeared to share one common characteristic—unquestioned loyalty to *her*. Many came, and almost as many
left quickly, having failed the loyalty test or in some other way having in-
curred Byrne's wrath. This led the press to dub her administration a
"revolving door" and to question her ability to govern effectively.

Early in her administration Byrne also caused a good deal of furor at
both local and national levels when she first apparently endorsed President Jimmy Carter for reelection and within ten days literally forced the
Democratic central committee to announce its support of the candidacy
of Edward M. Kennedy for the Democratic presidential nomination.
Comparisons with Daley's more astute approach to presidential nominating politics were inevitable, as the Carter fiasco not only cost the city
favorable federal grant consideration but raised anew serious questions
about the new mayor's capacity to govern effectively.

Shortly thereafter Richard M. Daley announced his candidacy for
Cook County state's attorney, a politically sensitive position then held
by Republican Bernard Carey. Thereupon Byrne drafted powerful
Fourteenth Ward Alderman Edward Burke to run in the primary with
the support of the central committee. The mayor, fearful that Daley was
positioning himself to mount a 1983 challenge to her reelection, openly
campaigned for Burke. Burke, and in effect the party organization, was
handily defeated by Daley in the March primary. Byrne grudgingly endorsed Daley, "as part of the Democratic ticket," and then dramatically
withdrew that support a short time before the general election. In an unprecedented maneuver she urged Democratic campaign workers to en-

courage Democratic voters to split their tickets and vote for Republican Carey! The maneuver failed, Daley was elected state's attorney, and Byrne's political stock suffered another severe blow.

It is expected that either Daley or someone handpicked by him will run for mayor in 1983. Byrne has already announced her intention to stand for reelection. And a number of blacks and independents are sending out feelers, although there are no obvious and compelling candidates within either group.

At this point, about halfway through Byrne's term, there are few political analysts who will give odds on the outcome of a Byrne-Daley confrontation in 1983. Byrne appears to have considerable popular support but no clearly identifiable constituency, and she does have the power of incumbency. Daley has been elected to a powerful political office despite Byrne's objections, he has a political name to conjure with, and a grass-roots campaign force not unlike that which elected his father to five terms as mayor.

During the fifty years since the Democrats captured city hall from Bill Thompson and the Republicans, the machine model that has dominated Chicago politics has undergone significant change, reflecting the shifting events, forces, and personalities of the period. Numerous studies, popular as well as academic, long and short, have dealt with this machine.[1] The exchange model of politics described so well by Harold Gosnell (rev. ed., 1968) in the 1930s continues to serve as the archetype of the machine—political support in exchange for services, jobs (patronage), and "facilitation." Later descriptions of Chicago's political process—such as those by Edward Banfield in 1961 or Milton Rakove in 1975—may have been more sophisticated, but they were fundamentally the same. Ted Lowi's introduction to the 1968 edition of Gosnell's work suggested a "new machine politics" based on the growing professionalism of Chicago's bureaucracy. Thomas Guterbock's more recent *Machine Politics in Transition* (1980) argues that the exchange function on which traditional machine politics was based has yielded to party loyalty and attachment, conditioned by public interest policies, attractive candidates, and a viable political process.

The essays in this book contribute to this rich body of literature on Chicago politics. While they have no common theme, they all reflect on the status of Chicago politics after the twenty-two-year Daley era. The authors come to their assignment with quite different approaches and methodologies. And some would doubtless disagree with one another. The extremes in approaches may be illustrated by the papers of Kenneth Mladenka and Rakove. Whereas the former uses a sophisticated quantitative approach, the latter comes to his conclusions as a participant-observer.

The chapters that follow can be grouped into three categories: electoral issues, the city's infrastructure, and external pressures and opportunities.

The first grouping comprises the bulk of the book. At the outset, several authors comment on the Chicago political machine and its ability to control and deliver the vote. Kathleen Kemp and Robert Lineberry talk about the need for the machine to get out those who are likely to vote for Democrats. The authors then classify certain wards into categories of controlled, deliverable, independents, and renegades. "The challenge the machine must face up to if it is to survive is how it can maintain its largely white ethnic base of support in controlled and deliverable wards at a time when whites are decreasing as a proportion of the electorate." As Michael Preston points out, there is the additional problem in the black community that "black voters are no longer the loyal, predictable, controllable, deliverable voters they once were; since 1975 they have become increasingly more unloyal, undeliverable." Moreover, the black wards have low voter turnouts. Preston suggests that "the reliance on low but controlled turnout means that black aldermen may win the election battle in their wards but lose the war at the city level. That is, the small turnout means that they have little power in the organization, and that they get the most menial patronage jobs the machine has to offer." Another segment of the voting population that has to be considered in the future is the Latinos. As Joanne Belenchia notes, they have not been terribly important to date as factors in elections. Besides, most Latinos live in wards where the machine controls the vote "very well." Finally, William Grimshaw describes the classic political machine, the Chicago version of which Daley headed. Such a machine depends on the inner city voters for "an exceptionally high and consistent degree of support for all of the machine's candidates for office. A second monopoly is also vital: control over the party's primary elections, and in this instance throughout the city. A classic political machine also depends on, and typically produces, a huge vote for all of its candidates." Whether the Chicago machine was failing in these regards is addressed by most of the authors in this section.

Although blacks tend to have low voter participation, another theme running through these papers is that they play a crucial role in the classic machine. Kemp and Lineberry tell us that "in the 1950s blacks accommodated to Chicago politics; in the 1970s Chicago politics has had to accommodate blacks. . . . Whatever electoral coalition the Daley organization built up over the years, blacks were the unreliable element in it. The result is a visible reversal of the relationship between deliverability and percent black, from strong positive correlations in the first half of the Daley era to strong negative correlations in the last half."

Preston raises a further issue when he states that "low voting turnout in both middle-class and non–middle-class wards is not only a result of economic poverty and the antipathy of middle class voters toward the machine, it also results from the lack of another important political resource—black leadership.''

Grimshaw suggests that blacks can be important in citywide elections and uses the Byrne primary victory as his example. Blacks formed one-third of Byrne's fifteen-ward primary support base, "and none of these five black wards had been among the party's top producers since 1963.''

There are obviously other ethnic groups in addition to blacks and Latinos that are important in understanding Chicago politics. The Poles are probably the most "politically noteworthy," as Joseph Zikmund indicates. But the Poles have had difficulty in trying to play a continuing and significant role in Chicago politics. In fact, "Polish frustration with the system may have been the highest in the city.'' The nearest that the Poles came to success was in 1963 when maverick Benjamin Adamowski garnered 44.45 percent of the vote against Daley. Alderman Roman Pucinski ran in the 1977 primary, but he carried no wards and his success was more regional than ethnic.

A discussion of electoral issues would not be complete without some reference to the role of the organized city employee, a point given considerable attention by Grimshaw. This will undoubtedly be a bigger factor in future elections with both the police and firemen now organized. The handshake relations between Daley and organized labor that Grimshaw sees breaking down is probably a thing of the past. Collective bargaining with or without state enabling legislation is the name of the game in the future.

What of the future of the Chicago machine? As our contributors suggest, the machine is not through. Preston claims that "a fragmented machine is still more powerful than an unorganized group of individuals," and Grimshaw, using a somewhat different metaphor, indicates that "while the party is unquestionably weaker and badly troubled now, under the circumstances it, like the fabled one-eyed man in the land of the blind, remains a force with which to reckon.''

Two of the chapters, those by Mladenka and Haider, deal with aspects of the city's infrastructure. Mladenka, harking back to the electoral issues discussed earlier, suggests that neither voting patterns nor race has had an effect upon the provision of city services, a notion with which others may well disagree. He concludes that "distributional outcomes are largely a function of past decisions, population shifts, technological changes, and reliance upon technical-rational criteria and professional values.'' Haider then takes a look at the total capital structure of the city. He develops a plan for dealing with the financial problems now facing it and that have already had such devastating effects upon other older, large cities. But he stresses the point that Chicago's financial problems are not on the scale of cities like New York or Cleveland.

The next group of chapters goes beyond the confines of Chicago and explores the impact of political development in the city on the broader community. Lawrence Hansen and Samuel Gove look at the suburbs and the Springfield-downstate situation. Hansen explores the expanding role of the suburban voter in Illinois politics at the expense of Chicago voters and describes this emerging new participant in the electoral process. In a concluding statement he suggests that those who "discard the assumptions and stereotypes of the past will prosper politically in the suburbs; those who do not will wither."

Gove offers insights into the special relationship that existed between Daley and successive regimes in Springfield, including all three branches of state government—the executive, the legislative, and the judicial. He also describes the statewide political scene and speculates about the effect on that scene of the present Chicago city government. He concludes it is too early to predict if past relations have fallen by the wayside.

In the final and concluding chapter Rakove looks to the new Chicago politics. He weaves into the fabric of his chapter many of the threads found in the earlier contributions—needs of the machine, the provision of services, the role of ethnics and blacks. He offers a view of the inner-most workings of the Daley machine in its heyday, suggests that it remained essentially unchanged under Bilandic, and then speculates about the long-range effects of the many fundamental changes made in the machine's operation by Byrne.

It is clear that Chicago politics has entered a new phase in the aftermath of Daley's death in 1976 and the advent of Byrne's administration. While it may be too early to assign a label to the new Chicago politics, factional conflict, accommodation, and realignment within the Democratic party organization appear to be the defining characteristics. How the conflicts are resolved, who gets accommodated, and what shape realignment takes may be the critical political questions of the 1980s. The answers may well determine whether machine politics will continue to dominate Chicago government or whether Chicago will move closer to the decentralized, pluralistic politics of other major American cities. The essays that comprise this volume are intended to assist the reader in understanding the transition from what has been Chicago politics to what it may become.

A final cautionary note: The essays contained in this volume were written in late 1979 and early 1980. While they were updated to some extent to take the November 1980 elections into account, they could not hope to remain current with the rapidly changing Chicago scene while the book was in press.

NOTE

1. The most popular book on Chicago politics, measured by sales, has been Royko's *Boss* (1971). However, it is a journalistic polemic laced with cynical half-truths about Daley and his political environment. O'Connor's *Clout* (1975) and Kennedy's *Himself* (1978) are interesting and occasionally insightful portraits of Daley but do not contribute much to an understanding of the political system.

REFERENCES

Banfield, Edward C. 1961. *Political Influence.* New York: Free Press.
Gosnell, Harold. 1968. *Machine Politics: Chicago Model.* Chicago: University of Chicago Press. Rev. ed.
Guterbock, Thomas M. 1980. *Machine Politics in Transition: Party and Community in Chicago.* Chicago: University of Chicago Press.
Kennedy, Eugene E. 1978. *Himself.* New York: Viking.
O'Connor, Len. 1975. *Clout.* New York: Avon.
Rakove, Milton. 1975. *Don't Make No Waves, Don't Back No Losers.* Bloomington: Indiana University Press.
Royko, Mike. 1971. *Boss.* New York: Signet.

KATHLEEN A. KEMP and ROBERT L. LINEBERRY

The Last of the Great Urban Machines and the Last of the Great Urban Mayors? Chicago Politics, 1955-77

TO CARL SANDBURG, IT HAD BIG SHOULDERS and was hog butcher to the world. But to political scientists, Chicago has had the most successful machine in any modern American city and has nurtured the most powerful mayor in recent urban history. Chicago is ethnicity, diversity, pluralism, industrialism, and proletarianism. Its 277 square miles are peopled by a declining population of something less than 3,000,000 citizens, most of whom are black or ethnic Americans. On the whole, the city has had a bad press. Its only citizen better known abroad than Richard J. Daley is probably Al Capone; Rudyard Kipling claimed that "having seen it, I urgently desire never to see it again." Sandburg's basically protective poem called it "wicked . . . crooked . . . brutal . . . [and] cunning"; and on the liberal imagination are indelibly stamped the ugly events of the 1968 Democratic convention.

Chicago's political system has an equally bad press. Known mostly as the big city with the big machine, it collects all the epithets and stereotypes of machine politics. In Chicago they still hold torchlight parades, they still color the Chicago River green on St. Patrick's Day, and the ward committeeman is still a good source of a job, a zoning variance, a sewer connection, or a tavern license. Locals used to call it "the city that works" and exhibited scarcely disguised satisfaction at New York's financial tumult. But if it "works," it works because, some suspect, the city runs on grease. The *Chicago Sun-Times* even operated a bar called the "Mirage" to catch the city in the act of being itself. If they talk of power elsewhere, in Chicago they speak of "clout."

Chicago was under the hegemony of Richard J. Daley from 1955 until his death in December 1976. Something of his public image can be gleaned by noting that the three major biographies of him are entitled *Boss, Clout,* and *Himself.*[1] It does not stretch a point to say that Daley *was* Chicago in a way that no other urban politician has ever symbolized his city. In fact, his name was so synonymous with Chicago that school children called his successor "Mayordaley Bilandic." Daley's leadership was hierarchical, but it was rooted in pluralist principles of bargaining and live-and-let-live. Even the machine one associates so closely with his name existed some time before Daley, but it was he who turned it into the powerful instrument known the world over. His successor, Michael A. Bilandic, is a testimonial to the power of that machine over a single man. An obscure, uncharismatic, Croatian newcomer to politics (he had been in politics only six years before his election to mayor), Bilandic inherited a Democratic organization that many proclaimed to be the last of the great urban machines.

An urban political organization is ultimately at the mercy of urban demography. In Chicago the machine has relied primarily upon a coalition of white ethnic voters, with increasingly lukewarm support from blacks. Yet the city's black population has rapidly increased. The 1980 census should show the city with a black-Latino near-majority. Maintaining white dominant–black subordinate power relations in a black dominant–white subordinate numerical reality is a signal challenge to any big-city political organization, Chicago's included. Historian John Allswang (1977: 153) remarks that "with a black population . . . the problem of the local Democratic organization [is] to avoid losing the political loyalties of this group. . . . And as the late 1960's witnessed increased tension between the major constituents of the Democratic coalition—the blacks and the immigrants and their children—while independent black leaders rose to contest the machine, it was not easy."

We suggest that machines have historically specialized in "divisible" or "non–zero sum" policy outputs, but that new racial dimensions of urban politics threaten to transform urban decision-making into "indivisible" or "zero sum" policy issues. Maintaining white ethnic support—holding down white exodus from the city—while simultaneously nurturing the city's fastest-growing constituency are the prime items for the agenda of the Chicago machine. We discuss here how a machine strives to maximize deliverability and control and minimize independence, and how well the Chicago machine succeeded at this task during the Daley years. We focus mostly on the Daley-Bilandic years, the heyday of the machine in Chicago. While we close with some notes on the Byrne era, a fuller analysis of that complex period requires more space than we have here—although scenarios about the future of the organization abound. What we hope to contribute to this debate is not answers but evidence, not definitive conclusions but decisive trends. The path of change depends not on the predictions of political scientists and journalists, however, but upon the character of political leadership and electoral choice.

CHICAGO POLITICS: AN OVERVIEW

All American cities have been profoundly shaped by the great demographic shifts and migrations of the last two centuries. Five of these migrations gave context and shape to the contemporary Chicago political system. We can most easily summarize that system by a brief inventory of these migrations and their implications for Chicago politics. Specifically, we refer to the urbanization of the population, ethnic immigration, both old and new, the movement of black Americans toward urban areas, the metropolitan population's migration to the suburbs, and the rise of the Sunbelt and corresponding decline of the Frostbelt.[2]

The urbanization of Chicago was rapid. It took New York City 236 years to reach one million people. Chicago telescoped that process into a brief sixty years, growing from fifty settlers in 1830 to 1,098,570 in 1890. It added its second million even more quickly, in nineteen years. The third million came in fourteen years, so that the estimated population of Chicago in 1923 was 3,010,850.[3] The population peaked in 1951 at 3,618,500 and has been eroding since. Chicago's growth has always been intimately linked to transportation technology, first as a portage point from Lake Michigan to the Mississippi and later as a railroad hub hauling cattle into Union Stockyards and industrial output everywhere. Franchise boodling had been a preoccupation of even the earliest Chicago businessmen-politicians. Swelling populations and burgeoning service demands were necessary ingredients for the emergence of a political machine, but they themselves were not sufficient conditions. Some would argue that the presence of a large and rapidly growing ethnic community was another condition for the birth of a political machine.

The immigrants came in waves, with the Irish and the Polish arriving relatively late.[4] These waves were cut to a trickle when a restrictive immigration law was passed in 1924, whose quotas were not to be repealed for half a century. It is probably no accident that after that date Chicago's population growth leveled off almost immediately. Counting ethnic groups is more difficult than might be imagined, largely because the U.S. Census Bureau does not count ethnic groups separately after the second generation. Yet ethnic patterns are persistent and powerful in Chicago politics. An ingenious study (Lorinskas et al., 1969) of a purely mythical election shows ethnic voters dutifully picking candidates for office on the basis of ethnic name even over the strength of party affiliation. There is some reason to believe that an ethnic resurgence is taking place today, as thousands of "weekend ethnics" who live in the suburbs slip back into the city to partake of "native" ways (at least of "native" food and drink).

Certainly among the older ethnic groups, the Irish have wielded a power beyond their numbers. One might not wish to go as far as Terry Clark (1975) in his assertions about Irish political dominance, but Chicago remains one of the finest flowers of the Irish ethic in politics. One in four male Irish Chicagoans reported to the 1970 census taker that he worked for the government; 22 percent of the Chicago city council since 1955 have been Irish; and Michael A. Bilandic broke a forty-five-year occupancy of the mayor's office by Irishmen, before returning it again to Jane Byrne. It will be a good many years, at the present rate, before the newest immigrants—the 10 percent of Chicago's population of Latin heritage—equal the weight of the Irish.

A third great immigration is seen in the growth of the black urban population. Black Chicago is the fastest-growing segment of the population. When St. Clair Drake and Horace Cayton wrote *Black Metropolis* in 1944, they described black Chicago as "the second largest Negro city in the world." Yet the city's population at that time was just over 9 percent black. A reasonable extrapolation of recent trends would predict a 40 to 45 percent figure in the 1980 census.[5] The rapid in-migration of blacks and the higher fertility rates of this group and the corresponding out-migration of whites may soon literalize the title of Drake and Cayton's volume. Blacks in Chicago are relatively recent entrants into the Democratic fold. The realigning elections of the 1920s, coupled with the big-city politics of the New Deal, switched the loyalties of black voters to the Democratic party in Chicago (Allswang, 1971). There they have remained, although with some waxing and waning in their support of the party's policies and politicians.

As is true of several major northeastern metropolitan areas, both suburbanization and the shift of population to the Sunbelt have aggravated local economic and political bases. These fourth and fifth emigrations set central city against suburb and North against South. Much has been made of the so-called Sunbelt-Frostbelt confrontation. Chicago and other northern urban areas supposedly suffer at the hands of the presumably more affluent and growth-hungry Sunbelt cities. There is now ample evidence that the Sunbelt-Frostbelt dichotomy is more myth than reality. Indeed, Frostbelt cities turn out to be better off on almost every dimension of well-being than Sunbelt cities (Dye and Ammons, 1978). Housing, crime, poverty, and other social problems are less serious in Frostbelt than Sunbelt cities. Nonetheless, the supposed gap between North and South may continue to shape location decisions by families and firms. It will also probably shape the coalition-building strategies of both northern and southern politicians.

Some of Chicago's suburbs are the very prototype of affluent dormitory suburbs, and this affluence gap between city and suburb increases with every passing census. Richard Nathan and Charles Adams (1976) of

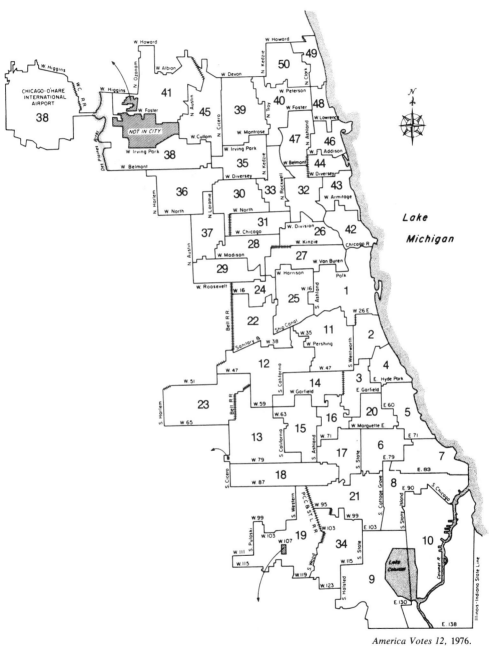

America Votes 12, 1976.

Map 1. Ward Map of the City of Chicago.

the Brookings Institution indexed "central city hardship" relative to each city's suburbs: only four other cities rated lower than Chicago among fifty-five SMSAs (standard metropolitan statistical areas). Chicago, however, is not Newark, and its economic and fiscal soundness is hardly matched among the great cities. But its whites, too, are clearly on the move both to the suburbs and the Sunbelt.

Chicago's political system and the impact of demography and geography upon it can best be explored in its fifty wards, which are depicted in Map 1. Each of those wards elects an alderman, giving Chicago the largest city council among major American cities. We have compiled for each ward the voting patterns in every election (national, state, and local) from 1955 through 1977 and, using the ward-by-ward census tabulation of the Chicago Planning and Redevelopment Department, matched ward demographic data with electoral outcomes. This correlation enables us to focus both on variations among the wards and on comparisons of ward behavior over time.

THE DALEY MACHINE AND ITS ELECTORAL COALITION

A machine can be distinguished from ordinary political organizations by its high degree of electoral control. As is true of other powerful organizations, it reduces uncertainty and maximizes predictability vis-à-vis its environment.

Predictability is manipulated through the skillful use of incentives. Banfield and Wilson (1963: 115) define a machine as a "party organization that depends crucially upon inducements that are both specific and material." Machines use selective and tangible incentives — jobs, gain, even payoffs — rather than ideologies or programs to attract voters. A machine, to put it bluntly, trades favors for votes.

But machines are more than decentralized, secular welfare agencies. Robert Merton and others have observed that a machine serves many functions. One of the most important is that of broker, handling diverse and often conflicting demands arising from a pluralist and spatially fragmented population. These demands cannot always be met by the distribution of patronage and other material benefits. To maintain hegemony, the machine must make decisions that will appease the groups comprising its electoral support while accommodating and/or neutralizing other groups. The challenge for a machine is to produce the benefits demanded by the diverse groups comprising its coalition. Machine control is achieved through the distribution of material benefits to poor ethnic and minority wards. Ethnic, working-class wards are mobilized by ticket-balancing, which reinforces ethnic identification with the machine, and by policies that maintain the cultural dominance of ethnic groups over their neighborhoods. But groups also place demands for benefits, such as school busing or control over police, that cannot easily be given as favors to every group. These demands place the greatest stress on the machine and are particularly costly when demographic changes alter the relative strength of groups.

Our major thesis is that the dominating concern of the Chicago machine has been to maintain its white and largely ethnic power base, while accommodating the city's growing black middle class, which has numerous intertwined and often symbolic demands. White ethnic wards have always comprised the machine's major base of support. For this reason the machine must be constantly on the lookout for an ethnic renegade, who could mobilize a significant proportion of the machine's coalition in opposition to it. In contrast, black support, also a significant component of the machine coalition, has been controlled until now. Recently, however, there have been changes in the black population. Not only is it increasing in size — while the white population is decreasing — it is also making increasing demands for benefits that conflict with those from the white ethnic population.

That Daley was able to balance all of these forces in an electorate of about one million voters — and one as pluralistic and demographically unstable as Chicago's — testifies to his political skill. His machine's success was based on two strategies: (1) maintaining its black and white ethnic coalition and (2) nurturing an image of invincibility in order to fend off any serious Republican or independent challengers. Although most of this chapter focuses on the first strategy — coalition building — the second strategy of gatekeeping deserves far more attention than it has received in writings on political machines.

In fact, we suspect that the image of control and invincibility may be as significant as real electoral control in explaining the machine's success. The first step in electoral control is to direct who gets on the ballot.[6] Chicago, like most northern big cities, is Democratic. It has turned out Democratic majorities in all presidential elections since 1928 — a feat not unique to Chicago. Because of the Democratic identification of blacks and white ethnics, Republican opposition, which is usually weak in any case, does not pose a threat to the machine. The danger lies rather in the possibility that a renegade, someone with a significant following from within the organization, will challenge the machine's candidate in a Democratic primary — the Jane Byrne scenario. As in many parts of the South, the primary in Chicago is far more important in terms of who will govern than the general election. Thus it is crucial for the machine to discourage primary opposition.

In only three of the seven mayoral elections held in the 1955-77 period was the machine unsuccessful in preventing opposition, and in only two was the challenger a renegade. In the three opposed elections (1955, 1975, and 1977), the machine was unable to maintain the image of invincibility. The 1955 primary, of course, was Daley's first mayoral election. He faced three opponents, including the incumbent, Martin Kennelly, who had been dumped by the machine, and a popular Pole and regular Democrat, Benjamin Adamowski. Daley won with only 49 percent of the vote. The machine was successful in gatekeeping until 1975, when Daley's health and the conviction of a number of Daley's men on corruption charges weakened the machine's image of invincibility. Daley faced three challengers — a black, an independent reformer, and a former machine-backed district attorney who had been dumped by the machine. Daley won with 58 percent of the vote, a strong showing in a race with four contenders. However, Daley's death made the machine appear vulnerable, and its gatekeeping function was unsuccessful.

In the special primary held in 1977, five opposition candidates ran against the machine's candidate, Michael Bilandic. The opposition included two blacks as well as a former machine congressman and then alderman of the heavily Polish Forty-first Ward, Roman Pucinski. In spite of these opposition candidates representing the two components of the machine's coalition, blacks and white ethnics, Bilandic won. But the victory was razor thin, based on only 51 percent of the Democratic vote.

These three elections tell us only part of the story; let us take a closer look at the Chicago ward map.

DELIVERABILITY, CONTROL AND A TYPOLOGY OF CHICAGO WARDS

There are two major dimensions of electoral choice: the decision to participate (turnout) and the candidate or party preference (direction of the vote). However distinctive those may be to a political scientist, from the point of view of a political organization they are not easily separated. Politicians try to ignore people who turn out but vote wrong. Banfield and Wilson (1963: 118) make the general observation that "the job of a precinct captain is to get out the vote for his party's slate and *to keep at home the vote for the other party's.*" Rakove makes the same point about Chicago in particular. Describing the precinct captain's efforts with a new voter (1975: 124), he observes that "if [the voter] is probably a Democrat, or might be encouraged to become one, he has to be registered. If he sounds like a Republican, *he had best be ignored.*" These observations suggest that machines are uninterested in high turnout, unless the direction can be guaranteed.

What the machine seeks, therefore, is deliverability, a term suggested by the old political cliche about "delivery" and "newspaper" wards.

We define deliverability as turnout plus voting right. Specifically, the delivery score of a ward (or any other unit) is the *proportion of the adult population voting for the machine's candidate or slate.*[7] Wards that score especially high on this measure we call the "deliverables." They can be counted on, year after year, to produce high turnouts that overwhelmingly favor machine slates. We argue that if the vote can be controlled, i.e., predicted, a machine will prefer a high level of deliverability, ceteris paribus. If it cannot, however, the machine prefers controllability.

Deliverability is not always easy to assure. A large electorate can be an unpredictable one. So machines turn to controllability. We define controllability as a relatively low turnout coupled with a high proportion of machine support.

Direction

		Low Proportion of Voters Voting Promachine	High Proportion of Voters Voting Promachine
Turnout	High Proportion of Adults Voting	^{A}Renegades	^{B}Deliverables
	Low Proportion of Adults Voting	^{C}Independents	^{D}Controlled

Figure 1. A Typology of Machine Politics.

To illustrate these distinctions, Figure 1 shows a simple two-by-two typology of wards, precincts, or other electoral units. One axis specifies turnout, the other specifies direction—the proportion of voters pulling the right lever. Cell B includes the deliverables. High on turnout, wards in Cell B also vote the organization's way. Controlled wards in Cell D, however, fit the classic machine model of low-turnout/high-support. Wards in Cell C are independents, who give the organization little support, but who turn out at fairly low levels. Wards in Cell A are independents-with-a-vengeance, turning out in droves to oppose the organization. We call them renegades because they are often Democrats mobilized against the machine's candidates. Any machine city will no doubt contain wards of all four types. A few independent and renegade wards can be tolerated if they do not become too numerous, but they can become a serious threat to the machine in contested primaries. In fact, it is in contested primaries that the full range of these political units are most evident. It is also in the contested primaries that the machine dilemma of maintaining both black and ethnic support is most evident.

The ward typology as applied to the 1975 and 1977 primaries is shown

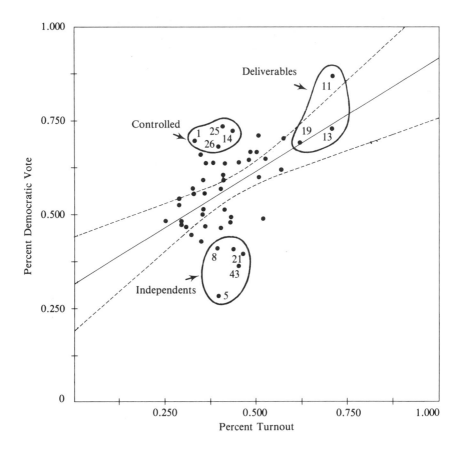

Figure 2. 1975 Primary: Deliverability.

in Figures 2 and 3. The major differences between the two primaries is the presence of renegade wards in 1977. These high turnout and low-machine support wards (Thirty-fifth, Thirty-eighth, Forty-first, and Forty-fifth) contain large numbers of Polish voters who were mobilized by the renegade regular Democrat and Forty-first Ward alderman, Roman Pucinski. The regression slope for 1977, which is steeper than the slope for 1975, shows that these wards pose the greatest threat to the machine's controllability and predictability. That is, greater turnout was not associated with greater machine support in 1977. While these renegade wards did not comprise the most deliverable wards in 1975, they all provided above-average machine majorities along with high turnout. Thus, in 1977 they contributed heavily to an anti-machine vote.

The independent wards pose the least threat to the machine because of

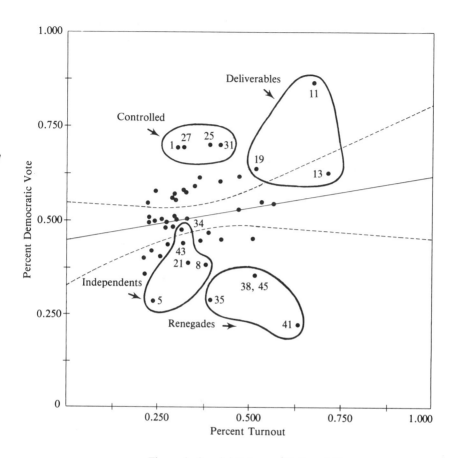

Figure 3. Special Primary: Deliverability.

their low turnout. Presumably, they are the most demoralized by the machine image of invincibility. Independents may be thought of as the proverbial strange bedfellows of politics. The Fifth Ward is the University of Chicago–Hyde Park area, consisting of a white middle-class and a poor population. The Forty-third Ward is a white middle-class ward that produces large Republican majorities whenever it is given a choice. The Twenty-first and Eighth wards are middle-class black wards. Because of their disparity of interests and apparent demoralization, they do not constitute a threat, at least in the short run. It is noteworthy that in spite of the presence of a black candidate in both the 1975 and 1977 Democratic primaries, the two middle-class black wards could not be easily mobilized.

The base of the machine's primary support consists of its controlled and deliverable wards. The controlled wards are typical inner-city machine wards. Their committeemen's talents are more geared to maintaining acquiescence and a small controlled electorate than in mobilizing large numbers of voters. Because all of the controlled wards have median family incomes below the city average, they are the most amenable to the use of material incentives. The Twenty-seventh Ward is all black, but the First, Twenty-fifth, and Twenty-sixth wards contain mixes of Poles, Italians, Ukrainians, Latinos, and blacks. The Fourteenth Ward, a poor Polish ward, became less controlled in 1977: it gave the machine a majority vote (61 percent), but that was 13 percent less than in 1974 (74 percent).

The deliverables, the basic source of machine strength and predictability, are working-class wards, comprising mainly eastern European and Irish ethnics. The Eleventh Ward, containing Bridgeport and the Back-of-the-Yards neighborhoods, has been deliverable in every election since 1955. Rakove (1975: 56) remarks that "if Virginia was the mother of presidents in the early days of the Republic, Bridgeport is the mother of mayors in recent Chicago history." Contrary to popular impression, the numerically (not politically) dominant ethnic group in the Eleventh Ward is Polish, rather than Irish. Every Chicago mayor from 1933 through Bilandic was from Bridgeport.

Bridgeport had a deliverability score of 60.3 in 1975—that is, sixty of every one hundred adults in Bridgeport turned out and voted for their native son, Richard J. Daley. (This is a staggering proportion if one recalls that the proportion of the U.S. adult population voting for *both* presidential candidates usually hovers about 60 percent.) It is an impressive feat, indeed, for a ward with a median education level of ninth grade and median income of $9,519. Even the impressive deliverability of the Thirteenth Ward (48.1 percent) and the Nineteenth Ward (38.5 percent) fades somewhat by comparison to that of the Eleventh. In 1977 the Eleventh Ward had a deliverability score of 57.2, turning out fifty-seven of every one hundred adults for Bilandic, who also resides, along with his extended family, in Bridgeport. "Upon the rock of the Eleventh Ward," one could have said, "I will build a machine."

The challenge the machine must face if it is to survive is how to maintain its largely white ethnic base of support in controlled and deliverable wards at a time when whites are decreasing as a proportion of the electorate. For the machine to keep even, it must somehow mobilize the deliverable wards even more, while preventing the defection and mobilization of renegade wards, since their loss could mean electoral defeat. But our scenarios of the machine's future would be incomplete without an analysis of the black electorate and how it has changed over time.

THE BLACKS: WAXING AND WANING

Chicago has been called the most segregated city north of the Mason-Dixon line. This is not strictly accurate. Karl Taeuber has carefully monitored patterns of residential segregation in 109 American cities since

Table 1. Population of Blacks in Chicago in 1960, by Ward.

Predominantly White Wards[a]		Integrated Wards[b]		Predominantly Black Wards[c]	
Ward No.	Percent Black	Ward No.	Percent Black	Ward No.	Percent Black
7	0.2	1	28.7	2	92.8
10	3.3	5	58.8	3	99.0
12	0.0	8	26.7	4	86.2
13	0.0	9	13.5	6	92.2
14	9.4	11	13.3	20	97.5
15	0.0	16	35.1	24	97.3
18	0.0	17	68.1	Population	
19	0.2	21	43.1	Black	408,561
23	3.4	22	30.3	6 wards	434,538
30	3.3	25	26.0		
31	0.1	26	12.7	Percent of citywide numbers	
32	1.4	27	61.3	Black	50.9
33	0.2	28	29.2	6 wards	12.2
34	0.0	29	57.1		
35	0.0	42	35.6		
36	0.0				
37	0.0	Population			
38	0.0	Black	363,674		
39	0.0	15 wards	1,061,214		
40	0.7				
41	0.0	Percent of citywide numbers			
43	4.3	Black	45.3		
44	0.1	15 wards	29.9		
45	0.0				
46	0.1				
47	0.0				
48	0.5				
49	0.1				
50	0.1				

Population
Black   30,157
29 wards   2,054,656

Percent of citywide numbers
Black   3.7
29 wards   57.9

[a]Wards with less than 10 percent of the population black.
[b]Wards with between 10 and 80 percent of the population black.
[c]Wards with over 80 percent of the population black.

1940. He computes a "segregation index" to show what proportion of the city's population lives in segregated neighborhoods. Taeuber's 1970 analysis (reported in Sorenson et al., 1975) finds Chicago's segregation index at 93.0, making it the second most segregated northern city (Dayton, Ohio, is first). The bulk of the city's black population has historically been clustered on the South Side, but has grown significantly in areas west of the Loop. The 1960 census showed that in six wards blacks were more than 80 percent of the population, in twenty-nine wards they

Table 2. Population of Blacks in Chicago in 1970, by Ward.

Predominantly White Wards[a]		Integrated Wards[b]		Predominantly Black Wards[c]	
Ward No.	Percent Black	Ward No.	Percent Black	Ward No.	Percent Black
10	9.2	1	35.7	2	94.2
12	5.3	5	56.9	3	99.0
13	0.0	7	26.8	4	91.0
14	6.1	8	76.7	6	97.6
15	8.3	9	28.3	16	92.0
19	2.2	11	11.1	17	98.0
23	0.0	18	28.2	20	97.4
26	4.7	22	23.7	21	86.5
30	0.1	25	36.2	24	98.5
31	1.4	34	66.7	27	89.7
32	3.9	37	12.4	28	83.9
33	0.3	42	39.1	29	88.2
35	0.0				
36	0.0	Population		Population	
38	0.5	Black	298,407	Black	758,508
39	0.6	12 wards	810,620	12 wards	815,654
40	0.1	Percent of citywide numbers		Percent of citywide numbers	
41	0.0	Black	27.5	Black	69.8
43	5.0	12 wards	24.1	12 wards	24.2
44	0.7				
45	0.0				
46	2.5				
47	0.0				
48	2.7				
49	1.2				
50	0.1				

Population
Black   29,838
26 wards   1,743,085

Percent of citywide numbers
Black   2.7
26 wards   51.7

[a] Wards with less than 10 percent of the population black.
[b] Wards with between 10 and 80 percent of the population black.
[c] Wards with over 80 percent of the population black.

were less than 10 percent, while in the remaining fifteen wards, blacks made up between 10 and 80 percent of the population. Table 1 shows the distribution of blacks in Chicago's fifty wards in 1960. Half of them lived in the six wards whose population was more than 80 percent black, while only 3.7 percent of them lived in the twenty-nine wards where blacks were less than 10 percent of the population. As the population of Chicago increased from less than one-quarter to more than one-third black between 1960 and 1970, residential clustering increased. By 1970 the number of wards with a population of more than 80 percent blacks had doubled (Table 2). These highly segregated wards contained almost 70 percent of the city's black population. At the same time, the number of integrated wards had declined, as had the number of so-called white wards—and the percentages of whites in the latter had also increased.

The recent history of Chicago politics is in large part a history of changing racial patterns. *In the 1950s blacks accommodated to Chicago politics; in the 1970s Chicago politics has had to accommodate to blacks.* The accommodationist era was the Dawson era. Congressman William Dawson held firm sway over a large segment of the South Side black community until his death. Five wards (the Second, Third, Fourth, Sixth, and Twentieth) were the core of the Dawson "sub-machine," as Wilson (1960) described his organization. Dawson's wards were an important key to Daley's first mayoral primary victory in 1955, giving Daley 81.6 percent of the vote, with nearly half the adult population voting. Only the First Ward exceeded the Daley vote of the Dawson wards. More generally Allswang argues that "Richard J. Daley bossed Chicago in part because of his ability to hold onto the black vote" (Allswang, 1971: 119), an observation based on "the overwhelming support of his machine by Chicago's poor blacks, who were served less well by his machine than any other group was" (Allswang, 1971: 134). Well into the 1960s, black wards, especially the old Dawson loyalists, fit nicely into our typology as controlled wards—turning out only modestly but solidly in the corner of the Democratic organization.

If the racial conflagrations of the 1960s provoked a confrontation between the city and the blacks in the streets, the 1975 mayoral primary provoked a confrontation at the ballot box, when state Senator Richard Newhouse entered the Democratic primary. Newhouse was the first major black candidate to seek the Chicago mayoralty, and blacks were nearly 40 percent of the Chicago population in 1975. In tandem with independent, anti-machine challenger William Singer, Daley was pressed on two fronts at once. After Daley's death, Bilandic had to fight a similar two-front war in his 1977 primary, confronting challenges again by a black, state Representative Harold Washington, and by Polish Alderman Roman Pucinski. With the city's two largest ethnic groups, blacks and

Poles, represented for the first time on the ballot, the Bilandic victory was testimony to the organization's ability to capitalize on deliverability and controllability. Just as Daley had turned back his black and independent challengers in 1975, so, too, did Bilandic defeat his black and Polish challengers in 1977.

There are several ways we can explore the pattern of black support for the Daley machine and its mayoral candidates. Because we are primarily interested in focusing on wards whose population is nearly all-black, one strategy is to pick some wards whose population has been consistently black since the first Daley election. The old Dawson wards—the Second, Third, Fourth, Sixth, and Twentieth—fit this description perfectly. These South Side strongholds were a key to Daley's electoral victory in 1955. In 1975, however, and again in 1977, a black candidate was in the race for the Democratic mayoral nomination. Table 3 provides a twenty-

Table 3. Machine Support, Turnout, and Deliverability in the Dawson Wards, 1955-77.

Election	Percent Daley/ Bilandic	Percent Turnout	Deliverability
1955 Primary	81.6	45.3	26.8
1955 General	71.8	54.5	36.8
1959 Primary[a]	80.3	31.7	21.4
1959 General	83.6	43.9	21.3
1963 Primary[a]	84.8	33.5	23.1
1963 General	76.7	49.6	38.2
1967 Primary	84.0	33.1	21.2
1967 General	81.2	41.4	32.1
1971 Primary[a]	90.2	27.4	18.5
1971 General	71.9	42.7	30.0
1975 Primary[b]	48.4	32.9	15.2
1975 General	83.0	23.6	18.9
1977 Primary[b]	49.7	25.6	11.9
1977 General	81.3	20.2	16.4

[a]Uncontested primary.
[b]Black candidate running in Democratic primary.

two-year overview of the patterns of deliverability, turnout, and machine support in these Dawson wards. As in most electoral time series, there are bumps, wiggles, and inconsistent patterns, but the general message seems clear. Except in two primary elections where a black candidate ran for mayor, *support for the organization candidate has remained strikingly high.* Support in the 80 percent range in the 1950s is matched by support in the 80 percent range in the 1970s. But turnout has declined dramatically. Turnout in the uncontested mayoral primaries of 1959, 1963, 1969, and 1971 exceeded the turnout in these wards in the 1975 and

1977 primaries. Either black voters feel pressures from several sources and choose to stay at home, or the appeal of a black candidate is not enough for them to reverse the trend of not voting in elections. The result is an irregular, but clear decline in the deliverability of black wards in Chicago.

Another way of assessing the patterns of political behavior among blacks is to look at the relationships between proportion of blacks in a ward and the ward's turnout, machine support, and deliverability. Table 4 shows Pearson correlations between the percentage of blacks in each of

Table 4. Correlations among Percentage Black, Machine Support, Turnout, and Deliverability, 1955–77.

Election	Percent Daley/ Bilandic	Percent Turnout	Deliverability
1955 Primary	0.78	0	0.68
1955 General	0.57	-0.23	0.44
1959 Primary[a]	-0.12	-0.11	0.30
1959 General	0.60	-0.18	0.23
1963 Primary[a]	0.22	-0.13	0.48
1963 General	0.78	-0.42	0.60
1967 Primary[a]	-0.30	-0.20	0.34
1967 General	0.56	-0.34	-0.02
1971 Primary[a]	-0.65	-0.42	0.07
1971 General	0.20	-0.49	-0.26
1975 Primary[b]	-0.50	-0.52	-0.48
1975 General	0.40	-0.57	-0.42
1977 Primary[b]	0.01	-0.50	-0.34
1977 General	0.43	-0.56	-0.40

[a]Uncontested primary.
[b]Black candidate running in Democratic primary.

the fifty wards and the three measures of machine strength. Not surprisingly, the relationship between percentage of blacks and turnout is consistently negative. Yet it becomes much more sharply negative over the years. Turnout in wards with a high proportion of blacks deteriorates with each passing election—even when a black candidate challenges the organization. The grip of the machine remains strong during all of the general elections (one finds it hard to imagine a strong positive correlation between percentage of blacks and voting Republican), but after Daley's 1955 primary victory, the blackness of a ward is weakly to negatively related to machine support. *Whatever electoral coalition the Daley organization built up over the years, blacks were the unreliable element in it.* The result is a visible reversal of the relationship between deliverability and percentage black, from strong positive correlations in the first half of the Daley era to strong negative correlations in the last half.

Here, then, is one paradoxical key to the future: *The electoral coalition of the Chicago Democratic organization has depended less and less on the growing black population and more and more on its declining ethnic elements.*

IMMIGRANTS' CHILDREN AND THE MACHINE

Support for the big city machine among newly arrived eastern European immigrants at the turn of the century is legendary. In fact, it is frequently assumed that a large immigrant population was a necessary condition for machine emergence and hegemony. The presence of a mass of immigrants with their pressing social, economic, and political needs has served as the basis for most theories of machine emergence and rule.[8] And the demise of the machine is most often attributed to the assimilation of these ethnics into the socioeconomic mainstream of American life, thus eliminating their material and social dependence upon the machine (Greenstein, 1964).

In Chicago immigrants did provide the most significant source of electoral support for the machine during its period of emergence. It is also clear that the immigrants' children and grandchildren do not have the material needs that made their parents a safe source of machine support. Second- and third-generation ethnics cannot be politically controlled in the same manner that their forebears were. White ethnics, however, continue to have needs and to make specific demands of the urban political system, but the basis of their demands has shifted from the economic sphere to the social and political ones. The machine's traditional use of material incentives is less effective. Today benefits that are social, symbolic, and status-oriented are the key to maintaining the support of the immigrants' children.

The expectations and demands of the ethnics fall into two major categories. The first are symbolic benefits characterized by demands for ethnic visibility in elective and appointive offices. The second category concerns what Downs (1973: ch. 9) has ominously referred to as the need for "cultural dominance," particularly over space (e.g., neighborhoods) and over culture-transmitting institutions (e.g., schools). Neither type of benefit is divisible in the same way that material benefits (such as jobs) are. That blacks are making demands for the same or similar benefits is the dilemma the machine must resolve if it is to survive.

ETHNIC VISIBILITY AND ELECTORAL MOBILIZATION

Meeting the demand for ethnic visibility in elective and appointive offices constitutes a more complex process than the term ticket-balancing implies. This complexity can best be explained in terms of the mobilization thesis. It was once believed that ethnic groups were assimilated into the political mainstream by the second and third generation, with class becoming more important than ethnicity in determining electoral choice. The evidence suggests otherwise. Ethnics become politically mobilized as ethnics in later generations.[9] The basis for this argument is that by the third generation, ethnics have a sizable middle class that constitutes a pool of talent and organizational skill necessary for ethnic leadership and political mobilization. Interpreted in terms of our typology, it can be argued that first-generation ethnics can be controlled, while second- and third-generation ethnics can be delivered. The risk is that the children of the immigrants can also become renegades.

Party mobilization and deliverability of a particular ethnic group are first achieved by selecting one of the group to run for a major citywide office, preferably for mayor, thus creating ethnic identification with the party. Machine selection of a fellow ethnic constitutes a major symbolic benefit, bestowing recognition and status benefits on the entire ethnic group. It represents the group's political coming of age. But in Chicago there are only a limited number of citywide positions, and the Irish maintained control of the mayoral position from 1933 until Daley's death, when the prize was given to an Eleventh Ward Croatian and Daley protégé. In addition, as Wilson (1973: 33-34) has observed, status benefits are relative. Not only can status benefits not be bestowed indefinitely, by definition, but their worth depends on who else gets them. If an office is given to an ethnic group held in low esteem and/or viewed as a threat by other groups, the status value of all offices is reduced in the perception of the other groups. The symbolic act itself may be perceived as threatening and result in the defection of the other groups, not only because of the threat but also because of the reduced status value of those offices they do hold.

In Chicago, the two groups most amenable to mobilization are the blacks and the Poles. They are the two largest groups in the city, and each has a sizable and politically restless middle class. In the aftermath of Daley's death, both blacks and Poles organized separately to pressure the machine power brokers for the mayoral position. Both lost but were given consolation prizes. Wilson Frost, the black alderman and committeeman from the black, middle-class Thirty-fourth Ward, was made chairman of the powerful council Finance Committee, a position involving more than ethnic visibility. The dean of the Polish aldermanic delegation was given the strictly symbolic position of vice-mayor, a position that was created specifically for the Poles and without much formal authority. The choice of a Croatian (Bilandic) as the machine's candidate to replace Daley was a practical choice, symbolizing the weakening of Irish control and bestowing status benefit for eastern European ethnics.

While Bilandic was a solution of sorts, the settlement failed to appease significant segments of the Polish and black communities. Both put opposition candidates in the 1977 special primary.

Polish renegades have imposed significant costs on the machine in contested primaries. In the 1955 and 1977 primaries, Polish opposition candidates won 133,173 votes (14 percent) and 368,400 votes (32 percent), respectively. To the extent that these votes were previously controlled, the machine had to compensate by mobilizing other voters, which is costly in terms of machine resources. The increase in the Polish renegade vote from 1955 to 1977 is partially consistent with the mobilization thesis, as the Polish middle class has undoubtedly grown during this period.

It is also comforting to the machine that a significant majority of the Polish electorate was not mobilized by the presence of a fellow ethnic on the ballot. Roman Pucinski, the renegade candidate in 1977, carried only the Polish wards in the northern section of the city (the Thirtieth, Thirty-fifth, Thirty-eighth, Fortieth, Forty-fifth, Fiftieth, and his own Forty-first). These are for the most part middle-class wards with median family incomes at or above the city average. He did not carry any of the inner-city wards with large, poor, and working-class Polish populations, although he was able to depress both machine support and turnout in some of them. For example, the machine vote percentage in the Fourteenth Ward decreased from 73 percent in the 1975 primary to 60 percent in the 1977 primary. The costs to the machine were not insignificant, but renegade Polish candidates obviously do not automatically have strong ethnic or even cross-class support within the Polish community.

CULTURAL DOMINANCE

According to Downs, a major impediment to racial integration is the perceived need of middle-class whites to maintain "cultural dominance" over their neighborhoods. Social and cultural groups fight to maintain the life-style and cultural dominance of their neighborhoods in order to eliminate the "unpleasant messages" created by the presence of other groups with conflicting life-styles and cultures (Williams, 1971). The presence of other groups constitutes a threat to one's way of life. But it is not only living space that becomes a source of cultural conflict; culture-transmitting institutions, such as schools and police departments, become the objects of conflict over whose values and norms are to dominate within the institution and to be transmitted and reinforced throughout the city.

Conflict between white ethnics and blacks, and even among white ethnics, over control of the schools has been a recurring theme in Chicago history and a persistent problem for the machine. Conflict over spatial dominance also marks ward and machine politics. Fear of losing cultural dominance over living space helps explain the ability of the machine to mobilize deliverable wards.

Maintaining the Democratic coalition requires satisfying the desires for cultural dominance of white ethnics. Occasionally, of course, this is manifested in thinly disguised anti-black schemes. One of the uglier examples is illustrated by a story, quoted in its entirety from the defunct *Chicago Daily News* (Apr. 16-17, 1977) during the peak of the primary election:

> *Save-the-neighborhood program:* Voters in the 54th precinct of the 38th ward received a form letter this week from the regular Democratic precinct captain, Joe Galiano, saying in part: "As you know April 19 is a special election for mayor of Chicago. The straw poll shows Mayor Bilandic with the largest number of votes. The second largest number of votes that the poll shows is the black candidate. May I urge you all to support Mayor Bilandic so that the white vote is not split causing a black to come out on top. I have property interests in this neighborhood as all of you do. So let's try to keep this area as nice as it is now."

Though worth noting, such stories present an unnecessarily pinched and intolerant perception of the Democratic organization. Political machines, like other electoral organizations, are in the business of winning elections. In Chicago this means meeting ethnic demands for cultural dominance while providing blacks with living space, freedom of movement, and political power.

This dilemma of black mobilization versus ethnic cultural dominance is played out not only in the city as a whole, but especially in the machine's backyard. Our analysis of the 1975 and 1977 elections demonstrated decisively that three wards—the Eleventh, Thirteenth, and Nineteenth—qualify as the deliverables. Yet it is also in those three wards that the dilemma of black mobilization and ethnic dominance is most visible.

The Eleventh Ward has a relatively poor working-class population. The median family income of $9,519 is below the city median of $10,242. Only 28 percent of the adult population has completed high school. However, the Eleventh Ward is above the city average in home ownership; 47 percent of all residential units are owner-occupied compared with the city mean of 44 percent. The Nineteenth Ward is the wealthiest ward in the city: the median family income in 1970 was $14,115. Sixty-five percent of the adults had completed high school, and 80 percent of all residential units were owner-occupied. The Thirteenth Ward fell in between, with a median family income of over $12,000, 47 percent of the adults having completed high school, and 70 percent of the homes being owner-occupied. The Eleventh Ward is an inner-city ward, while the Thirteenth and Nineteenth are periphery wards on the western boundary of the city. The characteristic shared by these three wards is that their populations are white, and they are surrounded by wards whose populations are all-black, or are becoming more nearly black, or are in the path of black migration (Table 5). The Eleventh Ward's eastern boundary

Table 5. Black Percentage of Population in Wards Surrounding Three Deliverable Wards.

Deliverable Wards	Percent Black (1970)	Surrounding Wards	Percent Black	
			1970	1960
		1	35.7	28.7
		2	94.2	92.8
		3	99.0	99.0
Eleventh	11.1	12	5.3	*
		14	6.1	*
		25	36.2	26.0
		12	5.3	*
		15	8.3	*
Thirteenth	0	18	28.2	0
		23	0	3.4
		18	28.2	0
Nineteenth	2.2	21	86.5	45.1
		34	66.7	*

NOTE. * = Ward boundaries changed substantially in the redistricting of 1970.

faces two black wards and the Nineteenth Ward's eastern boundary is shared with two wards that are becoming all-black. The Thirteenth Ward is just north of a westward path of black migration.

MACHINE POLICIES AND ELECTORAL SURVIVAL

Machines specialize in divisible public policies. Banfield and Wilson (1963: 115) describe a machine as an organization dependent on political incentives that are "specific and material," meaning that their outputs are both monetary or translatable into money (e.g., jobs or the fabled hods of coal) *and* capable of being given to some and withheld from others. Other political scientists use similar terms for roughly equivalent concepts. Some refer to "divisible" and "indivisible" goods and services. Others distinguish between public and private goods, following the economist's distinction between collective and non–zero sum policies. Whatever the concept, machines are assumed to specialize in policy outputs that are specific, divisible, private, and non–zero sum. Yet the issues involved in urban politics are far more complex. Racial issues, in particular, assume an indivisible cast. To be sure, some racial issues are themselves divisible. One may have a little or a lot of school busing for racial balance, a weak or a strong quota system for minority hiring, and a few or many black candidates endorsed by the party. Yet even they are so symbolic as to be virtually zero sum in the popular perception. The first school bus seems to imply that busing will soon become universal. One either does or does not have a black candidate slated for mayor.

The recent history of the Chicago Democratic organization can best be understood as an effort to pursue public policies designed to maintain its ethnic constituency while simultaneously guaranteeing enough divisible gains to black voters to keep them from independent or renegade status. In his later years, for example, Daley began to enforce stringently a municipal ordinance requiring municipal employees to live in the corporate limits of Chicago. But nowhere has the tightwire politics of coalition maintenance been more obvious than in the politics of school desegregation. Peterson's excellent account of Chicago's halting desegregation efforts stresses the desire to keep whites in the city. One school board member who cast the deciding vote in favor of a largely segregated attendance plan explained his vote by emphasizing that "in my mind [it] is the only way that we can prevent the exodus from the city" (Peterson, 1976: 175). Former School Superintendent Joseph Hannon (himself a white, chosen carefully over a prominent black candidate) stressed that the "bottom line" of his 1978 proposals was to prevent a middle-class exodus from the city.

What happened to the machine, then, in the Daley-Bilandic era was that it experienced increasing difficulty in reconciling the divisible non–zero sum politics, in which machines specialize, with the symbolic, largely indivisible demands of an emerging black majority. A thinner and thinner electoral base in deliverable and controllable wards was one horn of the organization's dilemma. The other was stiffer demands by blacks and diminishing turnout among the black wards. All these trends—not merely the politics of snow—constitute the backdrop for the election of Jane Byrne.

SOME NOTES ON BYRNE AND THE FUTURE OF THE CHICAGO MACHINE

When former Consumer Sales Commissioner Jane Byrne declared against Michael Bilandic, machine watchers gave her as much chance as the proverbial snowball in hell. But more snow than ever intruded on Chicago politics. The city that worked suddenly didn't. On February 27, 1979, Byrne defeated Bilandic by 412,919 to 396,134, a scant 17,000 votes. Local journalists fell over one another pronouncing the death of the much-venerated machine and attributing the Byrne victory to the politics of snow. How indeed, one may wonder in retrospect, could such a powerful organization—one that had weathered riots, racial transition, and even 1968—have been so easily beaten by the weather?

A serious assessment of the 1979 election would begin, not with the snow, but the machine's traditional gatekeeping function. Machines, we suggested earlier, not only mobilize votes; they play critical gatekeeping roles in the electoral selection process. It is best to have only your own name on the ballot. If, however, a renegade like Byrne appears, it is better to have other names as well on the ballot. For years factionalism among its opponents helped the machine outlast them. The presence of a black anti-machine candidate in 1975 (Newhouse) and 1977 (Washington) helped split the machine's opposition. Ironically, the absence of a black candidate in 1979 worked to the disadvantage of the machine itself. Had Democratic leaders engineered a black candidacy in 1979, one that could have drained away a mere 20,000 votes from Byrne (just 5 percent of her total and less than one-half the voted collected by Newhouse and Washington), no political pundit would be writing today about the death of the machine.

Politics in Chicago has long been dominated by the Democratic organization, and it may well outlive its analysts. Answers to two key questions will determine the future of Chicago politics and its electoral machine. Will blacks or white ethnics run the machine? Will the machine continue to monopolize power in the city, or will new elements emerge to challenge its hegemony? The first question asks who will run the machine; the second asks whether the machine will continue to run the city. There are four possible scenarios. In one, a continuation of the present situation, a white ethnic–dominated machine will continue to dominate, even monopolize, city politics. In a second, the machine is run by blacks, but continues to run the city. In a third, white ethnics continue to dominate a fragmented machine that shares power with other elements in city politics. In the fourth scenario, a black-run machine shares power in a fragmented system.

Only one of these scenarios is utterly implausible. The chances that a white ethnic–dominated machine will continue to monopolize power in Chicago is unlikely. To be sure, blacks have much mobilizing to do before they win a commanding place in Chicago politics. But that was also true at one time of blacks in Newark, Cleveland, Birmingham, Atlanta, and elsewhere. Every other large city with a black majority or near-majority has eventually yielded to black rule. Within the machine or outside it, blacks will shape the future of Chicago politics.

NOTES

1. Royko's *Boss* (1971) is characteristically ascerbic, so much so that Mrs. Daley once succeeded in getting the book removed from her supermarket shelves. Television newsman O'Connor wrote *Clout* (1975), which is scarcely more supportive. Most recently, Kennedy authored *Himself* (1978), which might be described as a paean to a fallen Irish chieftain.

2. These migrations and their effects on urban politics are discussed more generally in Lineberry and Sharkansky (1978).

3. An excellent source of data on population and other changes in Chicago is the study by Skogan (1976).

4. Some useful profiles of the city's immigrant groups today are found in several volumes published by Chicago's Department of Development and Planning in 1976 on its blacks, Poles, Spanish-speaking, German, Italian, and Irish populations.

5. A systematic telephone survey conducted by the Center for Urban Affairs at Northwestern University in 1977 found 40 percent of the respondents in Chicago to be black. Linear extrapolation of data reported in Skogan (1976) to 1980 suggests the 45 percent figure.

6. In politics, nothing succeeds like success, and nurturing the belief that a machine is invincible can go a long way toward scaring off potential opponents. Machine politicians in America are often Irish, and Irish blarney has been an important part of the myth of machine invincibility. Sacks (1976) even describes a very real machine in Ireland that maintained itself, in part, by "imaginary patronage," that is, by providing the appearance of aid to its constituents when its influence in acquiring such aid was limited.

7. To the best of our knowledge, the only other use of this measure in political science is by Przeworski and Sprague (1971). They define several measures of "mobilization," one of which is

$$V_i = \frac{\text{no. of voters for party } i}{\text{no. of adults}}.$$

8. See, for instance, Merton (1957: 71–81). The "center-periphery" thesis developed by Wade (1968) and the "community-society continuum" formulated by Hays (1975) as explanations of machine and reform conflict are also based on the differences in needs and social orientations of immigrants as opposed to the middle-class, Anglo-Saxon reformers, although they differ in terms of explanation.

9. A number of political scientists, such as Wolfinger (1965) and Parenti (1967), have found empirical support for the mobilization thesis.

REFERENCES

Allswang, John M. 1971. *A House for All Peoples.* Lexington: University of Kentucky Press.
———. 1977. *Bosses, Machines, and Urban Voters.* Port Washington, N.H.: Kennikat.
Banfield, Edward C., and James Q. Wilson. 1963. *City Politics.* Cambridge, Mass.: Harvard University Press and the M.I.T. Press.

Clark, Terry N. 1975. "The Irish Ethic and the Spirit of Patronage." *Ethnicity,* 2: 205-59.

Downs, Anthony. 1973. *Opening Up the Suburbs.* New Haven, Conn.: Yale University Press.

Drake, St. Clair, and Horace Cayton. 1944. *Black Metropolis.* New York: Harcourt Brace.

Dye, T. R., and J. Ammons. 1978. "Sunbelt and Frostbelt Cities." Paper presented at Annual Meeting of the Southwestern Political Science Association, Houston, Tex.

Greenstein, Fred I. 1964. "The Changing Patterns of Urban Party Politics." *Annals of the American Academy of Political and Social Science,* 353 (May): 1-27.

Hays, Samuel. 1975. "Political Parties and the Community-Society Continuum," pp. 152-81, in W. N. Chambers and W. D. Burnham, eds., *The American Party Systems.* New York: Oxford University Press.

Kennedy, Eugene E. 1978. *Himself.* New York: Viking.

Lineberry, Robert L., and I. Sharkansky. 1978. *Urban Politics and Public Policy.* New York: Harper and Row.

Lorinskas, R., B. Hawkins, and S. Edwards. 1969. "The Persistence of Ethnic Voting in Urban and Rural Areas." *Social Science Quarterly,* 49 (Mar.): 891-99.

Merton, Robert. 1957. *Social Theory and Social Structure.* New York: Free Press.

Nathan, Richard, and Charles Adams. 1976. "Understanding Central City Hardship." *Political Science Quarterly,* 91 (Spring): 47-62.

O'Connor, Len. 1975. *Clout.* New York: Avon.

Parenti, Michael. 1967. "Ethnic Politics and the Persistence of Ethnic Identification." *American Political Science Review,* 61 (Sept.): 717-26.

Peterson, P. 1976. *School Politics Chicago Style.* Chicago: University of Chicago Press.

Przeworski, A., and J. Sprague. 1971. "Concepts in Search of Explicit Formulation: A Study in Measurement." *American Journal of Political Science,* 15 (May): 183-218.

Rakove, Milton. 1975. *Don't Make No Waves, Don't Back No Losers.* Bloomington: Indiana University Press.

Royko, Mike. 1971. *Boss.* New York: Signet.

Sacks, Paul M. 1976. *The Donegal Mafia: An Irish Political Machine.* New Haven, Conn.: Yale University Press.

Skogan, Wesley G. 1976. *Chicago since 1840: A Times Series Analysis.* Urbana: Institute of Government and Public Affairs, University of Illinois.

Sorenson, A., K. E. Taeuber, and L. J. Hollingsworth. 1975. "Segregation Indices for 109 Cities." *Sociological Focus,* 8 (Apr.): 125-42.

Wade, Richard. 1968. "Urbanization," pp. 187-205 in C. V. Woodward, ed., *The Comparative Approach to American History.* New York: Oxford University Press.

Williams, O. P. 1971. "Life Style Values and Political Decentralization in Metropolitan Areas," pp. 56-64 in C. Bonjean et al., eds., *Community Politics.* New York: Free Press.

Wilson, J. Q. 1973. *Political Organizations.* New York: Free Press.

Wolfinger, Raymond. 1965. "The Development and Persistence of Ethnic Voting." *American Political Science Review,* 59 (Dec.): 896-908.

JOSEPH ZIKMUND II

Mayoral Voting and Ethnic Politics
in the Daley-Bilandic-Byrne Era

CHICAGO IS A CITY OF ETHNICS—it has always been that way, and it remains so today. From the beginning many of the city's residents came from abroad. In 1850 when the city contained a scant 29,375 inhabitants, more than half were foreign-born. The English, the French, the Germans, the Irish, and the Swedes all were present in considerable numbers. In the next half century Chicago's population increased by well over 1,600,000 persons. Many of these, too, came from overseas. In 1900 more than one-third of the city's people had been born in other countries; an additional 43 percent were native-born children of foreign-born parents—essentially what the U.S. Census Bureau calls people of "foreign stock." As the twentieth century progressed, the number of Chicagoans who fit the technical definitions of foreign-born and foreign stock has gradually declined. To some extent, this indicates a slow erosion in the ethnic character of Chicago. Ethnicity today is more a matter of attitude and behavior—the presence or absence of a self-conscious ethnic identification—than a matter of place of birth. Nonetheless, as late as 1970 Chicago still contained more than 370,000 people (out of a total of 3,362,947) who had been born in other countries and over one million whom the census bureau labeled as being of foreign stock (Department of Development and Planning, 1976a).

Table 1 shows the number of people in each major ethnic group in Chicago from 1900 to 1970. Here we find ample evidence of the social changes that have occurred in the city throughout the twentieth century. Concentrating for the moment on the period from 1900 to 1950, two important trends are apparent. First, the number and proportion of American blacks increased tremendously: from about 30,000 in 1900 to almost 500,000 fifty years later, or from 1.8 percent to 13.6 percent. While these increases both in raw numbers and percentages are large, it is important to note that in 1950 American blacks still constituted a relatively small

Table 1. Major Ethnic Groups in Chicago, 1900–70.

Ethnic Groups	1900	1930	1950	1970
Total city population	1,698,575	3,376,438	3,620,962	3,362,947
Total "foreign stock"	1,315,307	2,174,430	1,628,168	1,000,982
Major ethnic groups[a]				
Germans	428,201	337,975	229,230	99,413
	25.2	10.0	6.3	3.0
Irish	225,900	193,555	126,940	59,218
	13.3	5.7	3.5	1.8
Poles	111,506	401,316	315,504	191,955
	6.6	11.9	8.7	5.7
Swedes	103,220	140,913	85,684	26,988
	6.1	4.2	2.4	0.8
Bohemians/Czechs	77,343	122,089	78,135	30,492
	4.6	3.6	2.2	0.9
USSR[b]	40,546	169,736	139,504	64,179
	2.4	5.0	3.9	1.9
Italians	27,250	181,861	171,549	97,642
	1.6	5.4	4.7	2.9
American blacks	30,150	233,903	492,265	1,102,620
	1.8	6.9	13.6	32.8
Mexicans	. . .	19,362	24,335	82,097
		0.6	0.7	2.4
Puerto Ricans[c]	. . .	. . .	. . .	78,963
				2.3

SOURCE. Department of Development and Planning (1976b).
NOTE. Three dots = no members of group present in Chicago.
[a]Data for the "Major Ethnic Groups" are given as the total numbers that the U.S. Census Bureau counted as "foreign stock" (line 1) and the percentage of the total city population (line 2).
[b]Includes peoples from all parts of what is now the Soviet Union, many of them Jewish.
[c]Puerto Ricans are not "foreign," but are clearly "ethnic" in the general sense.

minority of the city's population and still were only 30.2 percent of the identifiable European foreign-stock population. Thus, while blacks had increased dramatically during the first half of the twentieth century, Chicago remained an overwhelming white ethnic city. Second, during this time the relative balance of numbers among white ethnic groups shifted. Poles replaced Germans as the city's largest countable group. The Irish dropped from second to fifth. However, these were not the only shifts. The size ranking of white ethnic groups in 1900 shows very poor correlation to the pattern in 1950.[1] In sum, the period from 1900 to 1950 shows major demographic shifts in Chicago's population, affecting both the blacks and the relative size of various white ethnic groups within the city. From 1950 to 1970 these same trends continued. Ultimately they were to alter the social balance within the city and to produce a Chicago radically different in composition from that which had existed seventy years earlier. During this brief twenty-year period Chicago's overall population—at least as counted by the census bureau—declined by 258,015. The total number of persons of foreign stock within the city went down by 628,186: 123,549 Poles were lost; 129,817 Germans; and 67,722 Irish.[2] In addition to these trends it is important to note both that the black population had expanded by 610,355 and that the Mexican and Puerto Rican peoples had increased by a combined total of about 135,000.[3] The first question one asks when confronted with these figures is where did all the white ethnics go? Many moved to the suburbs, especially during the 1950s. Others left the region; some, obviously, died. In any case, the trends of these two decades strongly suggest that as Chicago moves into the last years of this century, blacks will replace white ethnics as the dominant social group within the city.

Not only have the numbers changed, but the social geography of the city has changed as well. Two tendencies can be seen in the spatial distribution of ethnic peoples in Chicago over the past century. First, although certain ethnic groups have moved within the city, they have retained their basic, original ethnic homogeneity (see for instance, Department of Development and Planning, 1976b). Second, more and more areas have become ethnically mixed, with substantial numbers of persons from several identifiable groups present. Today, the only really ethnically pure portions of the city of any significant scale are either black or Latino—the latter, of course, potentially a mixture of various Spanish-speaking populations. Of these two trends the second has probably had the greatest impact on the character of the city and seriously complicates the problems of social-political analysis. When whole communities move, the implications are, at one and the same time, genuinely important and relatively easy to identify. When ethnic neighborhoods fragment and their peoples scatter throughout the city, ethnic attitudes and behaviors may still be present, but they are virtually impossible to isolate and identify. It is precisely this dilution of ethnic concentrations within defined areas that has occurred in Chicago over the past seventy years. It is not that there are no longer large numbers of ethnically conscious Poles or Irish or Germans. Rather the analytical problem is that these people are no longer geographically concentrated in great enough numbers to dominate a total neighborhood or community within the city.

This breakup of particular ethnic concentrations is not merely an analytical or research problem. It changes the whole social pattern and dynamic of the city. In the past, when each ethnic population was geographically concentrated into a separate, relatively homogeneous neighborhood, ethnic attitudes and behaviors were developed and reinforced by daily interaction and shared experiences. Ethnicity and geography were mutually supportive. The fragmentation of ethnic neighborhoods changes the situation in at least two distinct ways. First, ethnic identity must be consciously asserted and reinforced through ethnic-organization membership and activity, through retention of ethnic dietary, recreational, and religious patterns, and through contact with and use of the original ethnic language and local ethnic publications. Under these new conditions ethnicity can easily evolve from an inescapable fact of life to a latent aspect of one's personal background or family past. When this happens, ethnicity is not lost; rather, it becomes just one of several factors operating to influence a person's attitudes and behaviors. To re-emerge and, perhaps, become dominant, this latent ethnicity must be activated or stimulated from without, as the election of the new pope has done for many people of Polish descent. While this process appears on the surface to be similar to the melting pot notion of upward mobility for ethnics into the homogenized American middle class, the two are not identical. Here we are focusing on geographic mobility, not social-economic mobility. In the past the latter has frequently caused the former. However, geographic mobility occurs even when social-economic mobility is absent or is relatively modest in impact. When this geographic mobility does take place without parallel social-economic mobility, it has its own independent impact on ethnic identity and on the general patterns of ethnicity within the city.

The second and related consequence of the fragmentation of ethnic areas is to give peoples living in close proximity to each other a local or neighborhood—in the territorial sense—commonality of experience that in time comes to predominate over or, at least, compete with other factors influencing attitudes and behavior. Community areas, in effect, replace ethnicity and potentially even social class in structuring the individual's identification with people, groups, and public issues. Geography, in other words, may well be replacing ethnicity as the focusing element of urban identity for many city people.

THE MACHINE IN CHICAGO POLITICS

Urban machines have long been identified with the Americanization of our ethnic populations (Merton, 1961). Chicago, the city of ethnics, has been governed by bosses—both Republican and Democrat—and their political organizations for most of the last hundred years (Wendt and Kogan, 1967; Gottfried, 1962; Gosnell, 1937; Meyerson and Banfield, 1955; and Rakove, 1979). The current Democratic machine—whether one dates its origin from Cermak in 1931 or Nash and Kelly in 1933—has totally dominated the city's government and local politics for more than forty years. During this time the Democrats have continuously controlled the mayor's office, have almost always carried the city for local, state, and national party candidates, and have often provided the winning margins for Democrats in statewide electoral contests. The history of the machine is well known and the personalities who have made it function—especially Richard J. Daley—need no introduction (Banfield, 1961; Kennedy, 1978; O'Connor, 1975; Rakove, 1975; Royko, 1971). Our purpose is to explore the electoral base of this machine.

The advent of the Democratic machine in Chicago during the early 1930s did not happen by accident. The Great Depression, the New Deal, and the presidency of Franklin D. Roosevelt affected voter alignments all across the nation. Ethnics, white and black, responded to these events by shifting partisan loyalties from the Republicans to the Democrats. Local Democratic politicians everywhere benefited from this radical party realignment. Some groups shifted earlier than others, but eventually all of the major ethnic blocs stood with FDR and his party. The Chicago case, in other words, was not unique. Nor has it been atypical for these groups to continue voting Democratic in the post–World War II years. What is special about the Chicago situation is the ongoing political machine that came to power in the 1930s and continued to rule through the 1970s. John Allswang, in his book *A House for All Peoples* (1971), documents the voter shifts that occurred. In 1927 Bill Thompson, a Republican, won the mayor's office with 54 percent of the major party vote. In 1931 Thompson, seeking reelection, lost to Anton Cermak, a Democrat; this time he captured only 42 percent of the two-party vote. Among the largest white ethnic groups in the city at that time were the Poles, Germans,

Table 2. Percentage Point Change in Bill Thompson's Proportion of the Major Party Vote: 1927–31.

Ethnic Group	Percentage Decrease in Vote
Poles	–16
Germans	–21
Italians	– 5
Jews	–22
Swedes	–15
Czechoslovakians	–25

SOURCE: Adapted from Allswang (1971:161).

Italians, Jews, Swedes, and Czechs. Table 2 shows how each of these groups turned away from Thompson. Since the 1931 mayoral election, ethnics generally have been found in the camp of the Democratic machine.

However, ethnic loyalty at the polls did not necessarily lead to uniform satisfaction among all ethnic groups with the organization's reward structure. Cermak replaced the Irish contingent, which had dominated the local Democratic organization during the 1920s, with Czechs, Jews, Poles, and other eastern and southern European ethnics. When Pat Nash and Ed Kelly succeeded Cermak in 1933, the Irish reemerged. Even as late as 1970 Irish workers were more than 2.5 times as common in local government jobs as in the general, overall city population (Department of Development and Planning, 1976c: 2). Given this situation, it is not surprising that, although ethnic voters have tended to support the machine in general elections since 1931, primaries have sometimes reflected struggles for power among competing groups.

EMERGENCE OF THE DALEY ERA: 1955

In the twenty-four-year period from 1931 to 1955 three persons held the office of mayor in the city of Chicago—Anton J. Cermak (1931-33), Edward J. Kelly (1933-47), and Martin H. Kennelly (1947-55). Kennelly, a reform mayor backed by the Democratic organization in 1947 and 1951, ran into trouble when he sought reelection in 1955. The party withdrew its support from the incumbent, and a three-way contest for the party nomination developed among Kennelly, Richard J. Daley, and Benjamin Adamowski. The first two were Irish; Adamowski, Polish. Kennelly found support in the independent or reform faction of the party. Daley, while not the handpicked candidate of the machine, received

Table 3. Results of the 1955 Mayoral Primary and General Elections.

| Voting Results | 1955 Democratic Primary | | |
	Daley	Kennelly	Adamowski
Total votes	369,362	266,946	113,173
Percent of votes cast	49.0	35.0	15.0
Total wards won	26	20	4
Wards won by a plurality of 5,000 votes or more	15	3	0

| Voting Results | 1955 General Election | |
	Daley	Merriam
Total Votes	708,222	581,555
Percent of total vote	54.9	45.1
Total wards won	29	21
Wards won by a plurality of 5,000 votes or more	20	7

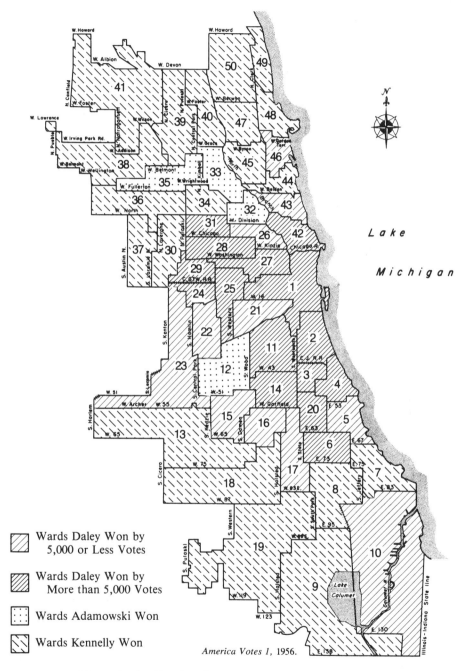

Wards Daley Won by
5,000 or Less Votes

Wards Daley Won by
More than 5,000 Votes

Wards Adamowski Won

Wards Kennelly Won

America Votes 1, 1956.

Map 1. Voting Results of the 1955 Democratic Primary.

most of his votes from organization regulars. Adamowski finished a poor third. Table 3 summarizes the results of this election.

Because census data do not fit the ward boundaries as they existed in 1955, it is impossible to correlate vote patterns in this year. However, the political geography of the election is illustrated in Map 1. Daley support is concentrated at the midsection, so to speak, of the city—the Loop (the First Ward) and its neighbors plus those portions of the city to the west-southwest of the Loop stretching all the way to Chicago's western boundary. By contrast, Kennelly's strength lay to the far south and to the north.

The general election of 1955 found Daley opposed by Republican Robert E. Merriam. Daley won the election, but not without a struggle, as may be seen in Table 3 and Map 2. The correlation between Daley's ward vote in the primary and in the general election was $r = 0.83$.

Another way to illustrate the similarity of geographic patterns between the 1955 primary and general elections is shown in Table 4. Here we see

Table 4. Comparison of Wards Supporting Daley in the 1955 Primary and General Elections.

		Primary Election	
		Daley	Not Daley
General Election	Daley	24	5
	Not Daley	2	19

NOTE. Phi = 0.72.

that very few wards switched either to or from Daley between the two elections.

In several ways the two elections of 1955 set the stage for the electoral politics of the entire Daley era. Daley's loyal strength remained concentrated in the city's midsection throughout the period. Similarly, his only effective opposition after 1955 came from a liberal reformer (William Singer, in 1975) and a dissident Pole (Benjamin Adamowski, in 1963). Aside from the rising black presence in Chicago politics after 1960, the Poles appear to be the most politically noteworthy ethnic voting bloc in the city during the Daley years. One reason is that Polish-Americans were the city's largest white ethnic group. At the same time, Polish frustration with the system may have been the highest in the city. Polish numerical predominance came at a time when black political strength was emerging and when the number of black residents, if not black voters, far outstripped the Poles. Polish politicians, in other words, probably have waited their turn only to find that turn now being usurped by blacks (Kantowicz, 1975: 219). In addition, the ultimate potential of Polish vote

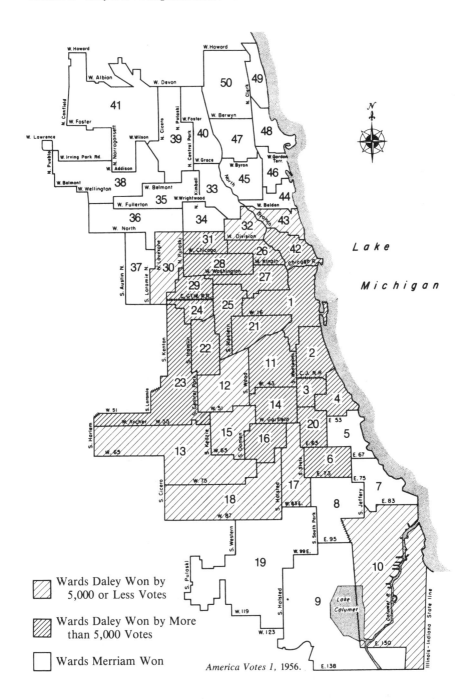

Wards Daley Won by
5,000 or Less Votes

Wards Daley Won by More
than 5,000 Votes

Wards Merriam Won

America Votes 1, 1956.

Map 2. Voting Results of the 1955 General Election.

power has become harder and harder to mobilize as Poles themselves have dispersed both into the suburbs and throughout the city. Recent neighborhood changes have served to weaken the attachment of some Polish voters to the Polish political cause.

ELECTORAL PATTERNS DURING THE DALEY YEARS: 1959-75

For purposes of analysis the elections from 1959 through 1975 are best considered in three distinct categories: first, those elections in which Daley did not face any serious opposition; second, the 1963 general election in which Daley was opposed by a strong alternative candidate of Polish background; and third, the 1975 primary election in which the mayor was opposed by a strong reform candidate from within his own party.

DALEY UNOPPOSED

In none of the Democratic mayoral primaries from 1959 through 1971 did Daley face any challenge to his renomination. When there was factional opposition to the mayor during this period, it never arose as a public contest within the Democratic party. In the one serious factional dispute—the Adamowski-Daley battle of 1963 to be discussed later—Daley's control over both the party organization and the regular Democratic primary voters forced that opposition into the Republican party.

The general elections of 1959, 1967, and 1975 found Daley opposed by a variety of token nominees representing the Republican party. In 1971 the Republicans nominated Richard Friedman, a reform Democrat from the Better Government Association in Chicago. All went down to crushing defeat. Still, the electoral patterns of these elections provide useful information for understanding political normalcy in the Daley years. The outcomes of these elections are presented in Table 5. In all cases opposi-

Table 5. Summaries of the 1959, 1967, 1971, and 1975 Mayoral General Elections.

Year	Daley Vote	Opponent Vote	Daley's Percenta	Wards Opponents Won	Wards Daley Won by less than 5,000 Votes
1959	776,806	Sheehan, 312,230	71.3	Sheehan—1	4
1967	792,238	Waner, 272,542	74.4	Waner—0	4
1971	740,137	Friedman, 315,969	70.1	Friedman—2	8
1975	542,817	Hoellen, 139,335	79.6	Hoellen—0	3

NOTE. Daley's opponents were Timothy Sheehan, John Waner, Richard Friedman, and John J. Hoellen.
aThis is Daley's percent of the major two-party vote.

tion strength concentrated geographically in the Hyde Park–South Shore area to the south and in the northern wards. While none did as well as Merriam in 1955, any strength these candidates did show was in areas where Merriam had been strong (except for John Waner's showing in the Twenty-third Ward in 1967). Conversely, one might say that Daley's areas of strength and weakness remained geographically stable for all five general elections from 1955 through 1975.

In sum, throughout much of the period between 1955 and 1975 Daley had no primary challenges within the Democratic party and little serious opposition from Republicans.

THE 1963 ELECTION

In both 1960 and 1970 Polish-Americans were the largest white ethnic bloc living in the city of Chicago. The U.S. Census Bureau put their numbers at 258,657 and 191,955 in these two years. Informal estimates suggest the figure for all people of Polish origin within the city today may be as high as 600,000 (Rakove, 1975: 151).[4] Given this potential electoral strength, it seems reasonable to assume that Polish candidates with considerable local reputation would do well in Chicago elections. Yet we have already seen that when Adamowski challenged both Kennelly and Daley for the Democratic party nomination in 1955, he came in a poor third. Eight years later he jumped to the Republican ticket and faced the mayor head to head in the mayoral general election.[5] The summary results appear in Table 6. Needless to say, this election more closely ap-

Table 6. Results of Mayoral General Election of 1963.

Voting Results	Daley	Adamowski
Total votes	677,497	540,705
Percent of votes cast	55.6	44.4
Total wards won	32	18
Wards won by a plurality of 5,000 votes or more	19	8

proximates the general election of 1955 than those discussed in the preceding section. Unfortunately, because of changes in ward boundaries, it is impossible to make direct statistical comparisons between the Merriam and Adamowski efforts. However, a visual comparison is possible by looking at Maps 2 and 3. Clearly, Merriam, the reform candidate, did better along the North Shore than did Adamowski, the Polish-ethnic, but Adamowski cut into areas to the southwest, where Daley had previously been strong.

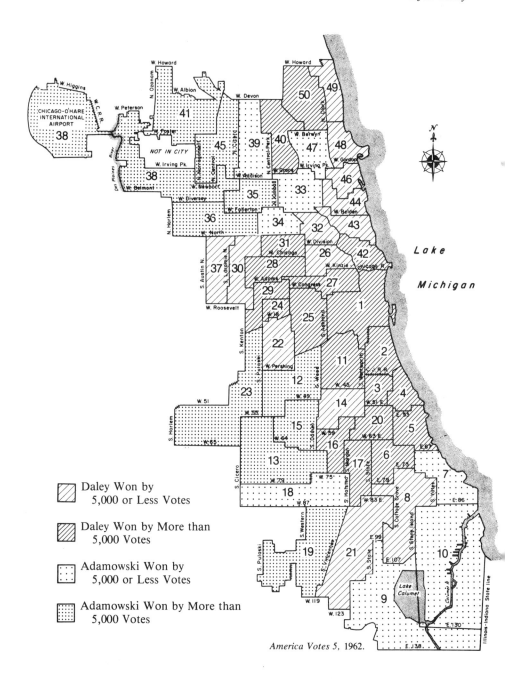

Map 3. Voting Results of the 1963 General Election.

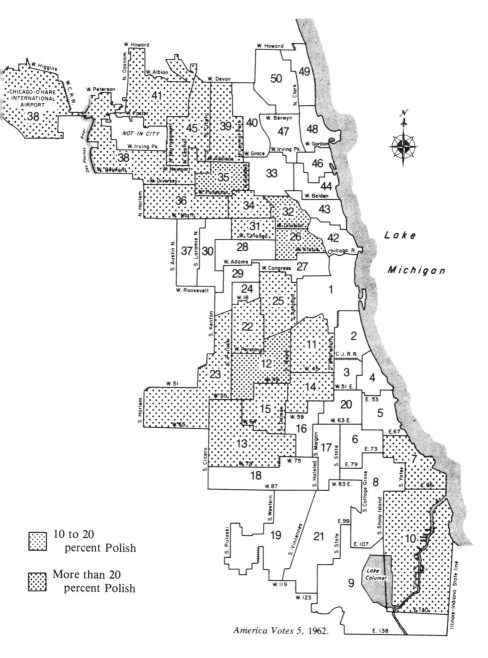

10 to 20
percent Polish

More than 20
percent Polish

America Votes 5, 1962.

Map 4. Polish Population by Wards: 1960. (Census figures for 1960 have been corrected to reflect 1963 ward boundaries.)

Our initial expectation might well be that Adamowski did well in those wards where the city's Polish population was concentrated. To some degree, as a visual comparison of Maps 3 and 4 indicates, this was indeed the case. What seems impressive here, however, is not that a general relationship exists, but rather that the relationship is not any stronger than it is. Put differently, Adamowski lost significantly in several wards that contained relatively large proportions of Polish residents: the Eleventh, the Twenty-fifth, the Thirty-first, and the Fortieth. Thus we can say that Adamowski was strong in Polish wards, but not all Polish wards went to Adamowski (Table 7). Where the machine was strong, the fact that a

Table 7. Polish Wards Won by Adamowski, 1963.

Polish Wards	Total Number of Wards	Wards Won by Adamowski
10.0 to 14.9 percent Polish	13	9
15.0 to 19.9 percent Polish	3	1
More than 20.0 percent Polish	4	2
Total	20	12

ward was heavily Polish did not seem to help Adamowski. Where the machine was weaker, Polish identity probably had some impact. But across the city as a whole, loyalty to the machine and traditional identity with the Democratic party won out.

THE 1975 PRIMARY

The only other election in which Daley faced serious opposition was in the 1975 Democratic primary, when reform Alderman William Singer challenged the regular Democratic organization. Four years earlier a liberal-reform Democrat, Richard Friedman, had bolted the party and run against Daley as a Republican in the general election. He was defeated soundly. This time the reform faction stayed within the Democratic party and attacked Daley in the primary. It was the first primary challenge Daley had faced in twenty years—since he had defeated Kennelly and Adamowski in 1955. Perhaps Chicago was tiring of the mayor, or the popular base of the machine had eroded in the ensuing twenty years, or Singer was a popular, effective candidate. In any case, the election turned out to be a real contest. Voter interest was also sparked by the candidacy of Richard H. Newhouse, a black, and Edward V. Hanrahan, a breakaway regular Democrat who had been dumped by the organization several years earlier. Daley got the fewest total votes he had received since 1955 and won with the lowest percentage of the total vote since that same 1955 primary.

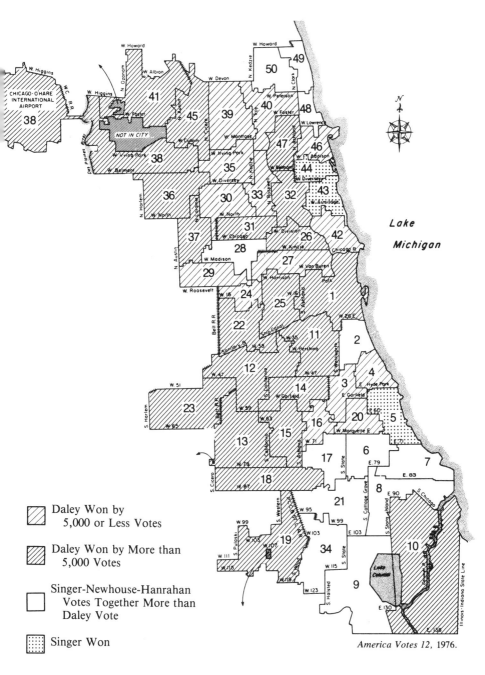

Daley Won by
5,000 or Less Votes

Daley Won by More than
5,000 Votes

Singer-Newhouse-Hanrahan
Votes Together More than
Daley Vote

Singer Won

America Votes 12, 1976.

Map 5. Voting Results in the 1975 Mayoral Primary.

An analysis of those wards in which Singer won outright and those in which the combined Singer-Newhouse-Hanrahan vote was greater than that of the mayor is very illuminating, as is the mayor's vote (Map 5 and Table 8). Singer won the reform Fifth, Forty-third, and Forty-fourth

Table 8. Summary of the 1975 Democratic Mayoral Primary.

Voting Results	Daley	Singer	Newhouse	Hanrahan
Total vote	463,623	234,629	63,489	39,701
Percent of total vote	57.8	29.3	7.9	5.0
Wards won (plurality)	47	3	0	0
Wards won by more than 5,000 votes	21	0	0	0

wards and the combined opposition did well on the North Shore in the Forty-eighth, Forty-ninth, and Fiftieth wards. All of the others in which the Singer-Newhouse-Hanrahan opposition together polled more votes than the mayor were wards with dominant black populations. Across the board, Daley did less well in black wards than he had previously. In 1971 he won by pluralities of more than 5,000 votes in eleven of the fourteen wards that had been at least 66.7 percent black in 1970. Four years later he did not get such pluralities in any of these wards. Both Singer and Newhouse cut into Daley's black support.

MICHAEL BILANDIC AND THE BEGINNINGS OF THE POST-DALEY ERA

When Mayor Richard J. Daley died in December 1976, Chicago had the rare experience of political uncertainty and perhaps even instability. For several days the competing factions jockeyed for power. Then the return to normalcy began. Out of the crowd emerged Michael A. Bilandic, alderman from the deceased mayor's own Eleventh Ward. First, there was the promise that acceptance of the appointment as acting-mayor would carry with it the assurance that Bilandic would not be a candidate for mayor in the special election. Next there was the awkward qualifier that Bilandic would not turn down a draft by the regular Democratic organization. Then Bilandic, as the slated candidate of the party, defeated two major and a host of minor challengers in the Democratic primary. In June Bilandic swamped another token Republican opponent. By September the signs at O'Hare Airport welcoming visitors to the city read "Michael A. Bilandic, Mayor." The transition into the post-Daley era was well under way.

THE 1977 PRIMARY

The story of how Bilandic became the nominee of the Democratic party need not be told here, and the general election in June was so routine that there really is nothing to tell about it, either. The Democratic primary, by contrast, is worth exploring in detail.

Three major candidates competed in the primary: Bilandic, the acting-mayor; Roman Pucinski, a highly visible Polish alderman from the Forty-first Ward; and state Senator Harold Washington, a black from the city's South Side. Singer, Daley's opponent in the 1975 primary, chose to abstain as did other potential reform candidates. Pucinski ran as a machine Pole, a candidate who sought to provide an alternative from *within* the organization. Washington, a Daley supporter in 1975, ran in many ways as a black from *within* the machine. The results of the election, especially when added to the patterns of the 1975 primary, go a long way toward defining the range of options open to electoral politics in Chicago in the years to come.

Perhaps the easiest way to describe the 1977 primary is to say that the organization's handpicked candidate (Bilandic) won with a smaller proportion of the votes than at any time since Daley's first contest for mayor in 1955—51.1 percent; that Washington took a higher percentage than any black candidate for mayor in recent history—10.7 percent; and that Pucinski fell far short of Adamowski's achievement in 1963—only 32.7 percent (Table 9 and Map 6). What happened and why?

Table 9. Summary of the 1977 Primary.

Voting Results	Bilandic	Pucinski	Washington
Total vote	368,400	235,790	77,345
Percent	51.1	32.7	10.7
Total wards won	38	7	5
Wards won by a plurality of more than 5,000 votes	11	3	0

Let us begin with Washington and the city's black wards. Census data from 1970 identify fifteen wards that were at least 50 percent black at that time. In addition, at least one ward—the Ninth at the far southern edge of Chicago—has probably become at least 50 percent black since 1970 (in 1970 it was 28 percent black). Of these sixteen wards, Washington won only five—the Fifth, the Sixth, the Eighth, the Ninth, and the Twenty-first, with 40.0, 42.4, 46.1, 40.8, and 45.5 percent of the total vote, respectively—and received at least 20 percent of the vote in ten of the remaining eleven wards. However, if we split these sixteen wards geo-

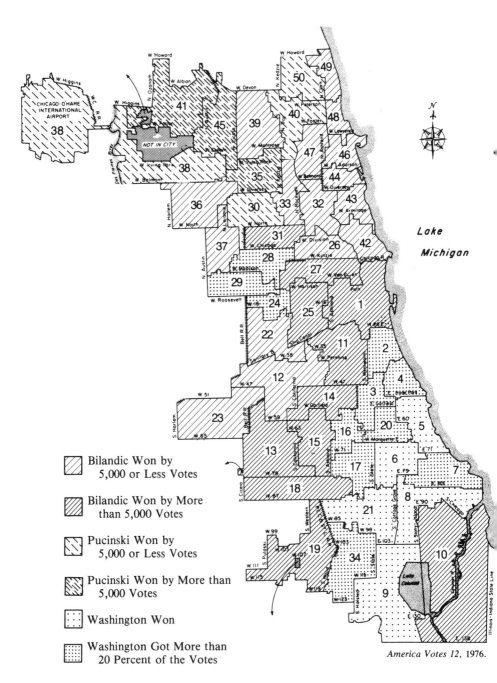

Bilandic Won by
5,000 or Less Votes

Bilandic Won by More
than 5,000 Votes

Pucinski Won by
5,000 or Less Votes

Pucinski Won by More than
5,000 Votes

Washington Won

Washington Got More than
20 Percent of the Votes

America Votes 12, 1976.

Map 6. Voting Results in the 1977 Mayoral Primary.

graphically between those south of the Loop and those to the west, it is clear that Washington's stronghold lay primarily to the south. Thus, geography definitely influenced the impact of the black-consciousness voting in this election.

Pucinski, by contrast, did worse than might have been expected. In 1963, it will be recalled, Adamowski won 44.4 percent of the vote against Daley, carried nineteen wards (eight by more than 5,000 votes), and generally gave the mayor a good run for his money (see again Map 3 for the geography of the Adamowski vote). It is true that most of Pucinski's support came from Polish wards. However, he carried no wards, Polish or otherwise, south of the Loop. Thus, Pucinski's power base was regional not ethnic, more approximating what one author (Key, 1950: 37–41) has called a "friends and neighbors vote." Pucinski was strong on the northwest side of the city. The farther one moves away from Pucinski's home base in the Forty-first Ward, the lower Pucinski's vote. Concentrations of Polish residents on the South Side had little pro-Pucinski impact on their ward votes. South Side Poles, as well as other South Side ethnics, apparently had concerns of greater import than ethnicity (race?). Table 10 shows even more starkly the impact of region versus Polish ethnicity in this election.

Table 10. Impact of Polish Ethnic Concentration Versus City-Region on the 1977 Democratic Primary.

	Wards with at least 10 percent Polish-Speaking	All Other Wards less than 50 percent Black
North[a]	49.3/40.8[b]	38.5/49.6
South-West	28.8/59.3	22.8/61.9

[a]Wards in each cell =
  North/10 percent Polish-Speaking: 26, 30, 31, 32, 33, 35, 36, 38, 41, 45
  North/not 50 percent black: 37, 39, 40, 42, 43, 44, 46, 47, 48, 49, 50
  South-West/10 percent Polish-Speaking: 7, 10, 11, 12, 13, 14, 23
  South-West/not 50 percent black: 1, 15, 18, 19, 22, 25
[b]Top figure in each cell is Pucinski's percentage of the total vote, the bottom figure is Bilandic's.

Bilandic's election in 1977 was hardly an overwhelming success. Bilandic did little better in the North Side, non-Polish wards than Daley had in 1975 against Singer, the liberal reform candidate. He did as well in the black wards as Daley had done two years earlier (certainly a negative qualifier to our preceding analysis of Washington's strength in 1977). Bilandic's real problem, however, was Pucinski. Although Pucinski did not do well, most if not all of his votes came from the ranks of traditional Daley supporters. In 1975 Daley received almost 65 percent of the vote in Polish wards; in 1977 Bilandic took less than 50 percent of the vote in these same wards. However, Bilandic lost votes in most of the other white-dominated wards as well. In sum, none of the major candidates did particularly well in the first post-Daley election.

ELECTORAL BASE OF MACHINE POLITICS IN THE POST-DALEY ERA

The 1975 and 1977 Democratic primaries provide an opportunity to develop an electoral picture of the machine and its citizen base. Because these two elections illustrate voting patterns at times when the machine was seriously challenged, they serve to highlight not only the areas of strength and of weakness for the regular Democratic organization but also the areas where political opposition to the machine is concentrated. These two contests, therefore, permit us to generate a map of the electoral geography of Chicago at the time of the post-Daley transition and to identify the major voting blocs within the city.

We suggest that electoral politics in Chicago in the mid-1970s must be understood in terms of six different area/voter blocs. These are the machine core (wards 1, 11, 25, 27, and 31); the black wards (wards 2, 3, 4, 5, 6, 7, 8, 9, 16, 17, 20, 21, 24, 28, 29, and 34); the reform/North Shore group (wards 40, 43, 44, 46, 48, 49, 50); the "Polish" northwest (wards 30, 32, 33, 35, 36, 38, 39, 41, and 45); the South Side ethnics (wards 10, 12, 13, 14, 15, 18, 19, 22, and 23); and a few white ethnic wards on the North Side (wards 26, 37, 42, and 47). Obviously, in a few cases the placing of a ward, for example the Fifth, into one category (black) rather than another (reform) is a matter of judgment. However, in most instances the classifications seem clear and reliable.

The reason for placing the five wards into the machine core is their geographic location in the middle of the city plus the fact that these were the only wards to go heavily for Daley in 1975 and to vote at least 70 percent for Bilandic two years later. The black wards all had significant black populations; all voted at least 10 percent for Newhouse and at least 20 percent for Washington. The "Polish" northwest wards are not all Polish. However, many did have a minimum of 10 percent Polish foreign-stock residents in 1970. More important, all of these wards on the North Side of the city voted 40 percent or more for Pucinski in 1977. The only two other wards to reach this level of support for Pucinski were the Forty-third and Fiftieth; both of these seem to fit better into the reform/North Shore category. The reform wards were those North Shore areas in which Singer won at least 40 percent in 1975. The last two groupings are those South and North Side wards populated largely by white ethnics, which fall into none of the above categories. The geography of these blocs is shown in Map 7.

This bloc analysis of Chicago electoral politics helps put the successes

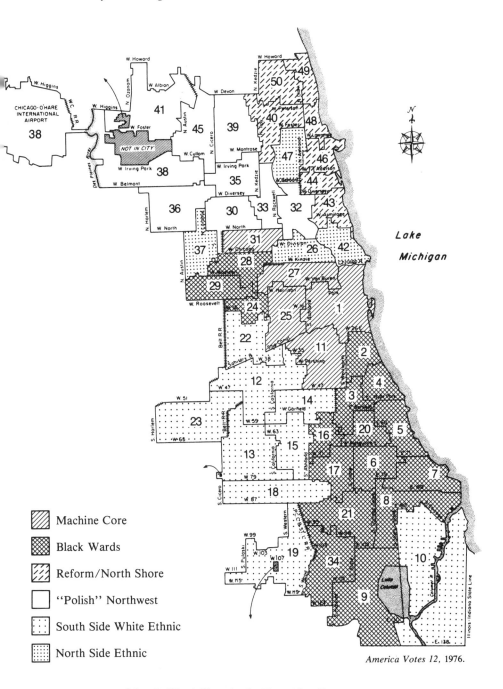

America Votes 12, 1976.

Map 7. Ward Blocs in the Transition Era.

of Mayor Daley and the machine in perspective. The last twenty years
have not seen a monolithic machine crushing a fragmented and terribly
weak opposition. Rather it has seen a relatively stable, but hardly monolithic, coalition of voter blocs uniting for victory in successive electoral
contests. Daley's coalition against Adamowski in 1963 was different
from that which had put him into the mayor's office in 1955. Neither of
these was identical to his coalition against Friedman in 1971. And finally,
Bilandic's coalition, perhaps the most tenuous of all, was like no other
before it. Yet, there are consistencies, and these, we argue, are reflected
roughly in the voter blocs specified above. Each election brought together different combinations of these blocs. When opposition candidates
were weak, the machine took everything. When opposition was stronger,
the machine developed a winning coalition of blocs, while the challenger
constructed a temporary minority alliance. Why did the machine's coalition always win? To begin to answer this question, let us become more
familiar with the social and political character of each bloc of wards
(Table 11).

Hypothetically, if all of the blocs were to unite against an isolated
machine core, the regular Democratic organization would go down to
defeat. As long as the machine kept major allies from among the
blacks—either "Polish" northwest or South Side white ethnics—it continued to win citywide electoral offices. One basic factor preserved the
machine in the face of electoral competition from within the Democratic
party. The machine, largely because of its organizational capacity, won
40 percent of the votes in all of the city's voting blocs. No one else, at
least until 1979, approached that general citywide level of voter support.
Put somewhat differently, the machine was everyone's second choice. If
there had been a widely popular first choice, second would have meant
defeat. Reform candidates were competitive in the reform wards, did
tolerably well in the black wards, and got killed everywhere else. Black
candidates were approaching competitiveness in the black wards, but
were wiped out everywhere else—including in the reform wards. Polish
and other non-machine ethnics cut into machine support in their own
areas but lost badly in the black wards. In sum, blacks did not vote for
Poles, Poles did not vote for blacks, and reform wards seemed to reject
any alternative except a reform candidate. The machine got its 40,000-
vote plurality from its core wards and then let all of the others cancel
each other out.

Thus, the electoral future of the machine rested with the machine itself. As long as its winning candidates continued to govern effectively,
the chances of defeat at the polls were very remote. Even a mayor who
intensified black-white tension could continue to get reelected if he retained the support of the machine's core wards plus a sizable majority of

Table 11. Characteristics of the Ward Blocs.

Voting Category	Number of Wards	Population, 1970	Mean Percent Black, 1970	Mean Percent Polish-Speaking, 1970	Mean Percent White Foreign-Stock, 1970	Mean Ward Turnout, 1975-77 Primaries
Machine Core	5	337,393	34.9	6.4	20.2	15,008
Reform/North Shore	7	471,378	1.8	4.3	39.7	16,043
Blacks	16	1,084,728	80.1	1.5	7.6	11,058
South Side White Ethnics	9	602,774	9.2	11.2	34.4	19,067
"Polish" Northwest	9	601,071	0.6	13.6	40.2	18,486
North Side Ethnics	4	272,015	14.2	7.0	33.0	14,741

Voting Category	Mean Percent Daley, 1975	Mean Percent Bilandic, 1977	Mean Percent Singer, 1975	Mean Percent Pucinski, 1977	Mean Percent Washington, 1977
Machine Core	71.0	73.6	18.8	16.6	6.6
Reform/North Shore	47.3	47.3	45.8	41.6	3.9
Blacks	47.2	46.2	32.3	15.3	34.8
South Side White Ethnics	67.9	58.1	19.4	29.1	6.6
"Polish" Northwest	60.8	40.1	28.7	53.2	0.8
North Side Ethnics	61.2	56.8	27.9	30.5	6.6

either the ethnic or black wards. However, if one could imagine blacks, reformers, and many white ethnics uniting on the same opposition candidate—for whatever reasons—the machine would be in serious trouble. And that is exactly what happened during the winter of 1978-79.

BILANDIC VERSUS BYRNE: 1979

Everyone was surprised when Jane Byrne upset Bilandic in the 1979 Democratic mayoral primary. Her victory, close as it was, represents another step in Chicago's political transition after Daley's death. Whether the people of Chicago wanted to set in motion such major changes is unclear. Unquestionably, they sought to protest both the incapacity of the city to cope with the winter's record snow and cold and Bilandic's refusal to admit that anything was amiss. Of the 809,043 total votes cast, Bilandic received 396,134 (49.0 percent), while Byrne got 412,909 (51.0 percent). In addition, the challenger took twenty-nine of the city's fifty wards.

In the preceding discussion we developed a model of electoral politics in Chicago for the mid-1970s. How useful is this scheme for analyzing the 1979 Democratic primary? Table 12 shows a breakdown of the 1979

Table 12. Ward Vote Patterns in the 1979 Primary.

Voting Category	5,000 Vote Plurality for Bilandic	Majority for Bilandic	Majority for Byrne	5,000 Vote Plurality for Byrne
Machine Core	1	4	0	0
South Side White Ethnics	3	5	1	0
North Side Ethnics	0	3	1	0
"Polish" Northwest	0	4	5	0
Reform/North Shore	0	0	7	0
Blacks	0	1	11	4
Total	4	17	25	4

results based on the six categories of wards identified previously. While the model did not allow us to predict a Byrne victory, the voting patterns in 1979 clearly do make sense within the basic structure presented.

The data necessary for an explanation of the Bilandic-Byrne contest are found in Table 13. The outcome of an election is determined both by the turnout of various constituent groupings and by the proportion of votes each gives to the several candidates. We have divided Chicago into six electoral blocs. How did each of these blocs respond in the Bilandic-Byrne primary? Three general observations appear to tell the story.

Table 13. Comparison of the 1977 and 1979 Democratic Primaries.

Voting Category	Mean Percent for Bilandic[a]		Mean Turnout[a]		Total Plurality for Bilandic		Mean Plurality for Bilandic[a]	
	1977	1979	1977	1979	1977	1979	1977	1979
Machine Core	73.6	69.8	14,840	14,618	38,811	33,200	7,762	6,640
South Side White Ethnics	58.1	56.6	18,907	20,465	28,567	25,945	3,174	2,883
North Side Ethnics	56.8	54.2	13,821	15,186	8,057	5,201	2,014	1,300
"Polish" Northwest	40.1	47.8	18,791	19,213	-40,324	-9,021	-4,480	-1,002
Reform/ North Shore	47.3	40.6	13,687	16,767	-5,794	-22,230	-829	-3,176
Blacks	46.2	38.8	9,775	12,545	-14,431	-49,870	-902	-3,117

[a]Mean for the wards in each category.

First, every voting bloc except the machine core showed an increase in turnout from 1977 to 1979. The average increase per ward was greatest among reform/North Shore and black wards—up 3,080 and 2,770 votes per ward, respectively. But, in descending order, turnout also increased in the South Side white ethnic, the North Side ethnic, and the "Polish" Northwest areas. The five machine core wards, by contrast, were down an average of 222 votes per ward, and the mayor's own Eleventh Ward dropped a total of 549 votes. Overall, more than 65,000 more people voted in the black and reform/North Shore wards in 1979 than in 1977. Across the city as a whole, the additional turnout from 1977 to 1979 was only 88,160. In other words, almost three-quarters of the increase in turnout came in those voting blocs that supported Byrne most heavily.

Second, every voting bloc except the "Polish" Northwest decreased its percentage of support for Bilandic from 1977 to 1979. Again, black and reform/North Shore wards dropped the most—7.4 and 6.7 percentage points, respectively. Even the five machine core wards fell from 73.6 to 69.8 percent for Bilandic, a loss of 3.8 points. By contrast, the "Polish" Northwest, which had gone heavily for Pucinski against Bilandic in 1977, moved back toward the mayor's side of the fence. However, the decrease in "Polish" Northwest vote against Bilandic was not enough to outweigh the other shifts across the city.

Finally, these data indicate that Byrne's victory came from a coalition of voter blocs, not from just one bloc. Blacks alone did not provide the pluralities needed to elect Byrne, nor did the reform/North Shore areas. And without the neutralization of the "Polish" Northwest, neither the black nor the reform/North Shore votes would have been great enough to carry the city. The Byrne victory was earned citywide. The black and reform/North Shore areas together provided the decisive pluralities, but they alone did not elect the winner.

GEOGRAPHY AND ETHNICITY IN THE POST-DALEY ERA

If the geographic patterns described above define the electoral base of mayoral politics in Chicago at the end of the Daley era, what has happened to ethnic politics in the city? Before we suggest some answers to that question, let us identify how ethnic politics has been manifested in the broader arenas of Chicago city politics. For over a century ethnic politics has involved at least three distinct dimensions or arenas of conflict among differing ethnic groups. First, the symbolic dimension of who held the visible public offices, both elected and appointed; second, the grass-roots dimension of electoral support for one party or candidate versus another; and third, the output dimension of who controlled and received the perquisites of power, e.g., jobs, payoffs, contracts, profitable inside information, policy benefits, city services, and the like. Our focus here has been on the second of these, but certainly the other two are also extremely important. Obviously, these three dimensions of ethnic politics interrelate in practice. Dominant electoral blocs support their candidates for public office, and victory at the polls brings the perquisites of power. However, the three must not always be seen as identical, for, in a complex political organization such as the Chicago Democratic machine, electoral support may bring symbolic victories but few, if any, perquisites of office to some groups within the organization while others use the threat of withholding electoral support as the basis for demanding concrete political benefits. In other words, in the organization these three dimensions of ethnic politics can be and often are manipulated separately to meet the political exigencies of the time.

Let us turn now to the first of these dimensions of ethnic politics—who holds public office. As indicated earlier, the struggle for power within the Democratic party in Chicago around 1930 was in large part a conflict over which ethnic group or groups would control the party organization. Cermak's election in 1931 meant not only a shift in the party in power—from Republican to Democratic—but also a shift of ethnic dominance within the Democratic party. Cermak was Czechoslovakian, not Polish or Italian. He took over from the Irish, and, when the Nash-Kelly faction reasserted itself after Cermak's untimely death, the Irish reemerged. The Irish have held the top public offices ever since, excluding Bilandic's brief term in the mayoral office. Below the level of mayor and chairman of the county Democratic central committee, ethnic plurality of a sort has emerged. Rakove (1975: 96) describes the situation as follows:

Putting a ticket together requires taking into consideration the interests of the various groups which make up the local Democratic party. Every ethnic, racial, religious, and economic group is entitled to have some representation on the ticket. Thus, in Chicago, the mayor's job has been an Irish job since 1933. The city clerk's job belongs to the Poles. The city treasurer can be a Jew, a Bohemian, or black. On the county ticket, the county assessor, the state's attorney, and the county clerk must usually be Irish, but the county treasurer, the county superintendent of public schools, or the sheriff can be a member of one of the other ethnic or racial groups. . . . The basic assumption behind building a ticket is that, when the Poles see a Polish name on the ticket, they will vote for the Polish name plus all the other people on the ticket . . . and so on.

How did Mayor Bilandic, a man of Croatian descent, affect the pattern of Irish dominance? Obviously, the forty-year tradition was broken. It is not that there would never be another Irish mayor or even that the Irish had lost an intraparty struggle, much as they did back in the 1930s. Whether Bilandic could have been Polish and still acceptable to the organization is questionable. The Poles are the one white ethnic group that behaves as though it still wants to rule the roost. However, with this exception, Bilandic might well have been from any group—as long as he was loyal to the organization, not likely to change traditional modes of operation, and not black. Geography, again, was more important than ethnicity. Bilandic was Daley's alderman from the Eleventh Ward. He was a trusted lieutenant of the late mayor. After her election, Byrne, while explicit about her own Irish background, was more concerned with destroying the power base of the Eleventh Ward—geographically defined—than with the remnants of ethnic consciousness.

The second dimension of ethnic politics—the electoral base—was analyzed at length in the body of this essay. Briefly summarized, electoral politics in Chicago today appear to be dominated by four factors: first, the general loyalty to and support for the Democratic organization throughout the city and from all kinds of people; second, the racial tension especially in the southern and western areas of the city; third, a residue of self-conscious Polish political identity, which sees itself as a white, intraorganizational alternative to the present leadership faction within the Democratic party; and, finally, a slight hint of anti-organization reformism concentrated north of the Loop and particularly along the North Shore. Here again, except perhaps among some of the Poles, ethnicity per se appears less important than geography, race, and other issues.

Finally, there is the question of real power and the advantages that come from the possession of that power. In earlier days the benefits of power tended to go to those ethnic groups within the dominant intraor-

ganizational coalition that produced at the polls. Today, as ethnicity becomes more latent and geographic patterns more diffuse, ethnic power
and ethnic benefits take on new and more complex forms. Several of the
Democratic organization's strongest wards (e.g., the First, Eleventh,
Twenty-fifth, Twenty-seventh, and Thirty-first) are in ethnic and racial
transition. The Democratic regulars continue to hold power, not for reasons of ethnic loyalty, but because of tradition and organizational effort.
Aldermen and committeemen stay in power because they serve the organization; they also serve the voters, whoever they may be; and they win
elections because it is in the personal interest of the voters to support the
organization that benefits them. In the strong regular organization wards
it is to everyone's benefit for voters to support the organization and its
candidates—except, of course, for members of excluded or manipulated
minorities. This is true even when it means voting against one's ethnic
group. After all, who controls the real benefits of power?

Robert Dahl (1961: 32–36) proposes a three-step sequence for ethnic
politics. The process is tied directly to social assimilation and economic
mobility. Dahl suggests that the final step before the total elimination of
ethnic politics is the latent ethnic consciousness of the assimilated middle-class person. There is much in this idea that parallels our own discussion. However, three factors operating in Chicago in the late 1970s serve
to alter the path of ethnic politics here at this time, in contrast to New
Haven two decades ago: (1) the presence of significant numbers of
working-class families of European descent, who are not upwardly mo-
bile, (2) the Democratic organization, and (3) race. Even when an ethnic
group assimilates through upward mobility, some of its people do not.
What happens to them? Although the old neighborhoods disperse, those
of the group who remain behind retain their ethnic identity and become
more and more vulnerable—both to the loss of their self-image as Polish
or Italian people and to the gains made by newly emerging groups. For
many years the regular Democratic organization in Chicago capitalized
upon this situation by offering ethnic accommodation and personal
benefits. Ethnicity was consciously highlighted; ethnic group representation and participation were encouraged. The organization preserved ethnic identity and protected the status quo for those who were vulnerable
to change in return for control over the perquisites of power. Race is the
confounding factor that challenges the very core of the idea of ethnic assimilation. Race is different from ethnicity in the minds of American
men and women. Middle-class assimilation may have provided a reasonable basis for the patterns of white ethnics in the first half of the twentieth century. It remains to be seen how well it fits black Americans or
Latinos in the second half of this century. Similarly, the politics of ethnic
accommodation practiced by Daley and Bilandic had its foundation in
ethnic plurality, not the numerical superiority of a single, largely ex-

cluded, majority group. All evidence suggests that race, not white ethnicity, will be the crucial factor for the regular Democratic organization in Chicago in the coming decade.

Mayor Byrne's election and first months in office appear to confirm this judgment. Blacks were essential to her victory and probably will be crucial to her successful reelection. If she is opposed by both the old Eleventh Ward/machine core regulars and the blacks, it is unlikely she can win again. Blacks have yet to reach the point where they can elect one of their own, but it is now clear that, when united, they can defeat a candidate who does not have the support of the entire white population. The politics of the post-Daley era remain in flux. Jane Byrne still has to prove that she will be the city's future.

NOTES

1. Spearman's Rho comparing the rank order of the seven white ethnic groups listed in Table 1 between 1900–50 is 0.25. This was well below the level necessary to show a statistically significant relationship between the two rank orderings.
2. Some would dispute the size of the ethnic populations reported here on the grounds that the census bureau category "foreign stock" does not reflect the total number of "ethnic" or "ethnic-identifying" persons in Chicago (see Kantowicz, 1975: 228); however, for the general survey presented here, these numbers provide sufficient estimates of the relative size of particular groups.
3. If we include all Spanish-speaking peoples within Chicago in 1970, the official figure becomes 247,343 or 7.3 percent of the total population (Department of Development and Planning, 1973: 1).
4. Census bureau numbers are for the category of "foreign stock."
5. Adamowski first contested a public office as a Republican in 1956 (Rakove, 1975: 150).

REFERENCES

Allswang, John M. 1971. *A House for All Peoples*. Lexington: University of Kentucky Press.
Banfield, Edward C. 1961. *Political Influence*. New York: Free Press.
Dahl, Robert A. 1961. *Who Governs?* New Haven, Conn.: Yale University Press.
Department of Development and Planning. 1973. *Chicago's Spanish-Speaking Population*.
———. 1976a. *Chicago's Irish Population*.
———. 1976b. *The People of Chicago*.
———. 1976c. *The Settlement of Chicago*.
Gosnell, Harold F. 1937. *Machine Politics: Chicago Model*. Chicago: University of Chicago Press. Rev. ed., 1968.
Gottfried, Alex. 1962. *Boss Cermak of Chicago*. Seattle: University of Washington Press.
Kantowicz, Edward R. 1975. *Polish-American Politics in Chicago, 1888-1940*. Chicago: University of Chicago Press.
Kennedy, Eugene E. 1978. *Himself*. New York: Viking Press.

Key. V. O., Jr. 1950. *Southern Politics in State and Nation.* New York: Alfred
    A. Knopf.
Merton, Robert K. 1961. "The Functions of the Political Machine," pp.158–67
    in S. Ulmer. ed., *Introductory Readings in Political Behavior.* Chicago:
    Rand McNally.
Meyerson, M., and Edward C. Banfield. 1955. *Politics, Planning, and the Public
    Interest.* New York: Free Press.
O'Connor, Len. 1975. *Clout.* New York: Avon.
Rakove, Milton. 1975. *Don't Make No Waves, Don't Back No Losers.* Bloom-
    ington: Indiana University Press.
————. 1979. *We Don't Want Nobody Nobody Sent.* Bloomington: Indiana
    University Press.
Royko, Mike. 1971. *Boss.* New York: Signet.
Wendt, Lloyd, and H. Kogan. 1967. *Bosses in Lusty Chicago.* Chicago: Bobbs-
    Merrill.

WILLIAM J. GRIMSHAW

The Daley Legacy: A Declining Politics of Party, Race, and Public Unions

CHICAGO'S POLITICS CONSTITUTE the exceptional case. So goes the conventional wisdom (for example, Lowi: 1968), although some reservations recently have been entered. Other big-city political machines have been unable to withstand a series of devastating developments. The reform movement dealt a mortal blow to many, and the civil rights movement finished off several others. The remaining machines found they were hardly better able to cope with insurgent public employee unions. Fiscal crises and increased dependency on intergovernmental aid and regulations put the final nails in each machine's coffin, if any nailing remained to be done. Yet through it all the Chicago machine under the leadership of Richard J. Daley appeared to persist as an exceptionally powerful and unfettered political party. Hence the fascination with Chicago's politics following Daley's death. Can the last of the great urban political machines survive the fall of its colossus?

The question is interesting and even significant, but it is difficult to answer, and more difficult still to answer in a fruitful way. For although several studies have been made of Chicago's politics, not much is known concerning just how and to what extent the city's politics are exceptional. Benchmarks, particularly of a comparative kind, are lacking. The studies have been primarily exotic treatments of the case-study variety. The unusual, the grand, and occasionally the bizarre have been accentuated.[1] Excessive reliance, furthermore, has been placed on interview data gathered from among the clout-heavy members of the city's political establishment.[2] The studies have also tended to treat the city's politics in an essentially static manner, either ignoring time and change or treating them unsystematically, thereby suggesting that little of significance had been altered during the twenty-one tumultuous years of Daley's reign.[3] So it is difficult to determine how much things have changed since Daley's death, and it is equally difficult to determine how much things in Chicago differ—now as well as before—from big-city politics elsewhere.

What is needed are more precise and reliable indicators of the Chicago political party's effectiveness, more information on how the party's effectiveness has held up over the years. Moreover, this should be done in such a way that Chicago's politics can usefully be compared with the politics of other big cities.

As a step in this direction, we shall examine some of the major developments that have occurred along three dimensions representing some of the severest problems the big-city political parties have had to confront during the past three decades: the maintenance of party organizational strength, the retention of black political support, and the containment of influence of public employee unions on political and governmental matters. This satisfies the comparative criteria, inasmuch as the Chicago party's effectiveness will be assessed in terms of coping with problems common to all urban political parties. In turn, we shall better meet the criteria of reliability and precision by making the assessment with electoral and similar forms of data, rather than by relying on interviews and other judgmental information. Finally, the analysis will span the length of Daley's mayoral term and the subsequent terms of mayors Michael Bilandic and Jane Byrne. This will inform us about how the party has fared over time and indicate just what changes have occurred and when.

In the process we hope to gain a clearer understanding of what may be termed the Daley legacy. To anticipate the analysis, in order to provide a framework for it, the three dimensions we shall examine—party strength, black support, and public union influence—covary to a remarkable degree. This enables the specification of three stages of the Chicago political party's effectiveness. During the first decade of Daley's reign, 1955-65, the party functioned very much like a classic political machine. The party was at the zenith of its strength, black electoral support for the party was solid, and public employee unionization was held firmly in check. By the mid-sixties, however, the first signs of deterioration had begun to appear, and they emerged along all three dimensions. The party's organizational strength showed the first earmarks of slippage, black voters displayed their first signs of discontent with the party, and Daley approved his first collective-bargaining agreement (and that with the city's largest public employee union, the teachers). Throughout the 1970s deterioration along all three fronts grew progressively worse.

The legacy left by Daley, then, was a declining politics of party, race, and public unions. This is not to say, of course, that Bilandic and Byrne have not made their own contributions to the party's decline. They certainly have. For one thing, Bilandic virtually drove black voters out of the party and into the camp of the independent mayoral challenger, Byrne. Byrne, in turn, is badly mishandling another traditional ally of the party, organized labor, disillusioning large numbers of black voters,

and creating potential opponents out of party hacks. Where the party
and its reenergized erstwhile allies are headed is obviously unclear at this
point. But it is important to recognize that the party began its decline and
shift in direction well before Daley's demise, and the course set for the
party during Daley's latter years is not likely to be easily altered now.[4]

THE CLASSIC POLITICAL MACHINE: 1955–65

PARTY ORGANIZATIONAL STRENGTH

A classic political machine relies for its maintenance on three basic
factors. It depends on the inner city voters to provide an exceptionally
high and consistent degree of support for all of the machine's candidates
for office. A second monopoly is also vital: control over the party's primary elections—and in this instance, control throughout the city. A classic political machine also depends on, and typically produces, a huge
vote for all of its candidates. According to these three criteria the
Chicago Democratic party began to function as a classic machine shortly
after Daley became mayor in 1955.

It merits recognition that the Daley party did not begin as a classic political machine; one chief characteristic was lacking. The Daley party was
able to produce a classically large vote from the outset, and the degree of
party support from the inner city was formidable indeed. However, the
party noticeably lacked the capability of monopolizing its all-important
primary elections. Reflecting the party's scandal-induced, brief fling
with a semblance of reform, in order to gain office Daley had to overcome the most difficult primary election challenge of his career in the
form of the popular, reform-oriented, and two-term incumbent Mayor
Martin Kennelly. The strength of Kennelly's challenge to the machine is
indicated by the twenty wards he managed to carry. In the subsequent
general election the Republican candidate, Robert Merriam, carried
twenty-one of the city's fifty wards, drawing on the same outlying middle-class areas of the city for his support.[5]

Daley's first two mayoral elections point up another cardinal characteristic of classic machine politics. The fundamental political division in
the city was socioeconomic. The "little man" in the inner city gave his
support to the machine, while middle-class voters residing in the outlying
areas of the city lined up solidly against the machine. The conflict existed
at the time within the Democratic party as well as along party lines. Both
Kennelly and Merriam geared their campaigns to attract the city's middle-class voters. But the strategy was virtually a preordained failure:
Chicago lacked a sufficient supply of such voters.

The principal task facing the early Daley party was well defined by the election returns. In order to secure internal and external stability, the party had to reduce the influence of the city's reform-oriented forces. The party's success is well reflected by the fact that not until twenty years later was Daley even moderately challenged by a reform candidate from within the ranks of the Democratic party, namely the lakefront liberal William Singer. The Republicans never again were able to field another reformer with any significant degree of backing to challenge Daley.[6] So, virtually as soon as Daley assumed office, the party began functioning as a classic political machine, and the party experienced no further opposition from the machine's classic enemy, the reformers.

The critical role played by the inner-city wards during the Daley party's first decade is shown by the returns from Daley's first three mayoral elections (Table 1). Map 1 graphically illustrates that the party's

Table 1. The Classic Inner-City Machine, 1955-63: Daley's Top Fifteen Plurality-Producing Wards.

Rank	Ward	Rank	Ward
1	24	9	25
2	11	10	4
3	29	11	31
4	2	12	26
5	3	13	14
6	1	14	6
7	27	15	16
8	20		

SOURCE. Grimshaw (1979).
NOTE. The wards were ranked separately for each election—1955, 1959, and 1963—and then combined into a composite score.

primary support base consisted of a contiguous cluster of inner-city wards.

As for the question of monopolizing the primary elections in general terms, J. David Greenstone and Paul Peterson (1968) analyzed state representative Democratic primary elections in Chicago for 1958 to 1964. Their findings amply justify characterizing the early Daley party as a classic political machine. In almost 80 percent of the primaries the party's candidates went unchallenged. Slating by the party was thus virtually tantamount to election. Even when opposition did surface, it constituted only a nominal threat. Only 8 percent of the challengers received as much as 20 percent of the vote, and in no instance did a challenger's vote exceed 39 percent. The early Daley machine's monopoly was absolute.

The early Daley party's ability to produce a sizable vote was also of classic proportion. From 1955 to 1965 the party produced its two largest

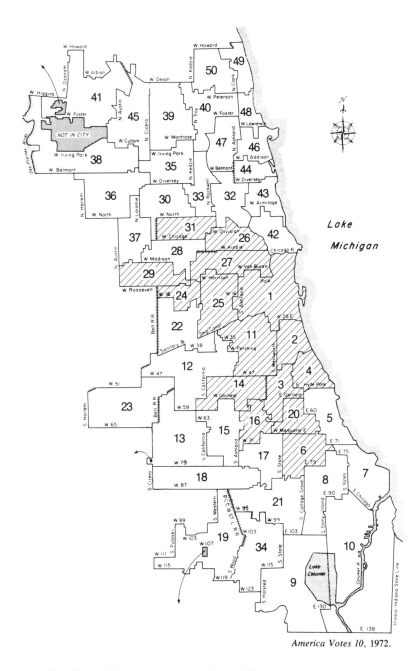

America Votes 10, 1972.

Map 1. The Classic Machine's Primary Base of Support: 1955–63. (Boundaries of these wards are as of 1970.)

presidential votes. John Kennedy's Chicago vote in 1960 tipped the one million mark, and four years later the Daley party produced an even larger vote for Lyndon Johnson: 1,141,148.

In all three respects, then—inner-city support, primary election control, and vote productivity—the Daley party functioned as a classic machine during its first decade. Rarely challenged and less rarely beaten, the party was at the zenith of its strength during its early years.

BLACK ELECTORAL SUPPORT

It is a commonplace among students of Chicago's politics that black voters were instrumental in putting Daley over the top in his first mayoral election. What is far less widely recognized, however, is that Daley's 1955 election constituted a critical turning point in the city's black politics. Prior to 1955 the city's black voters had been ardent supporters of the national Democratic ticket. Indeed, black voting percentages for Democratic presidential candidates had moved from 51 percent in 1940 steadily upward to 76 percent in 1952. At the same time, however, black voters had remained decidedly mixed in their evaluation of the local Democratic party. In 1939, 56 percent of the city's black electorate cast Democratic mayoral ballots, but then the Democratic edge fell to a bare 52 percent and remained at this level through the 1951 mayoral election.

The unprecedented outpouring of black support for Daley's mayoral candidacy in 1955 thus terminated a tradition of remarkably sophisticated split-ticket voting in the black community. Black voters finally had become local as well as national Democrats, and the shift was awesome. In the 1951 mayoral election the average black ward plurality for the Democratic nominee had been 931 votes. In 1955 Daley carried the black wards on average by nearly 12,000 votes. Table 2 tells the tale.

Once they entered the local Democratic fold, black voters remained consistently enthusiastic in their support of the party throughout the first

Table 2. Black Voting in Mayoral and Presidential Elections in Chicago: 1939–56.

Year	Mayoral Democratic Percentage	Presidential Democratic Percentage	Wards
1939/40	56	51	2
1943/44	52	63	2
1947/48	52	72	2
1951/52	52	76	2, 3
1955/56	77	65	2, 3, 20

SOURCE. Grimshaw (1980).

decade of the Daley administration. Indeed, in the only strong challenge to Daley's leadership—besides the initial ones by Kennelly and Merriam—that of Benjamin Adamowski in 1963, black voters proved to be the only voting bloc in the city that remained steadfast in their support of the beleaguered mayor.

Adamowski's challenge differed fundamentally from the ones by Kennelly and Merriam. Kennelly and Merriam had played for and received the great bulk of their support from the city's outlying middle-class wards. In turn, Daley had turned back both challenges with tremendous pluralities from the machine's primary base of support in the inner city. Adamowski's bid, in sharp contrast, cut heavily into all of the white wards making up the machine's inner-city stronghold of support.

Adamowski even cut into Daley's vote in the mayor's own Eleventh Ward. In 1959 Daley's plurality in the Eleventh Ward had been 16,355; against Adamowski it fell off to 10,685, a decline of 35 percent. The machine's other white inner-city wards lacked the "home town boy" element to offset Adamowski's appeal, and they accordingly experienced even more precipitous declines in their production of pluralities. Thomas Keane's invariably reliable Thirty-first Ward had its plurality for Daley cut in half, falling from 14,945 in 1959 to 7,503 in 1963. The equally reliable and formidable Fourteenth Ward, which bordered on Daley's Eleventh Ward, fell a phenomenal 67 percent, from 12,615 to 4,141. In addition to his extraordinary inroads into the machine's inner-city base, Adamowski carried eighteen of the city's outlying wards.

Accordingly, Daley's reliance on the black wards was greater than it ever had been, and, as it happened, the black wards came through for Daley as they never had before. Only five wards in the city increased their 1963 plurality for Daley over their 1959 performance, and four of the five were black. The three top plurality-producing wards in the city for Daley were black: the Third, the Twenty-fourth, and the Twentieth. These three were followed closely by the black Second and Fourth wards, which respectively ranked fifth and seventh. Through the hard times as well as the easy, then, no voting bloc in the city supported Daley in particular and the party in general better than black voters. Thus, in the space of a single decade, the city's black voters had indeed made a remarkable turnabout.

PUBLIC UNION INFLUENCE

The low estate of public employee unions in Chicago's politics is still another indication of the extent of the classic political machine's dominance during this period. No opposition to its hegemony was tolerated. Yet Chicago long has been properly regarded as a labor town, and organized labor, principally through the Chicago Federation of Labor, carries considerable influence within the city's political establishment. The city's endlessly elaborate, highly restrictive, and cost-escalating building code testifies to the considerable strength of organized labor, as do the guarantee of a prevailing wage for unionists in the city's employ and a labor presence on so many of the city's boards and commissions. From organized labor's point of view, Chicago is indeed the city that works.

It might be expected, then, that the city's public unions would have been in the vanguard of the public union movement for collective-bargaining rights that swept the country during the 1960s. Nothing could be further from the truth. While Daley did set aside some venerable traditions when he became mayor in 1955, replacing the handshake agreement in favor of a formal contract was not among them. The role of organized labor in the city's politics can be better appreciated by recognizing that one of the main reasons why Daley was able to keep the public unions in check was that there was little pressure exerted on him by organized labor to do otherwise.

The national AFL-CIO leadership often has acknowledged the limits of its influence by lamenting that "labor works a little differently in Chicago." One reason for the difference is a keenly developed understanding and respect for turf rights—perhaps because the labor leaders grew up in the old Chicago neighborhoods, which in many respects resembled sovereign nations. In his book on politics and labor J. David Greenstone (1968) roots the Chicago machine's success in its granting of exclusive rights over the domain encompassed by their interests to the city's major interest groups. This, of course, works both ways, and few interest groups in the city are willing to deny, much less make it stick, that the machine's claims on turf take precedence over all other claims. So it is that the Chicago Federation of Labor has displayed scant interest in contesting the machine for the loyalties and dues of the city's public employees. Since patronage is integral to the machine's survival interests and city employees constitute the bulk of the patronage, the machine's claims over city employees must take precedence.

It is not merely veneration for tradition or even coercion, though, that restrains organized labor from putting in a claim on the vast source of potential membership. The machine also takes excellent care of organized labor's interests. It is more a matter of accommodation and bargaining than coercion that keeps labor in line. Like many another conservative, Chicago labor supports the status quo for material rather than for sentimental reasons.

To a great extent this is true of several of the city's public employee groups. The salaries paid by Chicago generally rank near the top nationally, indicating that while a handshake from Daley may not confer the dignity labor desires, it has its compensations.[7] Of course, given the machine's influence in the city's agencies, for those employees who do prefer freedom over luxurious captivity, the organizing task is made difficult in more ways than one.

THE MACHINE IN TRANSITION: 1966-69

Organizational Strength and Black Support

A critical shift in the city's politics emerged during the mid-1960s, and, because party organizational strength and black electoral support are closely intertwined in the development, the two dimensions are considered together. The shift involves a change in the shape rather than the magnitude of the machine's organizational strength. The shift is of additional significance for its portent of greater changes to come. It may be said that the die are cast here. The classic shape of the machine begins to disintegrate, although the party remains basically intact and still formidably strong.

By comparing the 1967 mayoral election returns with Daley's preceding mayoral elections, one can detect the critical nature of the shift in the city's politics. Previously, the fundamental political division in the city had been along party lines, and the divide was based on socioeconomic differences. The lower classes residing in the inner-city wards constituted the main support of the Democratic machine; the outlying middle-class wards formed the backbone of the Republican party and independent challenges. Daley's elections against Kennelly and Merriam reflect the division in its classic form. Even Adamowski's challenge in 1963 demonstrated the division when he carried eighteen of the city's outlying wards. That Adamowski also ran well in the machine's white inner-city stronghold indicated for the first time that something unusual was afoot.

The 1967 mayoral election clarifies the nature of the shift. During the three preceding mayoral elections, the city's black wards invariably ranked among Daley's best plurality producers. In 1963 no voting bloc in the city provided Daley with greater support; all five of the black wards said to have been controlled by "Boss" William Dawson ranked among the top ten plurality-producers in that election. By contrast, only two of the Dawson wards remained among the top fifteen plurality-producers in the 1967 election. Even more significant, all four of the wards that were displaced among the top fifteen plurality-producing wards were black, and their replacements in each instance were white middle-class wards located on the edges of the city.

For the first time, then, the black electorate manifested discontent with the Daley machine. No less remarkable, the city's middle-class voters gave the machine an unprecedented measure of support. The significance of the shift is this: race had begun to replace class and party as the city's basic political division. So while the machine finally had won over its traditional enemy, the middle-class voter, in the process it acquired a new foe, the black voter. Map 2 and Table 3 provide details of the emerging transformation.

Table 3. The Disintegrating Classic Machine, 1966–69: Daley's Top Fifteen Plurality-Producing Wards.

Rank	Ward	Among 1955–65 Top Fifteen Wards	Rank	Ward	Among 1955–65 Top Fifteen Wards
1	50	No	9	40	No
2	11	Yes	10	26	Yes
3	3	Yes	11	49	No
4	27	Yes	12	20	Yes
5	25	Yes	13	18	No
6	29	Yes	14	1	Yes
7	24	Yes	15	14	Yes
8	31	Yes			

SOURCE. Grimshaw (1979).

As for the second distinguishing characteristic of a classic political machine—control of the primary election—two similarly small but portentous changes occurred between 1966 and 1969. During the Daley party's first decade an absolute monopoly had been maintained over state legislative offices; a similar monopoly had been maintained over federal legislative offices. In 1966 the party's state legislative office monopoly was finally broken; two years later the party also lost its monopoly over the city's congressional offices.

Running on the slogan, "A Vote for Chew is a Vote for You," a black independent senatorial candidate cracked the machine's lock on state office. Charles Chew's slogan indicates the racial appeal he made to swing black voters away from the machine. Two years later a machine renegade, Abner Mikva, who had held a state representative seat, ran against an elderly machine congressman and defeated him. Neither victory proved to have any long-term significance, however. Upon winning, Chew joined forces with the machine, while Mikva became the victim of redistricting, which forced him to move to a suburban district in order to retain his congressional seat.

Yet in another sense, the two victories were quite significant. They destroyed the myth that "you can't beat city hall." The victories set the stage for a large number of subsequent challenges to the machine, and, as

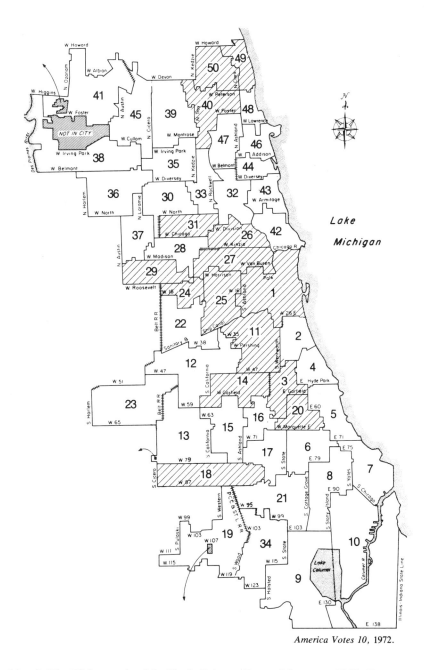

America Votes 10, 1972.

Map 2. The Disintegrating Machine's Primary Base of Support: 1966–69.
(Boundaries of these wards are as of 1970.)

we shall see, a number of the challenges in the 1970s were successful. By going against Committeeman Bernie Neistein's advice, "don't back no losers," the machine was to pay a heavy price throughout the seventies.[8] As for the size of the vote—the third characteristic of a classic political machine—the machine's fortunes were mixed. Presidential candidate Hubert Humphrey's Chicago vote was well below the one million mark that the party had provided for both Kennedy and Johnson, coming in at 874,113. But a part of the falloff can be attributed to the Humphrey candidacy, saddled as it was with the increasingly unpopular Vietnam war and the Chicago Democratic convention atrocities.

Daley's 1967 mayoral election performance is a further indication that a portion of the Humphrey vote falloff can be discounted. Daley's vote of 792,283 in 1967 represents the largest vote he ever received. Since the Republican candidate in 1967 presented only a token challenge, the vote can best be compared to Daley's 1959 election, a year in which the Republicans fielded another token candidate. That year Daley received 778,612 votes. Thus, while the Daley party had some difficulty delivering for Humphrey, no problem existed in regard to its main concern, reelecting Daley.

PUBLIC UNION INFLUENCE

A further indication that the Daley machine's iron grip on the city's politics was loosening occurred in 1966 when the mayor approved his first major public employee collective-bargaining agreement. The recipients of the good fortune were the teachers, the city's largest public employee group. While the mayor did not have formal jurisdiction over the schools, he did appoint school board members, and it was clear that Daley's informal approval was needed to effect the change. The following description by a board member at the time indicates just how much influence Daley carried with the school board: "All the good board members who normally vote as a block with the establishment were adamant against granting the union the right of collective bargaining. . . . In addition to wanting more money, they also wanted the right to hold an election to determine the sole bargaining agent. Bill Lee [president of the Chicago Federation of Labor] and one or two other top leaders very closely identified with the so-called 'power structure' of this city, were sent over to the Board meeting, and those Board members who were adamant against granting the union this right changed just like that" (Bacon, 1968: 167).

Here again it became clear that race was occupying an increasingly central role in the city's politics. In fact, racial conflict was at the bottom of the collective-bargaining development. The city's public schools were engulfed in racial turmoil at the time, and the turmoil grew increasingly worse as Superintendent Benjamin Willis persisted in his refusal to take any steps to integrate the schools or to equalize the distribution of school resources. By 1966 the racial strife had become so severe that it was spilling over into the city's politics and upsetting the political machine's delicately balanced biracial constituency. Then, just when Daley finally decided to enter the fray and appeared to be restoring order by arranging to dump Willis, the Chicago Teachers Union voted to strike unless the teachers were granted bargaining rights. The timing of this threat gave the union bargaining leverage that it had never before possessed.

The issue of racial strife was complicated by strife within the teacher union. For it was not the elected leadership of the union that was applying the strike pressure, but a radical faction, bent upon acquiring not only bargaining rights for the teachers but also leadership of the union. The narrow strike vote (90–80) by the union's delegate body indicated that the radicals were on the verge of ousting the conservative union leadership and setting the union on a more militant course.

Daley had a difficult decision to make. On the one hand, maintaining the status quo seemed to offer a low short-term risk, which would place the burden of pulling off an unprecedented strike on the radical faction, who could not expect any support in their effort from the city's conservative, machine-connected organized labor groups. Yet even a moderately successful strike would plunge the schools back into controversy, and the strike action would provide the radicals with a stronger platform for replacing the union's conservative leadership, making matters worse in the long term. Finally, there was no guarantee that the radicals would not escalate the conflict by adding the issue of race to their agenda, and the machine's leadership was determined to shelve that matter.

On the other hand, granting the teachers bargaining rights meant taking a step in a direction that the machine's leadership was equally determined not to take: setting the precedent for turning over the city's agencies and, worse yet, their personnel to the unions. While the teachers were no longer under the machine's patronage system of employment, virtually every other group of public employees was. Collective bargaining for the city's employees had to be resisted at all costs. Giving in to the teachers meant that every other public employee group would be demanding equal justice, and that could mean the end of the machine: no patronage, no machine.

Daley's decision to risk the dangerous precedent probably hinged on two considerations. Since the teachers were not a part of the machine's patronage system, giving the teachers bargaining rights did not constitute a loss of political workers, as would be the case with the city's other employee groups. Indeed, Daley may well have reasoned that granting the teachers a generous series of material benefits through collective bargaining would reduce their political independence. Material benefits would serve in place of patronage to secure the teachers' loyalties. In this regard the union did indeed come around. The Chicago Teachers Union gave Daley endorsements for reelection in 1967 and 1971—a jolt to some of the older teachers, who could recall when the union had been in the vanguard of the city's reform movement.

The other factor Daley probably banked on was the conservative leadership of the teachers' union. If it continued to bargain and behave in its traditional deferential style, the leadership would effectively blunt the edge of the bargaining weapon. There was reason to suppose that the leadership of the union would defer to the machine's leadership. At the time Daley was reaching a decision on the bargaining issue, the union's leadership was preparing to overturn the action of the delegates. It declared that the close vote favoring a strike for bargaining rights was the unrepresentative result of intimidation and packing the delegate meeting by a small band of radicals. The leadership intended to reverse the action of the delegates by polling the union's membership. But before the union leadership could act, Daley moved, and the leadership had collective bargaining thrust upon it.

If that was Daley's strategy, it certainly worked well initially. The first two collective-bargaining sessions ended in deadlock, and Daley was called upon to mediate in both cases. In turn, since a majority of the school board members was willing to defer to Daley, as was the leadership of the union, both mediations proceeded promptly and smoothly. This meant that the mayor was perceived by the public as an excellent mediator and by the teachers as the instrument of their good fortune. Thus, Daley and the teachers were benefiting from collective bargaining.

However, a flaw in the strategy surfaced three years later, in 1969. After producing two good contracts, the leadership settled for a third that contained no salary increase. It accepted the school board's position that there were no funds available to finance any increases. The union's delegate body, however, was unwilling to accept the board's argument. It rejected the leadership's proposed settlement and, again against the leadership's decision, went down before the state legislature to lead a mass demonstration for more state aid to Chicago schools. This action was capped by a strike that began as Daley was in the process of mediating still a third deadlock.

The teachers' strike managed to accomplish what both its detractor, the union's leadership, and its supporter, a majority of the union's delegates, said it would. Daley produced a settlement after the strike had run only a day; it was another generous one for the union. However, the union wound up losing a crucial aspect of Daley's support in its future negotiations with the school board. When Daley mediated these first three deadlocks, he accepted the responsibility of securing the additional funds required to float the settlements, thereby eliminating the deficits created by the settlements. Thereafter, while he continued to mediate when called upon to do so, he refused to accept the responsibility of securing the necessary funds.

Daley's refusal to perform the fetcher role any longer left the teacher union's leadership in a difficult position. The school board would obviously adopt a much tougher bargaining stance without Daley's willingness to bail the board out, and the board had not been an easy bargainer to begin with, as the three deadlocks demonstrated. This meant that the union leadership would have to adopt a much more militant bargaining posture in order to secure both the benefits and its position within the union. But that course of action would bring the leadership into conflict with Daley and the political machine, which the deferential leadership so far had been anxious to avoid.

To the extent that the union was willing to maintain a militant bargaining stance, the board was in an even worse position than the union. Just because Daley had set aside his financial responsibility did not mean he could ignore his political obligation to favor the union at the board's expense. This surely left the school board with a serious problem, for any deficits that developed were not likely to be easily eliminated without Daley's aid. But then Daley and the machine had problems of their own, which were much tougher. As Daley once informed the state legislature when it contended there were insufficient funds to support a program he sought: "You can make a budget say whatever you want it to say."[9] But votes are not so easily manipulated. That takes real money, and the teachers had quickly grown accustomed to receiving their share. Thus, political expediency led to budgetary gimmickry.

THE NEW POLITICAL PARTY: 1970–80

PARTY ORGANIZATIONAL STRENGTH

The Daley machine's organizational strength had experienced a moderate decline during the transition period of the late 1960s. During the 1970s the decline reached such proportions that by mid-decade the party no longer bore any of the basic characteristics of a classic political machine. Today the party no longer possesses a solid bloc of inner-city wards that can be relied upon to produce massive pluralities for any and all of the party's candidates. The party is no longer able to maintain any semblance of monopoly control over primary elections. As for the tremendous vote the classic machine had once been able nearly invariably to deliver, the new party is often hard pressed to produce a sizable vote, even under the best of circumstances.

The composition of the new party's primary base of support clearly indicates the extent to which race replaced class and party as the central division in the city's politics during the 1970s. Whereas the classic machine had relied on a contiguous mass of black and white low-income inner-city wards for its primary support, the new party receives the vast bulk of its support from the city's most racially threatened white wards. Over one-half of the party's new base of support comes from the southwest side, an area of the city in the most direct competition with blacks for housing, employment, and schooling. The bulk of the city's black population is located to the east of the area, and over the years blacks gradually and with considerable difficulty have been moving westward. Table 4, listing the new party's primary support wards, and Map 3 reflect

Table 4. The New Party, 1970–79: The Mayor's Top Fifteen Plurality-Producing Wards.

Rank	Ward	Among 1955–65 Top Fifteen Wards	Rank	Ward	Among 1955–65 Top Fifteen Wards
1	11	Yes	9	38	No
2	13	No	10	15	No
3	36	No	11	19	No
4	12	No	12	10	No
5	18	No	13	27	Yes
6	31	Yes	14	26	Yes
7	14	Yes	15	45	No
8	23	No			

SOURCE. Chicago Board of Election Commissioners.

how the Daley machine in 1970 attempted to dilute black voting strength by creating a fascinating variety of strangely shaped wards along what then was the South Side's racial dividing line. The narrow stretch of the Eighteenth Ward resembles a bowling lane, while wards Fourteen and Fifteen look like jigsaw-puzzle pieces.

The party's other classic machine characteristic—monopolization of party primary elections—also underwent a radical transformation during the 1970s. The party that once held complete control over its primaries for the state legislature has now been challenged in nearly all of the city's twenty legislative districts; half of the challenges have been successful. Independent candidates have won in ten legislative districts, and in three of these the independent challengers have captured the senate seat as well.[10]

That the southwest side has become the primary support base of the

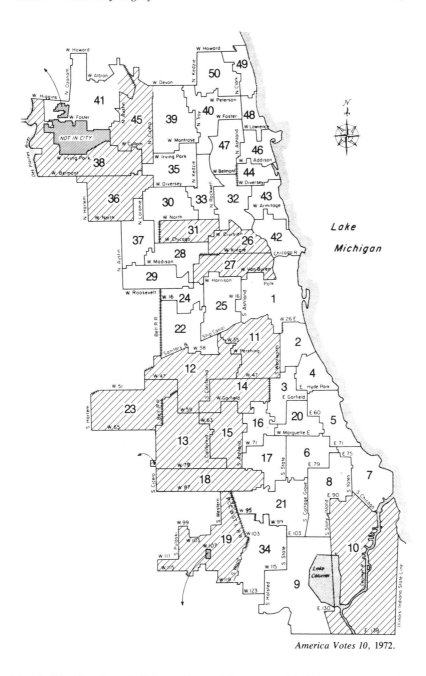

America Votes 10, 1972.

Map 3. The New Party's Primary Base of Support: 1970–79. (Boundaries of these wards are as of 1970.)

new political party is confirmed by legislative election data. Of the four legislative districts where the party has remained unchallenged, three are located on the southwest side of the city. Thus, the mayoral and state legislative evidence indicate that the new party finds its most loyal supporters in the most racially troubled white area of the city.

Even in vote size—the third aspect of a classic political machine—the 1970s data indicate radical changes. Whereas the Daley machine produced massive votes in nearly all of the major elections throughout the 1950s and 1960s, the new party is unable to produce anywhere near as large a vote even under excellent circumstances. Table 5 indicates the break that has developed in the mayoral election pattern.

Table 5. Voting in Mayoral Elections: 1955–79.

Year	Mayoral Candidates		Wards with less than 10,000 Democratic votes
	Democrat	Republican	
1955	708,222	581,555	2
1959	778,612	311,940	none
1963	679,497	540,705	5
1967	792,283	272,542	none
1971	740,137	315,969	3
1975	542,817	139,335	26
1977	490,688	135,282	32
1979	700,874	137,664	5

SOURCE. Chicago Board of Election Commissioners.

Clearly, the 1975 election—Daley's last—represents a major turning point in the party's productivity. Not only did Daley's vote fall off by nearly 200,000, but over half of the city's fifty wards failed for the first time to produce what once had been a standard 10,000 or more votes. The decline was as widespread as it was large. Daley's successor, Michael Bilandic, was unable to stop the decline. His vote fell off an additional 50,000, and this time nearly two-thirds of the city's wards failed to deliver the once standard 10,000 plus votes. His second time out, in the Democratic primary, produced the new party's well-known disaster at the hands of Jane Byrne.

Byrne's victory in 1979 should not be read as the return of the party's vote-producing ability. Quite the contrary. Her victory, both in terms of numbers and breadth of support, showed that there were large numbers of Democratic votes in the city that neither Daley nor Bilandic had been able to attract. The black wards, for example, formed one-third of Byrne's fifteen-ward primary support base, and none of these five black wards had been among the party's top producers since 1963. Byrne's numbers were thus a combination of machine and anti-machine support.

A similar pattern of progressive decline since the late 1960s is present in the presidential election returns (Table 6).

Table 6. Voting in Presidential Elections: 1956–76.

Year	Democrat	Republican	Candidates
1956	807,174	849,241	Stevenson vs. Eisenhower
1960	1,064,951	608,639	Kennedy vs. Nixon
1964	1,141,148	466,296	Johnson vs. Goldwater
1968	874,113	452,914	Humphrey vs. Nixon
1972	758,489	556,373	McGovern vs. Nixon
1976	776,539	375,165	Carter vs. Ford

SOURCE. Chicago Board of Election Commissioners.

Particularly instructive is the party's dismal performance for Jimmy Carter compared to the golden years of the early 1960s. Humphrey's poor showing in 1968 can be partially discounted, because he had the Vietnam war and the Democratic convention debacle draped around his candidacy. George McGovern had no less severe a handicap as far as many Chicago voters were concerned. The media and a number of regular Democratic party members gave credence to the suspicion that the McGovern people had supported the ouster of the party's delegates to the nominating convention in Miami. Carter, on the other hand, came into the city clean, and he wound up performing very well in several of the city's black wards. Nonetheless, Carter did worse than Humphrey had and hardly any better than McGovern. Even under favorable circumstances, then, the new party's ability to generate a sizable vote is a far cry from what the classic machine once produced as a matter of course.

BLACK ELECTORAL SUPPORT

The decline of the party's organizational strength throughout the 1970s is paralleled by, and is therefore partially attributable to, a decline in black support for the party. Black electoral support for the party's mayoral nominee reached its zenith in 1963, followed by progressive deterioration, the low point being reached in 1977. The same pattern obtains with respect to black support for the party's presidential candidate. Here the high point was reached in 1964, followed by a steady decline to a low point reached in 1976. The development becomes even more interesting when we place black electoral support for the party in a broader time frame, as in Figure 1.

The figure illustrates well the significance of Daley's 1955 mayoral election. It ended a decade and a half of split-ticket voting in the black

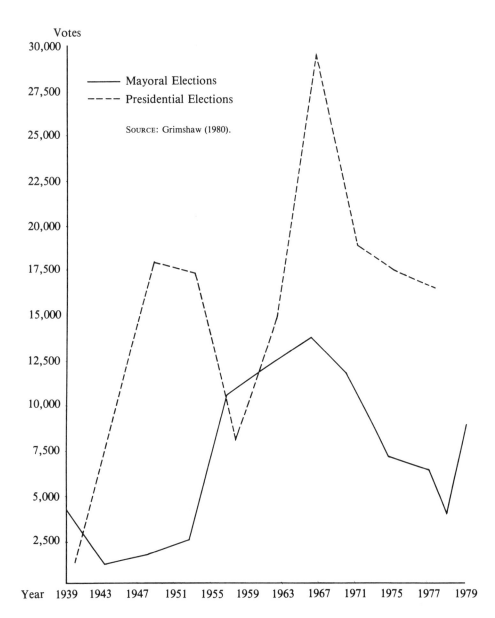

Figure 1. The Average Black Ward Plurality: Presidential and Mayoral Voting: 1939–79. (Wards headed by black committeemen were included in the calculation.)

community by finally bringing black voters into the local Democratic fold. A decade of intense support for the local and national party followed: the early Daley years when the party was viewed as the champion of the "little people," black as well as white, and the years of great expectations fostered by Kennedy's and Johnson's innovative social programs and civil rights rhetoric.

Then disillusionment set in, and it was founded on reality. Black voters understood well before Daniel Moynihan that the federally funded poverty program involved a great misunderstanding, and they apparently did not expect Humphrey, coming after the charismatic Kennedy and forceful Johnson, much less a McGovern or a southern presidential aspirant, to clarify the misunderstanding in their favor.

Things turned sour at the local level, too. Neither violence and protracted demonstrations nor dispassionate and well-documented studies managed to move the city's schools closer to integration. The city administration also fought to protect its policy of constructing public housing on racial grounds. When the city lost unanimously in the U.S. Supreme Court, it merely went out of the public-housing construction business. The city administration also fought all the way to the federal courts in an effort to maintain racially discriminatory personnel policies for its fire and police departments. After lengthy negotiations, these policies also were overturned by the courts. The schools now, too, seem on the verge of joining their racially discriminatory city brethren in the federal courts. Disillusionment is not difficult to appreciate.

What is additionally interesting about black electoral support for the local party is how consistently it declined across the board. Little differentiation can be found by social class, geographic location, or length of ties to the party (Table 7). The lower-income black wards on the near South Side, headed for so long by the so-called Dawson machine, have not generated much more support for the party during the 1970s than the newer, more affluent black wards. Even the support of the west side "plantation" wards, so-called because of lingering white control, cannot readily be distinguished.

As Table 7 indicates, there is one notable exception to the generalization that black support for the party during the 1970s generally cannot be differentiated by social class, locale, or duration of party ties: Byrne's election in 1979. Five black wards ranked among Byrne's top fifteen plurality-producing wards. At the same time, five other black wards occupied the very opposite end of the scale. The remaining five wards gave middling to low levels of support. This suggests that from a different perspective than that of support for the party, important distinctions can be drawn concerning black electoral behavior and, indeed, this is the case.

Black support for backing the party has deteriorated across the board;

Table 7. Chicago's Black Mayoral Pluralities, 1955–79: Rank-Ordered on a City-wide Basis.

Ward[a]	1955	1959	1963	1967	1971	1975	1977	1979
2	4	7	5	26	36	30	28	26
3	8	10	1	3	23	31	27	45
4	16	6	7	18	16	23	35	39
6	19	16	10	28	43	35	37	9
20	11	11	3	12	31	34	32	33
8				17	45	32	31	8
17			14	22	29	38	39	22
21			32	19	44	27	25	2
24			2	7	4	25	36	47
7					37	33	45	41
16					40	36	24	38
28						44	38	49
29					27	41	26	46
34						31	30	6
9								13
Below 50th percentile	0	0	13%	22%	75%	86%	86%	60%

SOURCE. Grimshaw (1980).
[a]Wards were included when they acquired a black committeeman or would acquire one the following year.

however, when it comes to supporting independent candidates, black voting behavior differs considerably. Hence the unusual voting pattern in Byrne's mayoral election. The exceptional voting surfaced because of the independent, i.e., anti-machine aspect of Byrne's campaign. Ordinarily the party's mayoral candidate is the party's choice; Byrne became the party's candidate by default after she defeated the party's choice, Bilandic, in the primary election.

Black support for independent candidates shapes up largely along social class lines. Since the 1960s a good many poor black voters have withdrawn from the electoral process altogether; little aid is given to the party's candidates, and they provide little support for independent candidates. The more affluent black voters have also withdrawn much of their support from the party; however, they have not withdrawn from the electoral process, but shifted their political support to independent candidates. From the party's point of view, the difference is, of course, critical: in one case the party survives; in the other, it does not. Table 8 shows how much more the black wards have supported independent candidates than they have the machine candidates.

Thus, to a critical extent, the future of the new political party is dependent on two developments, both of which are rooted in racial politics and neither of which bodes well for the party as it is presently constituted

Table 8. Black Support for Independent Candidates at the Ward and Mayoral
Levels: 1963-79.

Ward	Independent Alderman Elected	Rank by Plurality for Byrne	
		Primary Election	General Election
New "middle-class" wards (far South Side)[a]			
7		6	11
8	Cousins (1967)	2	3
9	Shaw (1979)	4	5
16	Langford (1971)	13	9
17	Chew (1963)	5	6
21	Sherman (1979)	1	1
34		7	2
Old Dawson wards (Near South Side)			
2	Hubbard (1971)	14	7
3		10	12
4		9	10
6	Rayner (1967)	3	4
20		8	8
Plantation wards (West Side)			
24		15	14
28		12	15
29	Davis (1979)	11	13

SOURCE. Chicago Board of Election Commissioners.
[a]In the absence of current census data, I can only speculate about the extent to which black wards are more or less middle class, hence the quotation marks. Moreover, the Sixteenth Ward is assuredly not middle class, as it is listed here; and the Sixth and Twentieth wards probably contain a larger middle-class population than other former Dawson wards. All schemes seem to have their virtues and drawbacks, and in this case I felt the former outweighed the latter.

and directed. As we have seen, the new party's primary base of support is in the white-populated southwest side wards, the area that has been diminishing throughout the 1970s. The city's more affluent black voters, the ones principally involved in the movement into the southwest side, have at the same time become the party's chief antagonists. The recent victories of independent congressional candidates Harold Washington and Gus Savage reveal how pervasive black dissatisfaction with the new party has become. As the city's black middle class expands and the white ethnic population on the southwest side diminishes, therefore, the party will have to alter its course radically by giving more consideration to black interests, or it will ultimately go the way of other big-city political parties: functioning as a ceremonial entity without much influence on the city's politics and government or on its own or the city's future.

PUBLIC UNION INFLUENCE

A third development also does not augur well for the new party's future role in the city's politics. Just as black disaffection with the party mushroomed during the 1970s, so too did public union discontent. The timing could hardly have been worse from the party's point of view. Paralleling the rise in union militancy was an increasingly stringent fiscal situation, which simply increased union dissatisfaction with the party's leadership. Not only were the public unions beginning to move away from the party's paternalism, but there were also fewer resources available to smother the smoldering discontent, to keep the unions bound to the party by the cash nexus that had served so admirably in the past.

The two unions that have given the party its greatest difficulties are the teachers and the transit workers. Leadership of both unions shifted during the 1970s from the hands of the conservative old guard to younger groups with weaker party ties. It was at that point that the party's public union problem began in earnest. Moreover, since Byrne campaigned on a promise to grant collective-bargaining rights to the city's employees, the rest of the employee organizations have begun to take an unprecedented independent and militant cast.

Among the newly insurgent public employee organizations, the fire fighters have made the biggest splash and most headway. As with the teachers and the transit workers, its shift to militancy involved a shift in leadership. Since the election of Frank Muscare to the union's presidency in 1978, the firemen have been fighting mayors as well as fires, and with about the same mixed degree of success. The leadership of the police, in contrast, is still badly split. Four employee organizations are competing with one another, and recently the Teamsters Union, headed by former police board member Louis Peick, has entered the tumultuous situation.[11]

The American Federation of State, County, and Municipal Employees (AFSCME) has made the least progress of all, and understandably so. Its territory encompasses those jobs providing the great bulk of the party's precinct captains with pay checks, and so it is a certainty that the party leadership will contest AFSCME to the bitter end. Muddying the situation even further, several private-sector unions have been contesting the AFSCME for jurisdictional rights; notable among these is the Service Employees International Union (SEIU). So, although Byrne already has had some dramatic confrontations, the severest are yet to come. Her easy campaign promise to grant bargaining rights has turned into a critical administrative problem, which may wind up sinking her or the party or both.

The Chicago Teachers Union is an excellent case of what a public union can accomplish once it comes under militant leadership. In 1972 a radical faction within the union leadership's party took over, following a controversial settlement by the incumbent leadership. This change in leadership dramatically changed the city's politics. The conservative leadership of the union had invariably employed a deferential negotiating style; it sought to accommodate the financial interests of the school board and the political interests of the party leadership along with the teachers' interests. The new union leadership defers to no interests beyond the union's. Confrontation has replaced conciliation, with even the political party's chief allies on the school board being subjected to scathing criticism. When Robert Healy, union president, was asked where the school board would secure the funds to finance a settlement it had just reached with the teachers' union, he replied, "I didn't ask" (*Chicago Sun-Times,* Jan. 26, 1973). When the union now strikes, no effort is made to compromise; the union leadership simply waits until the political pressure builds sufficiently, producing mayoral intervention and, in turn, capitulation to the union's original demands.

The teachers' union has become a new elite in the city's politics, and its new status is due chiefly to its power to strike. The conservative union leadership had not employed the strike effectively, and as a result it brought back modest gains and suffered constant criticism from within the ranks. The union's first strike in 1969 occurred over the leadership's objections and was settled far too soon for its internal critics. The leadership reluctantly supported a second strike in 1971, but only after it was endorsed unanimously by the delegate body. It, too, was settled within a few days. In 1972 the leadership brought back a settlement just before a strike deadline that involved cuts in the existing contract, arguing again that the strapped financial condition of the school board necessitated cuts. The settlement was narrowly approved, but it marked the end of conservative leadership of the union.

The union's next three strikes, under the new leadership, differed markedly. The 1973 strike lasted two weeks, as did the 1975 strike, and in neither instance did the union leadership make any effort to moderate its original demands. Both times the leadership's strategy paid handsome rewards. Daley intervened and the union received what it had originally demanded. Indeed, in 1975 Daley even abandoned any pretense of mediation; he disrupted a social gathering of the school board to dictate the terms of a settlement that amounted to the union's basic demands.

Daley's decision to allow the 1973 and 1975 strikes to run so long before intervening indicates his growing disenchantment with the teachers' union. Yet the settlement terms reveal that when Daley finally did come in, he came in on the teachers' side. Even with the enormous deficits involved—the 1975 deficit exceeded $100,000,000—Daley did not attempt to confront the union openly. The school board was not even allowed to seek an injunction, even though the strikes were illegal.

Not until Byrne assumed office was any effort made to combat the teachers' union, and this only came in the wake of a great financial scandal. Before that it had been business as usual. Two months earlier the board had approved a contract with the union that added a deficit of $40,000,000 to an existing deficit of $75,000,000. Moreover, even under the extraordinary financial circumstances, the board and Byrne were only partially successful in reining in the union.

When the board proposed a group of budget cuts in order to make the schools' scandal-tainted bonds salable once again, the teachers' union refused to go along with the other employee groups who were reluctantly accepting what they regarded as inevitable. The teachers' union struck over the cuts its membership was being asked to absorb. Healy sought to restore 800 teacher, teacher aide, and clerical positions—all of which are represented by the union—and he came away regaining nearly 70 percent of them.[12] This was accomplished by shifting the cuts to those areas where the representation was weaker: programs, supplies and equipment, maintenance, and other employees. So far, then, Healy has managed to persuade Byrne, too, if not as convincingly as he had Daley and Bilandic, that the teachers are the primary beneficiary of the city's schools.

The transit workers have also suffered at Byrne's hands in a way they had not under Daley and Bilandic. For some time the basic issue with the transit workers has been the cost-of-living adjustment that was written into their contract in 1951 in exchange for a reduction in the work force. At that time a shift was made from trolleys that required two people to operate to buses that required only one. The cost-of-living adjustment calls for a quarterly adjustment to keep wages in line with inflation and has become a heavy burden for the city to bear. The payoff was $12,000,000 in 1978, and it soared to $34,000,000 in 1979 (*Chicago Tribune,* Nov. 30, 1979).

As early as 1974 an effort had been made to have the clause modified through mediation, and, when the transit union became convinced that the city was serious, the city was hit by its first transit worker strike since 1919. The strike lasted only a few hours, however, because Daley sent the reliable Bill Lee, president of the Chicago Federation of Labor, to resolve the crisis. The upshot of Lee's mediation, needless to say, was that the cost-of-living adjustment remained firmly in the contract. The transit workers flexed their muscles even more after Bilandic became mayor. In 1977 the transit union demanded a salary increase in conjunction with the cost-of-living adjustment. The transit workers rejected two proposed settlements before narrowly accepting a third, which maintained their position as the second highest paid transit workers in the country.

However, when this three-year contract ran out, the transit workers came face to face with a mayor who was willing not only to take a strike, but to seek a court injunction to terminate it. The transit workers walked out shortly before the Christmas holidays in 1979, properly calculating that this would put the powerful State Street businessmen behind their cause. Byrne failed twice to mediate the city's way out of the crisis, the last time offering a 7 percent salary increase in exchange for sending the cost-of-living adjustment to a three-member mediation panel. After five days a court injunction ended the strike by ordering the transit workers back to work. The court granted the transit workers a retroactive salary increase under the terms of the cost-of-living adjustment; however, the court also sent the adjustment clause to mediation, where it was modified downward. Thus the transit workers won the battle, but lost the war.

Among those public unions still seeking recognition, only the fire fighters have managed to organize themselves sufficiently for battle. Unlike the police and AFSCME, the fire fighters had a leadership in place to respond to Byrne's pledge to grant city employees collective-bargaining rights. The fire fighters' leaders also had had some important organizing lessons as a result of their earlier confrontation with the wily Bilandic.

The fire fighters' efforts to secure collective-bargaining rights date back to 1977, when the political action committee of the union took the unprecedented step of bypassing the party's mayoral choice, Bilandic, by endorsing party maverick, Roman Pucinski. The endorsement was based on Pucinski's pledge to grant bargaining rights to city workers. After that strategy failed, the firemen resorted to the threat of a strike. However, the fire fighters' newly elected president, Frank Muscare, was unable to muster the votes to pull off the threat. Bilandic's counter-threat of mass firings and the failure of the Chicago Federation of Labor to support the fire fighters were, according to Muscare, the key factors figuring in the union leadership's setback.

The setback, in any event, set the stage for the fire fighters' endorsement of Byrne, who, as Pucinski had in 1977, dangled the collective-bargaining carrot before the city's employees. Although the fire fighters did back a winner this time, they wound up no better off than before. Byrne's promise of a contract was followed by reconsiderations, studies, and meetings, and 1979 slid into 1980 with little assurance that a contract was in the offing. Once again the fire fighers' leadership resorted to coercion, and, to everyone's surprise, they pulled off first a strike vote and then a strike.

The bitter strike ran for over three weeks and ended only because the black fire fighters intended to break ranks and return to work. A letter of agreement was signed by both sides, but several months after the strike's termination, its meaning was still subject to widely divergent interpretation. The fire fighters insist it is an interim contract and are demanding that the city begin honoring the terms of the letter. The city administration contends that the agreement must be approved by the city council before it can be implemented. The council for its part has yet to get a bargaining ordinance out of committee, and there is obviously a great deal of reluctance to do so. The aldermen understand better than most what the implications are for the party and their personal fortunes if the city's workers come under public union jurisdiction. So the fire fighters may well be back beyond step one: there is no contract, and the likelihood of pulling off another strike, given the outcome of the last one, has to be low indeed.

Dancing in the background of Byrne's confrontations with the public labor unions, and sometimes sweeping furiously to the foreground, is the city's organized labor establishment. While it is true enough that organized labor often has had to dance to a different tune under Byrne—hence its fury—it is important to recognize that each of the city's three mayors has understood and acted on an unusual premise underlying the city's public union problem. Elsewhere the problem may have pitted labor collectively against the party; in Chicago the struggle has been between the haves and the have-nots: the public union interlopers are up against the city's party-labor establishment.

The party-labor alliance has been rewarding for both sides, so both are anxious to maintain the status quo. Thus, when the public unions have sought the aid of their brethren in the labor establishment, little aid has been forthcoming, and some labor leaders have made publicly explicit the reason for their rejection of the public unions. After the fire fighters' union had called upon the Chicago Federation of Labor for support in its collective bargaining quest, Thomas Mayder, head of the Chicago and Cook County Building Trades Council and former member of the city's school board, observed that "his union would not support a strike that could jeopardize the relations of his union with City Hall" (*Chicago Tribune,* Oct. 8, 1980). The AFSCME is a greater pariah yet, because it represents a greater threat to the established order,[13] and even the powerful teachers' union has had to castigate the janitors for failing to honor its picket lines.

So while Byrne has reveled in what labor negotiators refer to as softening up actions with the labor establishment, she still has been just as careful as her predecessors to keep labor healthy. She has denounced the city's unionized employees as loafers and threatened to withdraw the prevailing wage agreement. It was the threat, however, rather than the agreement that was withdrawn on the eve of her big fund raiser in 1979, and established labor came through in its traditional grand manner. She horrified the labor establishment when she hired what labor regards as one of the outstanding union-busting law firms in the nation to advise her on labor matters, but it has only been the public unions that have suffered as a result. The sound and the fury directed at the labor establishment have humiliated it, but not materially affected it. If the public unions are going to make it, they are going to have to do so on their own against the city's long-standing party-labor alliance.

The public unions are thus in a situation similar to the city's black voters. Neither group has been able to avail itself of what might be considered its natural allies. The increasingly large number of independent black voters in the city are separated by racial considerations from the city's white independent forces, and the public unions are separated from the labor establishment by material considerations. So while the party is unquestionably weaker and badly troubled now, under the circumstances it, like the fabled one-eyed man in the land of the blind, remains a force with which to reckon.

NOTES

1. The case-study approach is not uncommon in urban political studies. But in Chicago, because it is the last of the machine cities, there has been a strong tendency to emphasize the distinctive at the expense of political features the city has in common with other big cities.

2. For example, Rakove's study of Chicago politics, *Don't Make No Waves, Don't Back No Losers* (1975), is subtitled *An Insider's Analysis of the Daley Machine.* Such an approach would be more acceptable if the interview data were corroborated by firmer forms of data. To a lesser extent, the same criticism may be made of studies such as Banfield's *Political Influence* (1961) and Wilson's *Negro Politics* (1960).

3. In my *Black Politics in Chicago* (1980), I criticized Wilson's study of black politics and Gosnell's *Negro Politicians* (1935) for this shortcoming, but virtually all studies of the city's politics are subject to the same criticism.

4. In the following account I have drawn upon two earlier studies of mine. Party organizational strength and the influence of the teachers' union are examined in *Union Rule in the Schools* (1979). Black electoral strength is treated in *Black Politics in Chicago* (1980). Additional materials and references will be found in these studies.

5. All references to electoral data are based on the files of the Chicago Board of Election Commissioner.

6. Benjamin Adamowski gave Daley a good run in 1963. But he was not a reformer and not really a Republican either; he switched parties to contest Daley in a general rather than a primary election.

7. Whether they have bargaining rights or not, most of the city's agencies rank at or near the top in terms of salary; this includes the teachers and the transit

workers, which have contracts, and the fire fighters and the police, which do not. But, of course, contracts confer more benefits than salaries alone.

8. Rakove borrowed Neistein's admonition for the title of his study of Chicago politics, *Don't Make No Waves, Don't Back No Losers.*

9. Daley made the candid observation while he addressed the full Illinois General Assembly in 1975, advocating an override of Governor Daniel Walker's vetoes of several education appropriation bills.

10. This was far more difficult for state senate candidates, since they did not benefit from Illinois's unique cumulative voting system, used only for the state house of representatives. The system permitted one vote for each of three candidates, or one and one-half votes for each of two, or all three votes for a single candidate.

11. Of 12,785 police on the force in 1979, 17,800 are listed as union members. So unions are either inflating their membership figures, or several police are carrying dual memberships. The largest union is apparently the Chicago Patrolmen's Association (5,500 members), while the smallest is the Confederation of Police (3,200 members). Shortly after it began an organizing drive, the Teamsters claimed a membership of 2,000 (*Chicago Tribune,* June 19 and 26, 1979).

12. The school board's position figures are about as reliable as its budget figures, which is to say little credence can be placed in them. In its negotiations with the union, the school board inflates and generally manipulates the figures in order to hide resources from the union. Thus the media regularly report larger deficits prior to a settlement than after, even when a sizable settlement has been reached, and positions are carried in the school budget even when there is no expectation of filling them. Given the union's adamancy and the party leadership's penchant for intervening on the union's behalf, the practices have been of little positive value; at the same time they have served to vastly undermine the board's credibility.

13. The Chicago Federation of Labor has submitted a model collective-bargaining ordinance to Byrne, which in part is designed to delimit sharply the potential might of the AFSCME. One of its provisions reads that there will be "no encroachment on existing unions for public employees" (*Chicago Tribune,* Nov. 7, 1979).

REFERENCES

Bacon, Warren. 1968. "Comments," in Sol Tax, ed., *The People vs. the System: A Dialogue in Urban Conflict.* Chicago: Acme.
Banfield, Edward C. 1961. *Political Influence.* New York: Free Press.
Chicago Sun-Times.
Chicago Tribune.
Gosnell, Harold F. 1935. *Negro Politicians: The Rise of Negro Politics in Chicago.* Chicago: University of Chicago Press.
Greenstone, J. David. 1968. *Labor in American Politics.* New York: Alfred Knopf.
――――, and Paul E. Peterson. 1968. "Reformers, Machines, and the War on Poverty," in James Q. Wilson, ed., *City Politics and Public Policy.* New York: Wiley.
Grimshaw, William J. 1979. *Union Rule in the Schools: Big-City Politics in Transformation.* Lexington, Mass.: Lexington Books.

_____. 1980. *Black Politics in Chicago: The Quest for Leadership, 1939-1979.* Chicago: Center for Urban Policy, Loyola University.

Lowi, Theodore. 1968. "Gosnell's Chicago Revisited via Lindsey's New York," foreword to the second edition of Harold F. Gosnell, *Machine Politics: Chicago Model.* Chicago: University of Chicago Press.

Rakove, Milton. 1975. *Don't Make No Waves, Don't Back No Losers.* Bloomington: Indiana University Press.

Wilson, James Q. 1960. *Negro Politics: The Search for Leadership.* New York: Free Press.

MICHAEL B. PRESTON

Black Politics in the Post-Daley Era

AFTER DOMINATING CHICAGO POLITICS for over twenty years under the late Mayor Richard J. Daley, the once powerful Democratic machine has been torn asunder by defection from its ranks of some of its
most loyal supporters. Today it is a fragmented and somewhat disorga-
nized party, in contrast to the highly organized structure it was in the
past. And it is safe to argue that whatever means of survival it adopts,
the machine will not again dominate city politics as it did.

The current internal power struggle (or as some might say, "civil
war") between the new Democratic administration of Mayor Jane Byrne
and one of the machine's "renegades," Richard M. Daley, is illustrative
of the kinds of political struggles that have erupted since Daley's death.
In addition to alienating a large number of regular Democratic politicians, Byrne has also managed, in a relatively short period, to alienate
the coalition that kept the Democratic machine in power for over twenty
years—the media, business and union leaders, fire fighters, teachers,
transit workers, Latinos, and blacks. By losing black voters, the machine
is losing some of its most loyal supporters; to be sure, the defection by
blacks was already under way before Daley's death, but it has intensified
under the administrations of Michael A. Bilandic and Byrne.

The sharp decline in black support for local machine candidates began
with the 1975 primary and general elections, the last elections in which
Daley ran. The decline continued in the special mayoral primary and general election in 1977, in which Bilandic was elected mayor. It accelerated
in 1979 when Byrne defeated the regular Democratic mayoral candidate,
Bilandic. Blacks voted anti-machine with a vengeance; they gave Byrne
over 63 percent of their votes. In the course of the year that followed,
black voters were disappointed to see Byrne embrace the very politicians
that they had helped her defeat in the primary. In the 1980 Illinois primary, black voters defeated almost all of Byrne's candidates for political
office.

The trend seems clear: blacks are seeking alternatives to machine candidates and policies. Black voters are no longer the loyal, predictable, controllable, deliverable voters they once were; since 1975 they have become increasingly more unloyal, unpredictable, uncontrollable, and undeliverable. As the black population grows, black voters may some day become the dominant force in Chicago politics.

One of the reasons why black voters are likely to become more influential in Chicago politics is seen in the demographic changes taking place in the city. In 1970 Chicago had a population of 3,362,825, which included 1,098,569 blacks. The 1980 census is likely to show that there are 1.4 million blacks in Chicago. Of this number, it is estimated that 950,000 are eligible voters and that 550,000 are registered. In 1980, then, blacks are likely to comprise over 40 percent of the city's population. The changing nature of the relationship between blacks and the political machine raises the question of whether blacks are likely in the future to challenge the regular Democratic machine for political leadership in Chicago. And, if they do, the question is: How successful are they likely to be?

There seems to be little doubt that there will be a black candidate for mayor in 1983. A recent survey of 540 blacks by state Senator Harold Washington in the First Congressional District indicates that of the people surveyed, 90 percent would vote for a black mayor. Also, a recent telephone poll of seventy-seven black leaders by the *Chicago Reporter* (1980: 1–3) yielded the names of fifty-six potential black candidates for mayor in 1983. Of these, seven emerged as the top choices of all participants. This suggests that black voters and some of their leaders are very dissatisfied with the regular Democratic leadership and are prepared to challenge them in 1983.

Despite the growing dissatisfaction of blacks with the political machine and despite their increasing numbers, it would seem that they still must overcome three major constraints if they hope to mount a successful independent challenge for the mayoralty in 1983. These constraints are: (1) the economic poverty of a large portion of the black population, (2) the underutilization of the black vote, and (3) the lack of a cohesive black political leadership group.

Stated differently, the lack of political resources or the slack use thereof will act as constraints on any black challenge in the immediate future. In our analysis we shall use Robert A. Dahl's (1961: 225) definition of political resources as "anything which can be utilized to sway the specific choice or strategies of another individual." One of the major political resources used in politics is the vote. But there are others as well. Dahl (1971: 82), for example, lists five: (1) income, (2) wealth, (3) status, (4) knowledge, and (5) military prowess. He then goes on to state that: "In allocating income, wealth, status, knowledge, occupation, organizational position, popularity, and a variety of other values every society also allocates resources with which an actor can influence the behavior of other actors in at least some circumstances. . . . Extreme inequalities in the distribution of such key values as income, wealth, status, knowledge and military prowess are equivalent to extreme inequalities in political resources.'' Blacks in Chicago suffer extreme inequalities in most of these political resources. Even the one resource which they should have in abundance by virtue of their numerical strength—the vote—is underutilized.

Low black voter turnout in local elections is a reflection of the lack of another important political resource—black leadership. While Chicago has more black elected officials than any other American city, the black community is now aware that representativeness does not necessarily equal responsiveness. Black machine politicians have been, and still are, more accountable to the machine's wishes than they are to those of their black constituents. Few black machine politicians have independent power in their wards, and they can be stripped of their positions if they refuse to follow the administration's line.

The underutilization of the black vote and the lack of effective black leadership is exacerbated by the economic poverty of a large portion of the black population. The high degree of poverty among blacks in Chicago means that they are likely to be more dependent and vulnerable to political control.

Given the fact that a large portion of the black electorate is poor, we shall begin our analysis by examining the socioeconomic conditions of Chicago's black population to determine their degree of dependency and vulnerability to political control. We shall then discuss the underutilization of the black vote in both the middle and non–middle class black wards. In addition, we shall discuss why blacks have become more national rather than local Democrats. Then we shall focus on the lack of black political leadership and discuss what the recent elections of black independent politicians is likely to mean for the future of Chicago politics. Finally, we shall discuss the future relationship of blacks to the political machine and speculate about the conditions that must prevail if blacks are to become leaders rather than followers in Chicago politics.

SOCIOECONOMIC CONSTRAINTS TO BLACK ELECTORAL PARTICIPATION

There seems to be little doubt that there is a significant link between participatory behavior and socioeconomic factors. For example, Verba and Nie (1972: 123-263) have demonstrated that (1) the higher a person's socioeconomic status, the greater his propensity to participate in politics (also confirmed by Morris, 1975: 146-78); (2) the stronger a person's feelings are about his capacity to influence public policy by his activities, the more likely that person is to participate; and (3) place of residence—the size of the community, whether it is rural or urban, or even its racial distribution—affects participatory behavior. The literature also suggests that a great deal of black electoral behavior can be explained by the fact that blacks in America are not only concentrated at the bottom of the economic scale in terms of annual income, but are also concentrated at the bottom of the educational scale. Furthermore, the evidence indicates that the lower voting rate among blacks is a result of low income and education (Campbell et al., 1960; Almond and Verba, 1965; Wilson, 1966; Matthews and Prothro, 1963). Given this evidence, one should not be surprised to find that the high degree of poverty in the black communities in Chicago acts as a depressant on black electoral participation. One should also not be surprised to find that the poor economic conditions in these communities create the opportunity for machine control over a large segment of this population. We begin by analyzing the degree of poverty, employment opportunities, and the rate of unemployment that exists in the predominantly black communities of Chicago.

THE SOCIOECONOMIC STATUS OF BLACKS IN CHICAGO

According to a 1977 Chicago Urban League report, there were twelve community areas in Chicago where the populaton was 95 percent or more black; this represents 46.7 percent of Chicago's total black community, or 624,942 people. Nine of these areas were below the citywide median income for black families. None was above the white median income. And eleven of these areas were in the city's lowest quartile of median family income. In addition, there are seven other community areas that contain 20.6 percent of Chicago's total black population, or 277,696 people. Some 25.3 percent of blacks in these areas had incomes below the poverty level.

A conservative estimate of poverty in the South and West sides, where most of these blacks are concentrated, suggests then that 35 percent or more of the families now fit the Social Security Administration's definition of poverty.[1] In contrast, the study found that of nonblack families in the city in 1970, only 6 percent fell in the poverty category (Chicago Urban League, 1977: 16).

Private Sector Employment and Unemployment

For blacks in the private sector, manufacturing, services, and retail trade account for 72 percent of national black employment, 71 percent of black employment in Chicago, and 81 percent in the outlying sectors of the Chicago SMSA.[2] Between 1969 and 1974, the city lost 212,000 manufacturing jobs (a drop of 12 percent), while suburban employment grew by 220,000 (an increase of 18 percent). The shift of manufacturing jobs to the suburbs and to the Sunbelt states has severely hurt black employment opportunities in Chicago.

Added to the decline in manufacturing jobs, blacks have also suffered from the effects of discrimination, especially by labor unions. In addition, the recessions of the 1970s hurt everyone but were devastating for blacks; while unemployment in predominantly black areas was between 8 and 12 percent in 1970, by 1975 it ranged from 11 to 32 percent in some areas. An even more discouraging development was the unemployment rate among black youth sixteen to nineteen years old, which in 1976 was 42 percent, compared to 17.3 percent for white youth. These figures represent the unemployment of about 350,000 black youth (Chicago Urban League, 1977: 103–4). In 1979 youth unemployment overall was 25.5 percent and for black youth, 40.2 percent (U.S. Bureau of Labor Statistics, 1979).

Most striking about unemployment in Chicago is not the large increase in the number of unemployed; rather, it is the shift in the kinds of individuals who are unemployed. In contrast to past recessions, this one produced a large segment of unemployed who possessed good skills and stable work histories. Moreover, as a result of limited resources in the face of high unemployment, the Mayor's Council of Manpower and Economic Advisors (1976: 1) decided to focus on the most employable groups, leaving the least employable without manpower assistance.

Municipal Employment

One might assume that since blacks have supported the Daley machine for over twenty years, they would be rewarded in some fashion. Yet, at no point have they received the patronage and other benefits (high-level administrative appointments, high-paying jobs, a halt to police brutality, or an end to day-to-day discrimination) one would expect from such overwhelming support (Wilson, 1960: 46; Walton, 1972: 212).

Furthermore, since blacks make up 33 percent of Chicago's population, one might expect the city work force to reflect a relatively high concentration of blacks. The real situation is mixed. In 1976 blacks were underrepresented in almost all functions, except for those supported by state and federal funds (community development, health, model cities, public libraries, and human resources). Since 1974, to be sure, the number of minorities employed in Chicago city government has increased, and in 1976 over one-third of the city's new employees were minorities (Pace, 1977: 1). More precisely, Chicago city government employed 44,165 workers in 1974 and 43,446 in 1976. Of this full-time work force, there were 11,765 minority employees in 1974 and 12,207 in 1976, a 3.8 percent increase. This increase is also apparent in the number of new employees hired in 1976. Of 2,816 new workers in 1974, 41 percent (1,155) were black and Latino, and of 3,393 new workers in 1976, 37 percent (1,452) were minority group members (Pace, 1977: 1).

Although prospects for municipal employment of minorites have improved slightly, minority employees generally earn less and are in lower level positions than their white counterparts. In 1976, 92.9 percent of the city's white employees, but only 71.9 percent of the blacks, earned $10,000 or more annually. At the same time, 7.1 percent of white—compared to 28.1 percent black—full-time employees earned less than $10,000 annually (Pace, 1977: 7).

POVERTY AND ELECTORAL PARTICIPATION

These data indicate clearly the striking level of economic poverty in most black wards. It seems reasonable to argue that such a high incidence of poverty offers at least a partial explanation for the low turnout in local elections. It is also a reasonable hypothesis that the high incidence of poverty leaves a large segment of blacks in these areas vulnerable to control by machine politicians. Indeed, one might well argue that those who receive welfare benefits, CETA jobs, and other low-level patronage jobs form the hard core of voters that will vote Democratic no matter who the machine runs for office.

A further explanation for the lack of participation among low-income

Table 1. Population Trends in Chicago and Suburban SMSA by Race: 1950, 1960, 1970.

Location	1950	1960	Percent of Change, 1950–60	1970	Percent of Change, 1960–70
Chicago	3,621,000	3,550,000	− 2	3,369,000	− 5
White	3,112,000	2,713,000	− 13	2,208,000	− 19
Percent total	86	76		66	
Nonwhite	509,000	838,000	+ 65	1,159,000	+ 38
Percent total	14	24		34	
Suburbs	1,557,000	2,671,000	+ 72	3,612,000	+ 35
White	1,512,000	2,558,000	+ 71	3,465,000	+ 35
Percent total	97	96		96	
Nonwhite	46,000	113,000	+ 146	147,000	+ 30
Percent total	3	4		4	

SOURCE. U.S. Department of Commerce, *Bureau of Census, General Social and Economic Characteristics, Illinois*, PC(1)-C15, 1970—*1960 Census of Population, Vol. 1: Characteristics of the Population*, Part 15, Illinois. (See also Chicago Urban League, 1977:22.)

voters may be found in the demographic changes taking place in black wards. The black population in Chicago is expanding rapidly. From 1950 to 1960 it increased by 65 percent, and from 1960 to 1970 it expanded by 38 percent (Table 1). A sizable portion of this expanding population is made up of rather young new voters, ages eighteen to twenty-four. And it is precisely this group that suffers most from high unemployment and low education. At the same time, many of them are not likely to find the low-level jobs offered by the machine very attractive. Thus, even though they may be enticed to register and vote in one election, the lack of adequate incentives may cause them to decline at another. Stated differently, the machine does not have, or is not willing to offer, the kinds of incentives necessary to induce this group to become regular machine supporters.

Many blacks do vote, however. Indeed, more and more are doing so. To understand more fully the extent of the decline in black voter turnout, let us examine the patterns of black middle and lower class voting behavior. Most of the literature on black voting behavior in Chicago begins and ends with aggregate analyses of the percentage that black voters give to machine candidates. Little attention has been paid to the difference between black middle-class and non-middle-class voters in local elections. An examination of their voting patterns will point up some important differences and will also be useful later in speculating about the chances of electing a black mayor in Chicago.

THE HIDDEN RESOURCE: BLACK MIDDLE- AND NON-MIDDLE-CLASS VOTERS

Two important questions must be considered if we are to understand electoral participation in the black wards. Does the voting behavior of the predominantly black middle-class wards differ substantially from the voting behavior of non-middle-class black wards in the mayoral primary and general elections? Second, is the voting behavior of middle-class and non-middle-class wards substantially different in local elections that it is in national elections?

To answer these questions, data from the primary and general mayoral elections and presidential general elections are considered for the period between 1971 and 1977.[3] The analysis begins with 1971 because numerous ward boundary alterations were made in 1970. It does not include the 1979 and 1980 elections, which are discussed later.

The figures for turnout as a percentage of registered voters are used to compare the extent to which registered voting potential is being exercised by middle-class and non-middle-class black wards. It is not intended to be a complete measure of voter potential or voter apathy, since it is likely

Table 2. Black Registration and Voting Turnout in Predominantly Black Wards: 1977 Special Mayoral Primary Election.

| Black Wards | | | | | | | | | |
Ward	Percent Black[a]	No. Registered	Total Applications for Ballots	Percent Voter Turnout	Democratic	Republican	Bilandic	Percent Turnout for Democrats	Percent Turnout for Bilandic
2	94.3	27,328	11,013	40.3	10,644	367	5,246	96.6	47.6
3	99.1	23,254	8,508	36.6	8,270	233	4,578	97.2	53.8
4	91.1	28,300	10,888	38.5	10,519	367	4,973	96.6	45.7
6	97.7	35,375	11,460	32.4	11,015	444	4,446	96.1	38.8
8[b]	76.8	38,313	14,908	38.9	14,501	264	5,436	97.3	36.5
16	92.0	26,242	9,785	37.3	9,562	222	5,335	98.0	54.5
17	98.0	28,276	8,667	30.7	8,381	286	3,517	96.7	40.1
20	97.5	28,450	9,589	33.7	9,273	314	4,622	96.7	48.2
21[b]	86.6	39,672	13,670	34.5	13,303	364	5,157	97.3	37.7
24	98.6	21,179	8,834	41.7	8,664	170	4,651	98.1	52.6
27	89.8	20,788	10,640	51.2	10,471	168	7,122	98.4	66.9
28	84.0	23,141	7,743	33.5	7,525	218	3,990	97.2	51.5
29	88.2	24,392	7,374	30.2	7,200	174	3,505	93.0	47.5
34[b]	66.8	36,258	11,870	32.7	11,607	253	5,430	97.8	45.7
Total[c]		400,968	144,949	36.2	140,935	3,844	68,008	97.2	46.9

SOURCE. Board of Elections, City of Chicago (1978).
[a]From Skogan (1976).
[b]Black middle-class ward.
[c]Average for percentage columns.

that at least some of the dissatisfied voters did not even register.

The Daley-Bilandic/Democratic percentages are used to give a measure of organization strength in black wards, and they also allow for comparison of Democratic strength in local and national elections. Table 2 presents a list of the fourteen black wards with registration and turnout in the 1977 special primary election. The black middle-class wards are the Eighth, Twenty-first, and Thirty-fourth. All have incomes at or above the city median of $10,242.

MAYORAL PRIMARY ELECTIONS: 1975, 1977

Turnout. When the fourteen black wards (out of the fifty wards in Chicago) are ranked according to turnout as a percentage of registered voters, the three middle-class wards do not fall in either extreme for local primaries in 1975 and 1977. In 1975 the three wards fell in positions four, five, and eleven. In 1977 they ranked four, eight, and eleven. Turnout for middle-class wards is not substantially different from that for non-middle-class wards in the 1975 and 1977 primaries.

Table 3 shows there was a sizable decline (13.67 percent) in the per-

Table 3. Turnout as a Percentage of Registered Voters in Black Wards: Mayoral Primary Elections, 1975, 1977.

Category for Comparison	1975	1977	Difference, 1977 − 75	Aggregate Average
Middle-class average	50.19	35.37	−14.82	42.78
Non-middle-class average	49.44	36.92	−12.52	43.18
Difference	0.75	−1.55	2.30	−0.40
Average for all black wards	49.81	36.14	−13.67	42.98

centage of registered voters turning out for the 1977 election. Put another way, on the basis of the 1975 primary turnout, one could have expected 52,206 more votes in the black wards in the 1977 primary than were cast. Of the 759,436 votes cast citywide, the black proportion was reduced from a probable 26.19 percent to an actual 19.32 percent.

Daley-Bilandic. Of the fourteen black wards, the three middle-class wards gave the organization candidate the least support in both mayoral primaries. In 1975 the middle-class wards ranked twelve, thirteen, and fourteen. In 1977 the Thirty-fourth Ward was in the nine-ten position, and the two remaining wards ranked thirteen and fourteen.

Election data reveal consistent levels of support from each class, but much higher levels from the non-middle-class blacks. To illustrate the effect of this difference, the aggregate average percentages may be applied to the actual turnout figures for 1977. In the middle-class wards 40,448 voters turned out for the primary, and 16,175, or 39.99 percent on the average, cast their ballots for the machine candidate. If the middle-class voters had supported the machine at the aggregate average level of the non-middle-class voters, 49.88 percent or 20,175 middle-class votes would have been cast for Bilandic. The machine would have gained only 4,000 votes. In 1977 the non-middle-class wards cast 285,815 votes. Therefore, if non-middle-class support had dropped to the aggregate level of the middle class, the machine would have lost 28,268 votes. Thus, the machine has a much greater stake in maintaining non-middle-class ward support than it does in elevating middle-class ward support levels.[4]

MAYORAL GENERAL ELECTIONS: 1971, 1975, 1977

Turnout. All three middle-class wards had relatively low turnout rates in the mayoral general elections between 1971 and 1977. Moreover, they were even lower in 1975 and 1977 than in 1971. Between 1971 and 1977, the Eighth Ward moved from position seven to ten, the Twenty-first from six to nine, and the Thirty-fourth from ten to thirteen.

The rankings indicate that, while there is a declining turnout in all black wards for mayoral general elections, the middle-class voter turnout is declining more rapidly. The significance of the trend may be tested by using data from the 1977 general election, when registered voters in black wards numbered 400,122. If the 1971 turnout level of 56.80 percent had persisted, 227,269 votes would have been cast in black wards in 1977. Instead, only 110,850 votes were cast. This decline of 118,220 votes represents a 106 percent decrease in black voting power.

PRIMARY AND GENERAL MAYORAL ELECTIONS COMPARED

The most significant aspect of black voter turnout is the decline in numbers for both primary and general elections. In the elections under consideration, black turnout decreased by 13.67 percent in the primary and 29.10 percent in the general election. The loss of black voting power in 1977 could have been as much as 52,206 votes in the primary and 118,220 votes in the general election.

Decline in aggregate proportional turnout has been somewhat larger for middle-class wards than for non-middle-class wards in both types of elections. In the primaries, the decline in turnout was 2.30 percentage points as compared to 5.03 percentage points in the general elections.

PRESIDENTIAL GENERAL ELECTIONS: 1972, 1976

Turnout. In both the 1972 and 1976 presidential elections, the three middle-class wards outranked all other black wards in terms of turnout

Table 4. Turnout as a Percentage of Registered Voters in Black Wards:
Presidential General Elections, 1972, 1976.

Category for Comparison	1972	1976	Difference, 1976 – 72	Aggregate Average
Middle-class average	73.66	71.29	-2.37	72.48
Non-middle-class average	66.20	67.01	0.81	66.61
Difference	7.46	4.28	-3.18	5.87
Average for all black wards	67.80	67.93	0.13	67.87

as a percentage of registered voters, although the difference was smaller
in 1976 (Table 4).

Democratic support. The ranking of black wards according to Democratic support in the 1972 and 1976 presidential elections reveals no clear
patterns (Table 5). In 1972 the black middle-class wards were in the lower

Table 5. Democratic Vote as a Percentage of Turnout in Black Wards:
Presidential General Elections, 1972, 1976.

Category for Comparison	1972	1976	Difference, 1976 – 72	Aggregate Average
Middle-class average	91.00	92.67	1.67	91.94
Non-middle-class average	88.30	92.27	3.97	90.29
Difference	2.70	0.40	-2.30	1.55
Average for all black wards	90.50	92.36	1.86	91.43

half of the fourteen-ward distribution, while in 1976 they were in the second third of the distribution. In the aggregate the proportional difference between middle-class and non-middle-class wards is small, 2.30
percent.

PRESIDENTIAL AND MAYORAL GENERAL ELECTIONS COMPARED

Turnout. Typically, turnout is higher in national elections than in local
elections. This trend is observable in the election data for black wards.
The aggregate average black turnout for the national elections was 71.54
percent and for the mayoral general 38.21 percent (Table 6). If black

Table 6. Percentage Gap between Aggregate Average Turnout in Black Wards:
Presidential and Mayoral General Elections, 1971–77.

Aggregate Average Percent Turnout	Middle Class	Non-Middle Class
Presidential general election	71.54	66.61
Mayoral general election	38.21	40.21
Difference	33.33	26.40

turnout in the 1977 mayoral general election had been proportional to the aggregate average in the national elections, 271,563 votes, instead of the actual 110,850 votes, would have been cast.

Political scientists have observed that middle-class voter turnout in elections is consistently higher than non-middle-class voter turnout. Among Chicago blacks, this is true for national, but not local, elections. Furthermore, the gap between turnout in presidential and mayoral elections is considerably higher for the middle-class wards than for the non-middle-class wards (by 5.87 percent). These data are of interest because comparisons among local elections also indicate that middle-class wards use less of their registered potential voting power than non-middle-class wards, which clearly suggests the existence of wasted voting power. For example, if the middle-class gap were equivalent to the non-middle-class gap of 26.40 percent, the middle-class turnout in the 1977 mayoral general election would have been 52,605 votes instead of the actual 27,221, or 46.01 percent. This would have been a 93.25 percent increase in black middle-class voting power.

Democratic support. Aggregate data on Democratic support also indicate a pool of unused black voting power. Many blacks are willing to support a Democratic presidential candidate, but not a Democratic mayoral candidate (Table 7). If black wards were to give the local mayoral

Table 7. Percentage Gap between Aggregate Average Democratic Support in Black Wards: Presidential and Mayoral General Elections, 1971–77.

Aggregate Average Percent Democratic Support	Middle Class	Non-Middle Class
Presidential general election	91.84	90.29
Mayoral general election	74.10	80.19
Difference	17.74	10.10

candidate the same degree of Democratic support that they give the national candidate, that candidate would receive approximately ten more votes out of every one hundred cast in black wards.

In summary, then, the data indicate that increasing numbers of qualified black voters are avoiding the system in mayoral elections. Considering the difference in Democratic support at the polls in national and local elections, the increased or steady machine support in local general elections, and the decreased black turnout, it would seem that many of the black voters who are staying away from the polls are potential anti-machine votes. Furthermore, the decline in voting is proportionally acute in black middle-class wards. It would seem, then, that the machine has a greater stake in maintaining the black non-middle-class vote than it does the middle-class vote: non-middle-class blacks are not only more numerous, but they also have been somewhat more consistent in their support. These trends serve the machine, not blacks. If turnout is low, but most votes are cast for the machine candidate, then the machine is in a strong position. If turnout should increase, and more votes are cast against the machine, then the position of the machine becomes shaky. Therefore, if large numbers of blacks are avoiding electoral politics because of their dissatisfaction with the machine or their belief in its invincibility, they are bypassing one of the most direct channels for altering that situation. Evidence suggests that blacks, especially middle-class blacks, have the potential for exercising much greater influence in local elections. And as will be discussed later, the increased voting among black middle-class citizens was an important factor in the 1979 and 1980 elections.

It is important to note that low voting turnout in both middle-class and non-middle-class wards is not only a result of economic poverty and the antipathy of middle-class voters toward the machine, it also results from the lack of another important political resource—black leadership.

LEADERSHIP AS A POLITICAL RESOURCE

Leadership is indispensable for groups seeking changes through politics. Effective political leadership can serve several purposes: (1) the creation of incentives for mobilization and organization; (2) the development of linkages or coalitions with other groups to further one's own goals; and (3) the skillful and selected pooling of resources to bring about the policies desired by constituents. Political leadership becomes a valuable resource when followers perceive that the leader's interest is similar to their own. Leadership becomes a limited resource, however, when elected officials are dependent on external forces rather than on their constituents. For blacks in America, and especially those in most urban areas, political leadership has been problematic. In Chicago, black machine politicians are illustrative of the type of leadership that depends upon external forces rather than its own constituents.

Much has been written about the history and development of black political leadership in Chicago (Gosnell, 1935; Patterson, 1974; Wilson, 1960; Banfield, 1961: 307; Banfield and Wilson, 1963: 115; Rakove, 1975; Royko, 1971: 149). For our purposes, Matthew Holden's definition of black leadership is useful (1973: 4) *"Black leadership thus generally means those who seek (or claim to seek) the interest of the 'whole' black population,"* and who purport to do so by defining for blacks how they should relate to whites (see also Thompson, 1963: Ladd, 1969: Wilson, 1960).

As a measure of black political leadership in Chicago, it is interesting to note that in 1979 there were fourteen black aldermen on the Chicago

City Council, a number that made them the largest bloc of ethnic politicians on the fifty-member council. Of this group, nine were also committeemen (committeemen have more overall influence in the Democratic organization than aldermen). Moreover, black Alderman Wilson Frost held the second most powerful position on the council as chairman of the Finance Committee and the administration's floor leader.

Black political leaders fall into two basic groups: (1) regular members of the Democratic organization and (2) independents. Generally speaking, the regular members of the Democratic organization represent the status quo, while the independents seek change.

THE BLACK DEMOCRATIC REGULARS

Since the death of Daley a major question has been whether black aldermen will take advantage of the greater level of freedom to gain more political influence. Paula Wilson of *The Chicago Reporter* (1978: 1–7) interviewed black aldermen and political analysts in search of an answer to this question. She found that both black aldermen and political analysts agreed: Black machine politicians have little power now and are not likely to increase it in the near future for three basic reasons—lack of cohesion, lack of political independence, and lack of popular support. We shall briefly discuss how these three conditions limit the amount of influence that black politicians possess.

Lack of Cohesion

Some black aldermen believe that blacks on the council should form a caucus; others do not. Alderman Eugene Ray, a long-time regular organization leader, has stated: "There's no need for a formal coalition because we meet together when it is necessary" (Wilson, 1978: 1). Wilson Frost, the most influential black alderman, feels the same way: "We have a coalition because we have the same skin color and represent people with the same concerns" (Wilson, 1978: 1). Alderman Clifford Kelley, on the other hand, believes that a formal coalition is necessary: "A formal black coalition would give us the concerted effort to collectively and systematically discuss the problems we have and then do something about them" (Wilson, 1978: 3).

Political analysts of Chicago politics do not believe that a formal organization is likely. Lu Palmer, a local black journalist, puts it this way: "Black politicians have been captives of the machine through the years. I don't expect any significant changes or the formation of a black coalition" (Wilson, 1978: 3). Don Rose, a white journalist, has a similar view: "The black alderman don't have enough power and they don't exercise the power they have . . . there is relatively no cohesiveness among them because some of them are responsible to white committeemen, some of them don't know what they want and some of them distrust the efforts of others" (Wilson, 1978: 3).

No one should be surprised about Wilson's findings or the statements made by analysts. The system of influence in Chicago under Daley was designed to keep power blocs from forming. Loyal committeemen controlled aldermen, and machine leaders controlled them all by dispensing patronage and rewards personally, not collectively. Cohesive action was viewed as disloyal (and disloyalty was the most serious offense a machine politician could commit), especially if it was not cleared and sanctioned by the top leaders. Black politicians were especially subject to individual control, given the increase in the black population and the growth in their numbers on the council.

Since the death of Daley, the machine's control has not been as tight. As different groups struggled to gain the upper hand, a cohesive black group might have been able to influence the future direction of the machine. More important, black politicians could now get the multitude of problems facing the black community on the political agenda and demand that something be done about them. The problems of poor housing, lack of jobs, poor police-community relations, segregated schools, and poor instruction, as well as the need for more appointments to top-level jobs in the city bureaucracy are all important problems facing the black community. It is clear that individual action will not be effective; a fragmented machine is still more powerful than an unorganized group of individuals. If black machine regulars remain fragmented, then they are also likely to remain relatively powerless.

Lack of Political Independence

Most of Chicago's black aldermen are loyal machine supporters. According to Wilson (1978: 3), black aldermen use three labels to categorize each other: (1) "maverick" or "dissident," (2) "controlled' (by the ward committeemen), and (3) "administration" (aldermen who have more freedom than the controlled aldermen, but who usually follow the administration's line). Political analysts note that few of the black aldermen can be characterized as dissidents. Some may exercise "voice" from time to time but seldom vote against the administration's line. Most are "controlled" aldermen, having little power of their own and usually following the wishes of their committeemen.

It should also be pointed out that white aldermen are also subject to control by machine leaders. However, the problems facing white politicians are not as acute as those facing the black politician and his constituents. Indeed, many of the things that constituents of white politicians desire are similar to what machine leaders are advocating. For example, the location of scattered-site public housing in white communities, which might attract a sizable number of blacks, has been opposed by machine leaders, white politicians, and their constituents. The same is true of busing to achieve racial balance. The point is that the administration determines what should or should not be on the agenda and that determination is more likely than not to exclude the concerns of the black community. Loyal black machine politicians are, therefore, forced to act as symbols rather than as representatives of the people they supposedly represent.

Lack of Followers

Most black aldermen agree that their power is undermined because blacks do not vote. Patronage and other rewards in Chicago are based on the size of the vote that each alderman and committeeman can deliver for the party, that is, the higher the vote for machine candidates, the higher the rewards and level of influence. For example, the power to influence who gets slated for federal, state, and city political offices is partially based on the number of votes that individual committeemen and aldermen produce from their wards. In addition, vote size per ward is supposed to determine the number and quality of patronage positions allocated per ward. Influence depends on productivity.

In her interviews Wilson came across several variations on this theme (1978: 4, 5, 7):

Alderman Marian Humes (Eighth Ward): Blacks don't have political power in Chicago . . . you get power through the exercise of the vote and blacks are not voting in significant numbers. My ward had 38,000 registered voters but only 11,000 come out to vote. Alderman Patrick Huel (Eleventh) got 20,000 out of 30,000 registered voters in his ward—now that's political power.

Alderman Bennett Stewart (Twenty-first): Until blacks start going to the polls and voting, we can forget about any kind of power in Chicago's political structure. The basis of political power is in the vote—that determines our influence—What kind of demands can I make with 39,000 registered voters in my ward and only 10,000 coming out to vote?

Journalist Lu Palmer: Blacks have voted and voted and voted in this town, but the more they vote, the worse things get. It doesn't matter if they vote for a white or a black. . . . Sometimes I think black people who don't vote are more sophisticated than those who do, because the black voter has to choose between the lesser of the two evils. If a person decides not to choose any evil, he's more sophisticated.

Political analyst Don Rose, arguing that what rebellion there was in the 1960s has been replaced by silence and withdrawal from the political process by blacks and black leaders, concludes that "whites in power can basically write off the black vote. They don't need it, they don't want it. In fact, they snicker about black committeemen not being able to deliver the votes from their wards'' (Wilson, 1978: 7).

Black aldermen, it would appear, then, face a dual dilemma. On the one hand, they do not have power because blacks do not vote, while on the other hand, black voters do not vote because nothing seems to change when they do vote. Put another way, Chicago has an increasing number of black elected leaders, but ever fewer followers.

THE INDEPENDENTS

Disaffection within the black community, caused in large measure by the regular Democratic organization, should have been enough to stimulate the development of a large independent black movement. That has not been the case. Until recently, independent movements among both blacks and whites have been sporadic and not very successful. The problem is that while some blacks have mounted successful efforts against the machine (e.g., Renault Robinson of the Afro-American Patrolmen's League, the late Congressman Ralph Metcalfe, state senators Harold Washington and Richard H. Newhouse), only Metcalfe was backed by a sustained effort in the black community.

The 1977 special mayoral election in which Washington ran as the black candidate was typical. He was not the first choice of most leaders because of his income tax problems some years earlier. Black leaders were so divided that two search committees were operating to select a black mayoral candidate. Ultimately, there were two black Democratic challengers—Washington and Ellis Reid, a black lawyer. While Washington's campaign attracted the support of some leaders—such as the Independent Voters League—he did not have the endorsement of all—e.g., Representative Metcalfe (Jarrett, 1977).

The regular black Democratic organization used everything at its disposal to bury the Washington challenge: patronage, fear, and inducements were all part of the arsenal. One reason may have been the memory of what had happened in the 1975 primary: Daley won in the black wards—but not as big as usual. In 1977 the machine took no chances and mounted an all-out effort not only to beat Washington, but also to crush all independent challenges. It succeeded.

To run and lose is not all bad. Losing can set the stage for a new politics. But here, too, there are differences of opinion. In 1977 many black leaders felt that the time was not ripe for a black mayor. Others, like mayoral candidate Robert Tucker, argue that no opportunity should be passed up: "If running for mayor now is insane, it will be insane in 1979. The inaction . . . only demonstrates our capacity to do what we do best . . . wait, hope, and pray" (Cose, 1977). If black independents ever hope to challenge the regular Democratic machine, they must develop unity among themselves and seek the support of independent white groups. Leon Finney, executive director of the Woodlawn Organization, has summed up the need for political unity among blacks: "There are two sources of power: money and people. Either one, unorganized, remains merely a source of power. . . . There is no black cartel working as a disciplined force in an organized way. . . . The regular Democratic Organization is not going to concede anything unless there's an organization to force it to" (Cose, 1977).

In summary, it is fair to argue that blacks in Chicago do not have effective black political leadership. Black politicians, in their roles as committeemen and aldermen, put the interest of the regular Democratic organization first and end up being merely officeholders rather than representatives of their constituents. This point is reenforced by Alderman Cousin in an interview with *The Chicago Reporter* (1979: 2): "Most black aldermen do not provide political leadership or deal with issues which are of interest to black people. . . . There has been more control over the black community than over the white. The administration has been able to select people to represent the interests of the administration who have been very effective. They've been given the patronage they needed to keep the people in line, to engender fear in the community of reprisals or of not receiving any consideration."

A concluding note is in order: black politicians are not the only leaders in the city of Chicago. Indeed, there is no one group of leaders. There exist other civic leaders such as the executive directors of the Urban League, the National Association for the Advancement of Colored People, and the Woodlawn Organization. In addition, there are black press, business, and religious leaders. All of these leaders and their organizations are part of the overall leadership structure in the black community of Chicago, and it is likely that they do exert influence in their areas of competence; however, an in-depth analysis of their influence is beyond the scope of this paper. We focus on political leaders not because they are more powerful, or because they supposedly speak for the black masses to the exclusion of others, but because in Chicago the name of the game is politics. Black political leaders in Chicago are uniquely situated to influence policies and decisions relevant to the black community. That they have failed in most instances to exercise that power or influence has had definite negative implications for the black community and their own potential political influence.

BYRNE AND BEYOND

Jane Byrne's defeat of the regular machine candidate, Michael A. Bilandic, for mayor in the 1979 primary election was one of the major political upsets in the nation's history. Black voters gave Byrne over 63 percent of their votes in the primary and a much larger percentage during the general election. If there ever was any doubt that a new black voter had emerged in Chicago, it has been dispelled by this and subsequent elections.

One of the most consistent patterns in black wards since 1975 has been the increasing size of the anti-machine vote. Table 8 shows a continua-

Table 8. Anti-Machine Vote in Black Wards.

Year	Votes for Machine Candidate	Votes against Machine Candidate	Percent against	Percent against Machine, All Wards
1955	73,366	17,775	19.5	51.0
1975	85,668	92,090	51.8	42.2
1977	71,427	74,757	51.1	48.9
1979	74,805	110,683	59.7	51.0

SOURCE. *Chicago Reporter* (1979).
NOTE. Black wards in 1955 were: 2, 3, and 20, which were more than 80 percent black in 1950, and 4, 6, and 24, which were racially mixed in 1950 and more than 85 percent black in 1960. Black wards in 1975 to 1979 were: 2, 3, 4, 6, 16, 17, 21, 24, 27, 28, and 29, which were more than 80 percent black in 1970, and 8, 9, and 34, which were more than 80 percent black by 1975.

tion of this trend: a majority of black voters rejected the regular Democratic candidate in the 1979 mayoral primary. In fact, *since 1975 black voters have voted in greater percentages against the machine than have voters in all other wards combined.*

Black voter dissatisfaction with regular machine candidates in 1979 was not due solely to the Bilandic administration's act of closing the rapid transit stops in black neighborhoods during the blizzard of 1979. Its roots were planted long before this event, some preceding Bilandic by many years. Among them could be included Daley's attempt to punish Metcalfe by slating cabinet member Erwin A. France to run against Metcalfe in the primary; the issues of police brutality and the shooting death of Black Panther leader Fred Hampton by police assigned to State's Attorney Edward V. Hanrahan; the total disrespect shown Alderman Wilson Frost (Thirty-fourth Ward) when, as president pro tem of the city council, he was passed over as acting mayor after Daley's death; and the disregard and disrespect shown the black community with the slating of Bennett Stewart for Metcalfe's seat in Congress. Of course, large groups of white voters were also dissatisfied with the Bilandic administration over the breakdown in city services (i.e., snow removal), cronyism in city government, corruption, and the apparent condoning of the condominium hustle by real estate interests that tended to drive up rents. This combination of factors led to Bilandic's defeat.

Another interesting aspect of the 1979 election was the defeat of three incumbent machine aldermen by black independent candidates; voters also elected two former regular Democrats who had been dumped by the machine over two machine-slated candidates. The three new black independent aldermen are Danny Davis (Twenty-ninth), Niles Sherman (Twenty-first), and Robert Shaw (Ninth). Whether these three will remain independent is an open question. If they do, it may signal to black voters in other wards that it is possible to elect people who will be responsible to them and not to some external source. Indeed, this may well be a more significant victory for black voters than the election of Byrne. Black voters may now realize that they can "beat the machine."

According to Vernon Jarrett (1979), Richard Barnett, the campaign manager for Davis, explained the strategy for beating the machine this way: "We discovered that Cross [the incumbent in the Twenty-ninth Ward] had around 3,200 votes that he could depend on. . . . That meant to us that there were nearly 17,000 registered voters waiting for the right movement—not to mention the thousands not registered." This statement is significant for several reasons. First, it points out the weakness in the machine's strategy of relying on low turnout in elections. When the voters are given a viable alternative, and the candidate is serious and well organized, the regular machine candidate is vulnerable. Second, this statement suggests a more fundamental flaw in machine strategy in black wards—the weakness of the ward organization. Most black aldermen do not have the resources (or, if they do, they do not use them) to build strong ward organizations. Moreover, black aldermen are not encouraged to build too strong a base in their wards because it would lessen their dependence on the machine leader. Thus, the reliance on low but controlled turnout means that black aldermen may win the election battle in their wards but lose the war at the city level. That is, the small turnout means that they have little power in the organization and that they get the most menial patronage jobs the machine has to offer. Third, this statement points out a gap between "leaders" and "followers." It suggests that most black leaders have only a few followers and that a large segment of black voters are not led by and do not follow regular machine candidates.

Another significant development was the return of the black middle class to local politics. In 1977 these wards had the lowest voter turnout in both the primary and general elections. In 1979 they showed the greatest percentage increase in voter turnout in both the general and primary elections when compared to the turnout in the 1977 elections. If we look at just the wards defined as black lower class, ethnic middle class, and black middle class, the latter group was the only one to have an increase in voter turnout from the primary to the general election in 1979. In 1977 they had shown the greatest decrease (11 percent) in voter turnout from

Table 9. Black Registration and Voting Turnout in Predominantly Black Wards: 1979 Mayoral Primary Election.

Black Wards		No. Registered	Total Applications for Ballots	Percent Voter Turnout	Bilandic	Democratic				Percent Voter Turnout for Democrats	Total Republican Vote
Wards	Percent Black					Percent	Byrne	Percent			
2	94.3	27,328	12,326	45.1	5,948	49	6,088	51		97.6	290
3	99.1	23,254	9,980	42.9	4,405	45	5,427	55		98.5	148
4	91.1	28,300	10,972	38.8	4,471	42	6,241	58		97.6	260
6	97.7	35,375	14,695	41.5	4,431	31	9,927	69		97.7	337
8	76.8	38,313	17,602	45.9	5,117	30	12,208	70		98.4	277
16	92.0	26,242	10,915	41.6	5,059	47	5,684	53		98.4	172
17	98.0	28,276	11,357	40.2	3,453	31	7,695	69		98.2	209
20	97.5	28,450	10,522	37.0	4,351	42	5,920	58		97.6	251
21	86.6	39,672	17,198	43.4	4,880	29	12,033	71		98.3	285
24	98.6	21,179	8,787	41.5	4,352	51	4,325	49		98.7	110
27	89.8	20,788	10,391	50.0	7,006	69	3,216	31		98.4	169
28	84.0	23,141	8,647	37.4	3,861	46	4,591	54		97.7	195
29	88.2	24,392	9,204	37.7	4,014	44	5,055	56		98.5	135
34	66.8	36,258	16,595	45.8	7,244	44	9,079	56		98.4	272
Total[a]		400,968	169,191	42.2	68,592	41	97,489	59		98.2	3,110
5[b]	57.0	32,871	14,053	42.8	3,521	26	10,189	74		97.6	343
7[c]	81.0(est.)	30,645	11,346	37.0	3,947	35	7,190	65		98.2	209
9	97.0(est.)	29,185	13,715	47.0	4,486	33	9,041	67		98.6	188
10	49.0(est.)	35,591	20,888	57.7	12,608	61	7,926	39		98.3	354
37	78.0(est.)	31,523	13,062	41.4	5,770	45	7,165	55		98.3	227
15	90.0(est.)	33,413	15,816	47.3	8,071	52	7,468	48		98.2	277
Total		193,228	88,880	46.0	38,403	44	48,979	56		98.3	1,598
Combined Totals[a]		594,196	258,071	43.4	106,995	42	146,468	58		98.2	4,708

SOURCE. Unofficial returns for the mayoral election in 1979, *Chicago Sun-Times*, Apr. 5, 1979.
[a]Or averages, for percentage columns.
[b]The Fifth Ward was not included in the *Chicago Reporter* survey.
[c]These estimates are based on information from the *Chicago Reporter* (1976) and were derived from elementary and secondary school enrollment data of 1975.

the primary to the general election. The other two groups still had a decline in voter turnout in 1979, although it was less than that of 1977.

It is important to note that Byrne won all but two (the Twenty-fourth and Twenty-seventh) of the predominantly black wards in the primary. In addition, she won five other wards (7, 9, 10, 15 and 37) that have a black majority (*Chicago Reporter,* 1976: 1–6, 7). Nonetheless, in 1979 each had a white alderman, and four of the five had white Democratic committeemen. If we add the Fifth Ward with its estimated black majority (57 percent), there were in 1979 twenty black wards but only sixteen black aldermen and fourteen black committeemen (see Table 9). It has been suggested by Don Rose, a journalist and Byrne's campaign manager, that a ward has to be 70 percent black before the machine lets it have a black representative (*Chicago Reporter,* 1976: 7). These figures indicate that while the black population is expanding, its representation is not.

The 1979 mayoral primary election also provided a clear picture of the gap that has developed between black political leaders and the majority of black voters. Although all of the black politicians supported the regular Democratic candidate, only two of the fourteen predominantly black wards and none of the majority black wards voted for the regular machine candidate for mayor. This is a clear signal that black machine leaders have lost touch with their followers. And it also seems clear that leaders that lack followers are not likely to be leaders very long.

THE 1980 PRIMARY

If the Democratic organization was surprised by the large anti-machine vote by blacks in the mayoral election of 1979, its members must have been astounded by the results of the 1980 Illinois primary. Byrne, who only one year earlier had received overwhelming support by black voters, saw her choices for political office soundly defeated by those same black voters. Her betrayal of their trust may well mean that the relationship of black voters to the machine has suffered a permanent rupture—or certainly one that will take a major effort to repair.

There seems little doubt that a large percentage of the anti-machine vote in the primary can be directly attributed to Byrne's record while in office. Among the events that led to grievances listed by black political and community leaders, seven are especially glaring:

1. *Appointment of Police Superintendent.* Mayor Byrne had informed black police board member, Renault Robinson, that she wanted to bring in a new police chief from outside the department. Robinson supported the mayor in this move and did not insist that Sam Nolan, a black assistant chief in the department, be considered. With Robinson's

assurance of no backlash about Nolan, the mayor then turned completely around and appointed a white from inside the department, Richard J.
Brzeczek (the only white on the list of recommendations from the police
board).

2. *Transit Strike.* The Reverend Jesse Jackson asserts that during the
week-long strike by city transit workers that shut down the Chicago
Transit Authority and most of the city, the mayor tried to break the
striking unions, both of which are headed by black men. Her policy of
refusing to negotiate with striking unions had a devastating impact on
blacks who depend on public transportation (*Chicago Tribune,* Mar. 24,
1980).

3. *School Board.* In 1979 Byrne bypassed the black deputy superintendent of public schools, Manford Byrd, in consideration for superintendent; instead she appointed his subordinate, a white woman, Angeline
Caruso. (It is important to note here that the city schools are predominantly black.) A year later, after a major financial crisis that threatened
to shut down the entire system, the mayor appointed a new school board
more representative of the city's school population. At the same time,
she attempted to install a white man, Thomas G. Ayers, as president.
When the board chose a black, the Reverend Kenneth B. Smith, instead,
Byrne refused to swear in the members (although she did do so at a later
date).

4. *Teachers' Strike.* As in the transit strike, minorities in the city suffered disproportionately during the teachers' strike. Especially hard hit
were young children, whose only adult supervision had to go to work and
for whom there is a lack of alternative day care.

5. *Fire fighters' strike.* The third major strike of 1979 also affected
minorities more harshly than others, in part as a consequence of poor living conditions. The majority of deaths during the strike were among residents of the black community. This situation was not resolved until the
Reverend Jackson stepped in and served as a mediator.

6. *CTA Fare Increase.* The mayor supported Governor James
Thompson's transit package which resulted in a fare increase.

7. *Sales Tax on Food and Medicine.* Byrne failed to support legislation that would have removed all of the state sales tax on food and medicine (*Chicago Sun-Times,* Mar. 24, 1980).

In addition, Byrne had promised to strike down the patronage system
dominated by Eleventh Ward jobholders in order to provide more and
better jobs to the black community. Instead, after her election she began
to dominate rather than dismantle the system. Moreover, there was no
change in the quality or quantity of patronage jobs available to blacks.
Probably the most serious blow to black voters was the realization that
Byrne was neither anti-machine nor a reformer, for after the election she

embraced the very machine politicians whom she had criticized earlier. The results of the primary election reflected their degree of dissatisfaction. A brief review of the 1980 races will illustrate the depths of black dissatisfaction with Byrne and her candidates.

The Presidency. Daley was famous for the way he and his machine could bring out huge numbers of voters to support the Democratic party's candidate for president. Prior to the Illinois primary, both candidates Jimmy Carter and Edward Kennedy felt that they needed the endorsement of Byrne. After reneging on what appeared to be support for Carter ("if the convention were today"), the mayor threw her support—and what she thought to be the city's support—to Kennedy. Kennedy lost badly in both black and white wards. In fact, he managed to take only two black wards, the Twenty-fourth and the Twenty-eighth.

Of special note here are the large turnouts in the middle-class wards (Eighth, Twenty-first, and Twenty-fourth), which usually have a low turnout for primary elections. This new interest among black middle-class voters could change the face of Chicago politics if it continues.

The question asked in this, and the other four races, was whether Kennedy's defeat was more anti-Byrne or pro-Carter. Jackson argues that it was pro-Carter, while Don Rose argues that it was anti-Byrne. The evidence in black middle-class and lower-income wards suggests that Rose is correct. Both voted heavily against all Byrne-endorsed candidates, including Kennedy. The election of Richard Daley as state's attorney over Bernard Carey in the November 4, 1980, election gives even more credence to Rose's argument, since Byrne had opposed Daley's election and implicitly supported Carey. It may be that Jackson's response is based on his unhappiness at Kennedy's reliance on Byrne to deliver the black votes rather than his going directly to Jackson and other black community leaders. Whatever the case, the result proved that the mayor's endorsement was a burden and not a blessing.

State's Attorney. There is a great deal of argument about whether or not this race was the important contest in Cook County in terms of the future of the Chicago machine. Upon the announcement of Senator Richard M. Daley's candidacy, Byrne approached several prominent Democrats to oppose the late mayor's son. It is interesting to note that according to several articles by Mike Royko and Basil Talbott in the *Sun-Times,* she views Daley as the chief threat to her continued party dominance. Byrne and the organization finally endorsed Alderman Edward Burke to represent the party against Daley, who then ran outside of the machine that his father had been so instrumental in developing. In spite of a strong effort to disassociate his campaign from the mayor, Burke was apparently perceived by voters and the media as her hand-picked candidate. Daley, who was endorsed by both major newspapers, stressed his recently progressive record in the state senate and obviously benefited from his family name. The results in the primary were unequivocal. Burke was able to carry only three black wards (Three, Twenty-four, and Twenty-eight); again the machine-endorsed candidate had been thoroughly defeated.

While Senator Daley was rather successful at portraying himself as an independent, his family heritage and past performance suggest that his conversion may be short-lived. His candidacy better fits Kemp and Lineberry's definition of a "renegade" Democrat (see Chapter 1 herein). Daley ran against the machine only to increase his power within the machine—not to reject it. His victory over Carey can be attributed, according to both Rose and Carey, to Byrne's support of Carey.

U.S. House. In the First and Second Congressional Districts, black independents mounted strong challenges against black candidates endorsed by the regular organization. The widespread dissatisfaction felt among blacks toward the Democratic machine was translated into independent victories in both contests. In the First District, Harold Washington (who garnered almost 50 percent of the vote) easily won over machine-endorsed incumbent Bennett Stewart and Ralph Metcalfe, Jr. In the Second District, Gus Savage took 45 percent of the vote in a four-person race, soundly defeating machine-endorsed Reginald Brown for the seat vacated by white machine Congressman Morgan Murphy. The popularity of Washington and Savage may have a profound impact on the future of Chicago politics. It also means that Chicago is the only city with three black U.S. congressmen.

Ward Committeemen. The most significant development of the 1980 primary, from the standpoint of black voters, came in the races for ward committeemen. Five black regular Democratic organization committeemen lost their positions to independent challengers. Again, the anti-Byrne vote appears to have been a determining factor. All of these wards supported Byrne in the 1979 primary. Three of the victories were registered in South Side black wards (Nine, Seventeen, and Twenty-one), continuing the independent trend of Chicago's black community. In the predominantly black Seventh Ward, Ray Castro became the first Mexican-American to become a committeeman in the city of Chicago.

Independent aldermen Shaw (Ninth), Sherman (Twenty-first), and Tyrone L. McFolling (Seventeenth) who became aldermen in 1979 solidified their strength by capturing their respective ward committeemen positions. What is especially significant in these races was that, despite the drop in turnout, their electoral support increased. Traditionally the machine counted on a low turnout with predictable results where a high proportion of voters "pay the machine back." According to Kemp and Lineberry, machines "thrive on low-turnout elections." In this instance, however, the most active voters in the Ninth, Seventeenth, and Twenty-first wards were apparently also the most independent. The party organization's use of benefits and incentives to control low-turnout elections failed. It should also be noted that Shaw and Sherman had been thorns in the side of the mayor. In their campaigns for the post of committeemen, they faced a serious organizational effort to defeat them. That effort failed. The election of these three black committeemen increased their number to fourteen of the fifty-member body.

The results of the 1980 Illinois primary may prove to be a watershed in Chicago politics. The election results indicate the birth of an extremely sophisticated black voter, a voter who is beginning to reward political friends and punish political enemies.

THE FUTURE OF BLACK POLITICS

The future relationship of blacks to the regular Democratic organization is highly uncertain. The decline in machine support since 1975 by black voters, culminating in their almost complete rejection of machine candidates in the 1980 primary, means that black voters may have outgrown any need for the regular Democratic party. In fact, there is some indication that the Democratic party needs them more than blacks need it.

The 1980 primary may well signal something even more important than simply a strong anti-machine vote by blacks: that is, it may signal an increasingly pro-independent sentiment. If this movement continues to grow and is able to form coalitions with other dissatisfied groups, the Byrne era may prove to have been the catalyst for a revolutionary development in Chicago politics. It could become the greatest threat to the machine in decades. Little wonder, then, that machine politicians are considering dumping Byrne in 1983.

The future relationship of blacks to the regular Democratic party will depend not only on the responses of the new black independent leadership but also on the responses of the machine itself.

One of the consequences of the rise in independent black voting behavior is the fact that blacks may have less political influence in the short run. The Democratic party is still in possession of most of the political rewards that blacks seek. The autonomy of black voters may deprive regular black political leaders of whatever bargaining influence they previously held. That these leaders can no longer deliver even a minimal number of votes may strip them of the only political trade important to the Democratic party. The result could be that blacks will be locked out of that aspect of the political process to a greater extent than ever before. Yet given the past behavior of black machine politicians, this does not seem to be too high a price to pay. Over the long run, black voters may gain political independence and more accountability from their elected politicians.

This discussion suggests that leadership will be the key variable for the future development of black politics in Chicago. The power void that may result from the emergence of black independence can only be stemmed by a cooperative effort on the part of black political leaders. Black machine politicians will have to accommodate to the new attitudes of their constituency, and black independents will have to accommodate to the realities of politics.

Black political and business leaders are aware of the need for political cohesion, especially as it pertains to the mayoralty of 1983. They have already organized some fund-raising activities that will allow a black mayoral candidate to enter the race. A recent telephone poll by the *Chicago Reporter* should help identify potential candidates. The top seven choices were: state Senator Harold Washington (D., Chicago, state senator at the time of the survey), who received thirty-two votes (with twenty as first preference); state Comptroller Roland W. Burris, with twenty-seven votes (twenty as first preference); state Senator Richard H. Newhouse (D., Chicago), with twenty-four votes (with three as first preference); Alderman Wilson Frost (D., Thirty-fourth Ward), with twelve votes (none as first preference); city Treasurer Cecil A. Partee, with eleven votes (with one as first preference); and Inland Steel executive and former Chicago School Board member Warren H. Bacon, with eleven votes (with one as first preference). Of the seven candidates named, only two can be considered regular machine candidates; the rest are independents. And the chances are that an independent will be selected.

We return to the question we started with: Can blacks successfully elect a black independent candidate for mayor in 1983? Such an independent challenge is likely only if the independent candidate can first unify blacks and develop a coalition with other dissatisfied white ethnic groups, Latinos, and, yes, even Republicans. The evidence in this chapter suggests that this is not likely.

First, the current fragmented nature of black leadership militates against a unified black challenge in 1983. Black Democratic regulars will want the leadership position because they feel they have paid their dues. The failure to agree on a single leader will result in a divided black electorate. Second, the poor voting turnout of the black electorate in general, and especially among lower socioeconomic voters, will make it essential that the independent candidate form a coalition with other groups.

Coalition politics is easier said than done. For example, a coalition with Latinos would seem to be highly advantageous to both groups. Yet an effective black-Latino coalition is not likely because of cultural/religious differences and the belief by Latinos that blacks have been getting more than their share of rewards. Indeed, the 1979 elections showed that Latinos supported the machine rather than Byrne. Finally, even if Latinos did join blacks, their voter registration and turnout have been so low that it would make them undependable allies. An alliance with independent white voters is possible, but their past support for black independent candidates has been very low.

The white ethnic–black coalition (Poles-Croations, Irish, etc.) that survived throughout the Daley era now appears destined for dissolution—especially if the candidate for mayor is a black independent. The likelihood is that Richard M. Daley will be the candidate of the white ethnics, and, if this is the case, a black–white ethnic coalition to elect a black independent is not possible.

The most intriguing possibility would be a black–independent Republican coalition. The Republicans have suggested this possibility, and black independent leaders seem interested. The chance of such a union is remote, because Republicans simply do not have the political organization and the numbers to be helpful allies. It is also unlikely that a sizable number of black voters would make the switch to the Republican party in time for the election (if they would switch at all).

Finally, a fragmented and weakened machine is still more powerful than a politically unorganized and fragmented group of voters.

In the long run, however, recent developments in the black community are more important than the election of a black mayor in 1983. The emergence of a new sophisticated black voter means that politicians who are not responsive to black needs will not be elected or, if elected, will be defeated if they do not perform. The new black voter is likely to be interested in more than symbolic recognition. Whether the mayor is white or black will be less important than his/her ability to respond to the needs of black people. That is the real issue facing Chicago voters. A black mayor with these qualities will be a double bonus to black voters. It would be a desirable, but not an absolutely necessary condition, for their support.

NOTES

1. The federal government defines an area as a poverty area when more than 20 percent of its residents are below poverty levels. On the Social Security Administration's definition, see Chicago Urban League, 1977: 11-12.

2. The Chicago SMSA consists of Cook, DuPage, Will, McHenry, Lake, and Kane counties.

3. The data in this section are based on information from the Board of Elections, city of Chicago; Scammon, 1973: 110; and Scammon and McGillwray, 1977: 114.

4. Uses of data across time are extremely risky propositions, since the compo-

sition of the population living in black wards in 1977 is not the same as in 1971. We use specific figures from particular elections simply to provide us with numbers to use in our speculations. In this way the speculation is grounded in something fairly concrete—but no extraordinary accuracy beyond this should be inferred.

REFERENCES

Almond, Gabriel, and Sidney Verba. 1965. *The Civic Culture.* Boston: Little Brown.
Banfield, Edward C. 1961. *Political Influence.* New York: Free Press.
———, and James Q. Wilson. 1963. *City Politics.* Cambridge, Mass.: Harvard University Press and the M.I.T. Press.
Board of Elections, City of Chicago. Primary and general mayoral election data, 1971–77.
Campbell, A., Donald Stokes, and William Miller. 1960. *The American Voter.* New York: Wiley.
Chicago Reporter. 1976. 5 (July).
———. 1978. 7 (Jan.).
———. 1979. 8 (Apr.).
———. 1980. 9 (Aug.).
Chicago Sun-Times, Apr. 20, 1977.
———. Mar. 24, 1980.
Chicago Tribune, Mar. 24, 1980.
Chicago Urban League. 1977. *The Current Economic Status of Chicago's Black Community: A Mid-1970's Overview Report.*
Cose, E. 1977. "Can city's blacks get it together?" *Chicago Sun-Times,* Feb. 27, 1980.
Dahl, Robert A. 1961. *Who Governs?* New Haven, Conn.: Yale University Press.
———. 1971. *Polyarchy.* New Haven, Conn.: Yale University Press.
Gosnell, Harold F. 1935. *Negro Politicians: The Rise of Negro Politics in Chicago.* Chicago: University of Chicago Press.
Holden, Matthew, Jr. 1973. *The Politics of the Black "Nation."* New York: Chandler.
Jarrett, Vernon. 1977. "Washington train picking up steam." *Chicago Tribune,* Mar. 9.
———. 1979. *Chicago Tribune,* Apr. 11.
Ladd, E., Jr. 1969. *Negro Political Leadership in the South.* New York: Atheneum.
Matthews, D. R., and J. Prothro. 1963. "Social and Economic Factors and Negro Voter Registration in the South." *American Political Science Review,* 57 (Mar.): 25–44.
Mayor's Council of Manpower and Economic Advisors. 1976. "Unemployment Labor Force Policy" (Special Report, Apr.).
Morris, M. 1975. *The Politics of Black America.* New York: Harper and Row.
Pace, I. M. 1977. "Employees in top salary range jump 500 percent in two years, over one-third of city hall's new hires are minority in 1976." *Chicago Reporter,* 6 (June-July): 1–7.
Patterson, E. 1974. *Black City Politics.* New York: Dodd, Mead and Company.

Rakove, Milton. 1975. *Don't Make No Waves, Don't Back No Losers.* Bloomington: Indiana University Press.
Royko, Mike. 1971. *Boss.* New York: Signet.
Scammon, Richard M., ed. 1973. *America Votes 10.* Washington, D.C.: *Congressional Quarterly.*
————, and A. V. McGillwray, eds. 1977. *America Votes 12.* Washington, D.C.: *Congressional Quarterly.*
Skogan, Wesley G. 1976. *Chicago since 1840: A Time-Series Data Handbook.* Urbana: Institute of Government and Public Affairs, University of Illinois.
Thompson, Daniel. 1963. *The Negro Leadership Class.* Englewood Cliffs, N.J.: Prentice Hall.
U.S. Bureau of Labor Statistics. 1979. Unpublished Reports.
Verba, Sidney, and Norman Nie. 1972. *Participation in America: Political Democracy and Social Equality.* New York: Harper and Row.
Walker, J. 1964. "Negro Voting in Atlanta: 1953-1961." *Phylon,* 24 (Winter): 379-87.
Walton, H. W., Jr. 1972. *Black Politics.* Philadelphia: Lippincott.
Wilson, James Q. 1960. "The Negro in American Politics—the Present" in J. P. Davis, ed., *The American Negro Reference Book.* Englewood Cliffs, N.J.: Prentice Hall.
————. 1966. "The Negro in American Politics—the Present" in J. P. Davis, ed., *The Negro American Reference Book.* Englewood Cliffs, N.J.: Prentice Hall.
Wilson, Paula P. 1978. *Chicago Reporter,* 7 (Jan.): 1-7.

JOANNE BELENCHIA

Latinos and Chicago Politics

LATINOS ARE THE SECOND LARGEST MINORITY group in Chicago, yet they are not represented by Latino aldermen in the city council and have few appointed officials to reflect their presence in the city. Some of the reasons for their lack of political presence may be found in studying Latinos' unique situation in American society. But one must also consider the political structure of Chicago to develop an explanation for their weak position in the city.

The 1970 census counted nearly 250,000 persons of Spanish language in Chicago. By 1977 it was estimated that the population had more than doubled. Latinos are thought to make up 25 percent of the city's population and account for 15 percent of the greater metropolitan region. Of the estimated 500,000 persons of Spanish language in the city, 72,596 are registered to vote, comprising 4.5 percent of the city's electorate (Walton and Salces, 1977).

"Latino" is a purposely vague term denoting any number of groups sharing in a variety of Spanish-influenced cultures in the Western Hemisphere, and it is appropriate for describing Chicago's second minority. Chicago is the only U.S. city to contain significant numbers of the three largest immigrant Hispanic populations: Mexicans, Puerto Ricans, and Cubans. There are also smaller populations of Central and South Americans in the city, representing nearly every country. Within the context of Anglo (Western, non-Hispanic) society, the shared problems of attaining recognition and moving from disadvantaged positions may allow use of the group identification. But to understand more about those problems the group label should be abandoned, for it disguises more than it illuminates. Each distinct ethnic group within the larger Latino population of Chicago has characteristics that place it in a different position vis-à-vis the established Chicago political organization and practices.

SPATIAL AND SOCIAL CONSIDERATIONS

Chicago prides itself on being a city of neighborhoods. Despite population shifts and changes in land use throughout the metropolitan area,

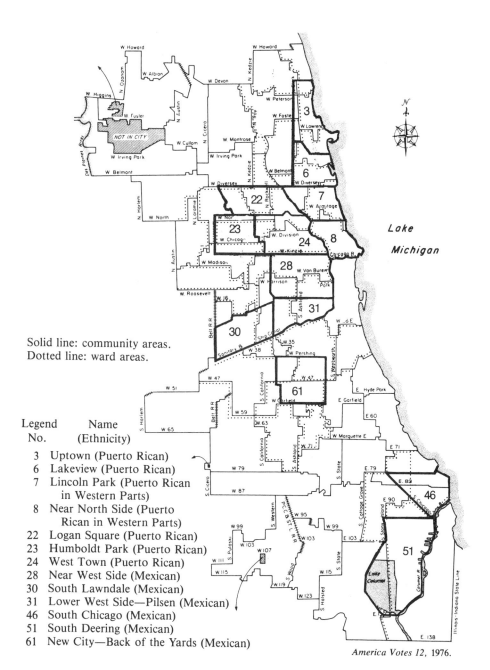

Solid line: community areas.
Dotted line: ward areas.

Legend   Name
No.   (Ethnicity)
  3 Uptown (Puerto Rican)
  6 Lakeview (Puerto Rican)
  7 Lincoln Park (Puerto Rican
       in Western Parts)
  8 Near North Side (Puerto
       Rican in Western Parts)
 22 Logan Square (Puerto Rican)
 23 Humboldt Park (Puerto Rican)
 24 West Town (Puerto Rican)
 28 Near West Side (Mexican)
 30 South Lawndale (Mexican)
 31 Lower West Side—Pilsen (Mexican)
 46 South Chicago (Mexican)
 51 South Deering (Mexican)
 61 New City—Back of the Yards (Mexican)

America Votes 12, 1976.

Map 1. Latino Community Areas and Intersecting Ward Boundaries.

ethnic as well as social status group enclaves persist in the city. But there is no single Latino section. Instead, Latinos are found throughout a number of separate communities, usually with one nationality predominating. Map 1 illustrates the spatial distribution of Chicago's largest Latino groups, Mexicans and Puerto Ricans. Together, these two nationalities comprise portions of the populations of ten of Chicago's designated community areas, and of nineteen city wards.

The history of Latino settlements in Chicago can help explain the differing positions of the major Latino groups in the city. We will explore some of the major Latino neighborhoods in the following sections, beginning with the first Latino immigrants, the Mexicans.

MEXICANS IN THE CITY

Mexicans are the oldest Spanish-speaking group in the Midwest. Their numbers increased to nearly 30,000 throughout Illinois between 1910 and 1930 (Taylor, 1932). The possibility of jobs in transportation (the railroads needed construction and maintenance crews), industry (especially in steel manufacturing), and agriculture drew them, mostly young men, from dusty and dormant border towns of the Southwest and northern Mexico. Political and social unrest in Mexico during and after the Revolution added to pressures to relocate. Three Mexican settlements took shape in Chicago during this period: Pilsen, South Chicago, and Back of the Yards.

Pilsen

Pilsen grew from a seasonal stopover for farm workers into a busy year-round settlement, the first Mexican settlement in Chicago. The early population was composed of former farm-worker families seeking new occupations in an urban market and single men who were most often employed by the railroads as unskilled laborers. Living arrangements were often crowded, with the single men renting rooms with families to save what money they earned and to ease the loneliness of separation from relatives and friends left behind. Pilsen was, and continues to be, the poorest Mexican community. The farm-worker families were a feasible economic unit in agriculture, where everyone's labor was productive. In an urban setting, however, they were at a disadvantage. Forced to rely upon only the father's and sons' incomes, large families that had once been independent suffered from the costs of life in the city and sought relief from agencies such as Hull House. Social workers reportedly argued for Mexican families to remain in town for the educational and health benefits Hull House could provide, but the economic difficulties presented by urban life drew many back to a migratory existence (Jones,

1928). Despite these difficulties, Pilsen continued to grow and remains the area of first settlement for most Mexican immigrants.

Whites moved to the suburbs during the 1950s and 1960s, thus opening sections of Chicago to Mexican residency, especially in the Little Village area near Pilsen. This neighborhood offered somewhat better housing and amenities than the more deteriorated Pilsen. Both areas are now predominantly Mexican and are often considered by social service agencies to comprise one target area, as evidenced by several hyphenated community services organizations (e.g., the Pilsen–Little Village Mental Health Clinic).

South Chicago

South Chicago's steel mills provided Mexicans their first means of entry into the world of blue-collar heavy industry. One might say that they entered through the back door. For Mexicans, steel became a way of life only with the beginning of labor disputes in 1916, when groups of young men were shipped much like cattle from the Southwest to Chicago. Once here, many of the Mexicans became strikebreakers. Controlled by the labor contractors to whom they owed their jobs, they probably could not make the decision to work. Kerr (1975) has noted that numbers of Mexicans, when made aware of the strike, joined with the protestors. By 1928, approximately 2,600 Mexicans, mostly young men, lived and worked in South Chicago.

As Kornblum showed in this study, *Blue Collar Community* (1974), the area is now dissected by ethnic groups, with separate areas in the community set aside as the property of one or another ethnic group. There are two separate Mexican neighborhoods within the South Chicago community, the result of restrictive housing policies and the more or less accidental opening up of new housing. These residential patterns have had immense importance for ward politics, a subject that we shall investigate below. Within the community, the shared experience of mill work serves as a bond that unites different ethnic and neighborhood groups and creates a complex network of primary relationships that combine in politically significant ways.

Back of the Yards (New City)

Back of the Yards has a history similar to that of South Chicago. The difference lies in the type of industry involved. Upton Sinclair's *The Jungle* (1906) described the life of meat packers in the slums surrounding the city's slaughterhouses and stockyards: poverty and ignorance, horrifying work conditions, and a general acceptance of the exploitation of immigrants as business-as-usual. Again, labor disputes in 1919 generated an increased interest in employing Mexicans in the stockyards, many of whom lost their higher-paying positions once the disputes were settled. Those who stayed on lived in areas dominated by the Irish or Polish, working out a coexistence with the frequently hostile Anglo groups.

Two sets of events have shaped the growth of the Latino population in Back of the Yards. The first, at a time when the Mexican population was only about 0.2 percent (1,500) of the community, was the organization of the Back of the Yards Council, Saul Alinsky's attempt to bolster the growing unionization movement in the stockyards by creating a sense of mutual dependence in the workers' neighborhoods. The council emphasized territorial boundaries and minimized ethnic differences. This institutional support for unity, strengthened by common work experience and, possibly, the lack of a separate Mexican settlement of sufficient size to warrant its own businesses and newspapers (as existed in Pilsen and South Chicago), appears to have resulted in greater assimilation of Latinos into the neighborhood. The second set of events followed the closing of the stockyards and points up the degree of assimilation that had taken place. With the loss of their major employer, many of the community's residents, often the second and third generation of original settlers, have sought other employment and other neighborhoods. While the Back of the Yards community has continued into the 1970s, it is the least visible or distinguishable of the three Mexican areas.

Legal Problems of Mexican Residency

Until the 1930s the experiences of Mexicans in the Midwest were similar to those of other European immigrants. However, the ease of entrance along land borders, much less carefully controlled than immigration from abroad, worked to create unique legal problems for Mexicans, problems that had major repercussions in the Great Depression and that, in the 1980s, could again become important to the political future of Mexicans in the United States.

The border between the United States and Mexico was established through military efforts and perpetuated by bureaucratic and legal distinctions. In few ways does it reflect real distinctions between ethnic or cultural traits. The border has been largely a legal fiction that by its existence has interrupted but not dissolved the social organization of the Southwest. Innovations and exceptions in immigration law since the 1920s have served to show the exceptional economic interdependence of U.S. farmers and industrialists, on the one hand, and Mexican workers, on the other. Numerous formal and informal arrangements have provided legal entry to thousands, perhaps millions, of Mexicans while denying them the ability to apply the time spent in the United States to the residency requirements for citizenship. Among the better known are: green cards, passes for workers who live in Mexico but work in the

United States; visitor passes, often used for the same objective as green cards but easier to obtain; and the *bracero* programs, which enabled a U.S. employer to hire entire crews of farm workers for seasonal needs. (The green cards are also used by many migrating French-Canadians, but their numbers are few compared to the overwhelming majority authorized for Mexicans.)

Many of the Mexicans who came (and still come) to the Midwest were legal permanent immigrants, the category into which most European immigrants also fell in the early 1900s. But many more were either green carders or illegal alien workers, meaning that they either had no papers at all, held forged documents, or had entered with passes that did not allow them to work (such as visitors' visas).

In 1930 these legal distinctions among immigrant categories were used to repatriate nearly 22,000 Mexicans from Illinois, leaving only about 7,000 in the entire state (Taylor, 1932). Some left voluntarily, as the general hardships of the Depression were compounded by new welfare policies that limited aid to citizens. Others were forcibly deported, including families whose children had been born in the United States and were therefore eligible for relief and certainly would have been excluded from deportation in more prosperous times. (From the 1940s to the 1970s, parents who had entered illegally but who had children born in the United States were often allowed to remain in the country while resident visas were prepared for them. These "baby cases" were a primary means of establishing legal residency until new immigrant laws ended the procedure in January 1977.)

It was not until World War II that Mexicans were again officially welcomed to the United States as needed workers. Then in the 1950s Operation Wetback, coincident with the recession of that decade, repeated the mass roundups and deportations of the Depression. The hard times of the 1970s have likewise been accompanied by intensified efforts at removing illegal immigrants. A difference in this latest effort has been a dual emphasis on urban industrial areas as well as agricultural areas, a reflection of both the increasing concentration of jobs in metropolitan areas and the increasing proportion of Mexicans in urban areas. This "job liberation" action, as it has been unofficially nicknamed, was of such fierce intensity that mass protest demonstrations took place in Chicago in 1974 and again in 1976. Indeed, local resentment among Latinos (not only Mexicans but Puerto Ricans—who are U.S. citizens—and other Latinos who had been stopped by Immigration and Naturalization Service [INS] officers) caused the INS to establish the first community relations committee in its history in Chicago.

This excursion into international relations points out a major problem facing Mexicans and other Latinos, the problem of justifying and main-

taining their presence. Anyone who speaks Spanish and does not appear
to be well off financially (two key items of identification used by the
INS) risks interrogation by that agency. Two police organizations, the
local police and the federal agents of INS, "protect" Chicago Latinos. In
a recent poll, 60 percent of Latino respondents rated the actions of the
INS as Bad-to-Very-Bad, and 58 percent rated the local police department in the same category of least acceptable performance (Walton and
Salces, 1977). What are the implications of ambiguous citizenship status
on local politics?

   Those who are citizens among the Latino population are, of course, eligible to vote. They may participate in political activities. Noncitizens,
however, who have worked for radical organizations may be denied citizenship. But consider the potential trade-offs for participation of any
sort. While one may be a citizen, one's friends, relatives, or business associates and clients may not be. And while some political influence
achieved through diligent political work may help them, the risk of a
failed campaign or an unwise endorsement may very well jeopardize de-
fenseless acquaintances. It is not surprising, then, that Mexican voters
are largely strong supporters of the Democratic organization, the organization most likely to win elections. This should not be taken as a causal
statement, but it does highlight an interesting possible correlation. Before going into the current political situation, we must consider the second largest Latino group, the Puerto Ricans.

PUERTO RICANS IN CHICAGO

   The 1970 U.S. census for Chicago estimated the Mexican population
in Chicago at 82,000, constituting 43 percent of the city's Latino population. Puerto Ricans, with an estimated 79,000 persons, accounted for 32
percent of that same population. While one should use caution in speculating about the 1980 census, it is possible to predict that the proportion
of Puerto Rican Latinos will increase. This is in part due to limitations
put on Mexican immigration and in part because Puerto Rican migration
to Chicago began thirty years later than that of Mexicans; there is no tell-
ing where the peak of the Puerto Rican movement may lie.

   The presence of Puerto Ricans in Chicago makes it difficult to compare the city's politics with another city, such as Los Angeles or San
Antonio. Similarly, the large number of Mexicans in Chicago creates differences that cannot be explained by a comparison with New York's
Spanish Harlem.

   The border between the United States and Mexico is penetrable. There
is no border at all between the mainland and Puerto Rico. Direct daily
flights from Chicago to San Juan and the absence of complicated immi-

gration forms make movement only a question of money. And it does not cost much.

The first large-scale immigration into Chicago from the island occurred in the late 1940s via contract labor agreements similar to the *bracero* program. The Commonwealth discontinued the program when suits were filed for misrepresentation by a legal aid society in Chicago on behalf of the workers (Padilla, 1947). But Chicago had been made part of the consciousness of many Puerto Ricans, and immigration has continued, sometimes in family units, but more often in the familiar pattern of the single or recently married pioneers who then amass the necessary funds to bring over wives, brothers, and parents.

Residence in the city has been in tandem with the requirements of the immigrant family unit. The earliest arrivals found rooms in the worn-out tenements close to downtown that were being abandoned by more prosperous former inhabitants, especially in the near North Side area. As families were reunited or newly created, apartments and houses were sought, and the Puerto Rican settlement moved westward and northward from the Loop to Lincoln Park and the near West Side. As if to offset the advantage of citizenship, Puerto Ricans found themselves beset by another form of federal intervention: urban renewal. The history of settlement for Puerto Ricans has been one of forced movement and desperate attempts to maintain their neighborhoods. Unlike the Mexicans, whose earlier arrival enabled them to establish neighborhood institutions before the massive cleanup campaigns of the 1950s and 1960s, Puerto Ricans appear to have been shifted from place to place, each seemingly worse than the previous, with subsequent loss of institutional ties. Arson and abandoned buildings, poor service, and land competition from well-endowed hospital and educational groups were frequent complaints of Puerto Rican respondents in a recent survey (Walton and Salces, 1977).

The usual pattern of movement out of first settlement areas as fortunes increased has been accelerated by housing demolition. Persons unable to move upward are forced to move outward, reestablishing homes and contacts, often in more crowded conditions. Adding to the problem is the continued increase in the Puerto Rican population, as more people arrive from the island and those here maintain a higher birth rate than the general U.S. population. Thus the newer Puerto Rican neighborhoods (West Town, Lakeview, Uptown, and now Humboldt Park and Logan Square) endure the pressures of overcrowding and high dependency ratios in a city losing employment possibilities and suffering with a constricted low-cost housing market.

The 1970 census figures provide the most recent estimates of the social condition of Latinos. Profiles of the communities we have so far discussed have been compiled by the Council for Community Service in

Table 1. Selected Chicago Community Area Profiles: 1970.

Comparative Categories	City Median	Pilsen		South Chicago	Back of the Yards (New City)	West Town	Lakeview	Uptown
		South Lawndale	Lower West Side					
Percent Latino of total population	7.3	31.9	55.0	26.1	12.8	39.2	13.5	10.9
Persons below poverty level (percent) (rank in city)	14.5 (—)	13.3 (20)	17.7 (22)	11.7 (28)	12.3 (24)	21.5 (4)	12.1 (12)	14.3 (6)
Unemployed adults 16 years old and older (rank in city)	2.6 (—)	2.1 (45.5)	3.5 (14.5)	2.5 (34.5)	2.9 (22.5)	3.6 (13)	2.4 (37.5)	2.4 (37.5)
Median years of school completed: 25 years of age and older (rank in city)	12.2 (—)	9.1 (5)	6.7 (1)	10.3 (22.5)	9.2 (6.5)	7.0 (2)	12.1 (55.5)	12.1 (55.5)
Housing units lacking plumbing facilities (percent)	3.9	3.4	8.2	6.2	6.0	8.3	4.4	6.5
Overall ranking[a]	(—)	54	59	47	53	61	46	52

SOURCE. Council for Community Service, *Community Analysis Project: Report #1.* Sept. 1975, Chicago, Ill.
[a]Overall ranking is based on a composite index of well being that includes 31 indicators. The index ranges from 1 (Best Community) to 76 (Worst Community).

Chicago. Some indicators used by the council to establish a rank order for seventy-six community areas are shown in Table 1. Considering the general downward momentum of the economy, the continued suburbanization of industry and housing construction, and the greater numbers of Latino youths to be served by an ailing school district, it is unlikely that these indicators will show much improvement in 1980.

Puerto Ricans are citizens, eligible for all rights and duties thereof after one month's residency in the mainland. Participation in politics then does not have the negative potential of deportation that it has for some Mexican residents. However, there is a good deal of racial prejudice against Puerto Ricans, many of whom are of mixed Spanish and black descent. Sixty-seven percent of the Latinos polled in a local study felt that Puerto Ricans are highly discriminated against. This was the largest percentage (strongest general agreement) found regarding the question of discrimination (Walton and Salces, 1977). (Blacks were determined by the survey sample to experience high levels of discrimination by 64 percent of the sample.)

An additional constraint on Puerto Ricans is the aggressiveness of the INS. That organization, until stopped by federal injunction, often detained persons on the streets of Chicago on the basis of speech and appearance, demanding proof of citizenship. At the same time such people were often refused the opportunity to collect such documents and were required to remain in custody until someone arrived with the necessary papers.

CUBANS

Among Latinos there is yet another ethnic group that requires consideration. It stands between the Mexicans and Puerto Ricans in terms of citizenship: the Cubans. This group comprised 7 percent of the Spanish-speaking population canvassed in the 1970 census. Many of them entered as refugees, a special immigrant status that entitled them to immediate social services, including employment and housing placement services throughout the country. Chicago was one of the first major resettlement areas for Cubans after Florida. Thus Cubans have had relatively few legal problems in regularizing their presence in the United States.

Cubans have not settled in one particular area of Chicago, but are dispersed throughout the city. There are small groups in most Puerto Rican neighborhoods, but many Cubans have chosen housing on the basis of social and economic factors rather than ethnicity.

Added to their advantaged immigrant status is the fact of a selective migration from Cuba, resulting in a largely white-collar population. If one looks at the local communities that have become small centers of

Cuban residence, male labor force participation shows the following percentages of Cubans in white-collar employment (Walton and Salces, 1977): Near North—55.3 percent; Uptown—49.9 percent; Lakeview—44.6 percent; Lincoln Park—34.7 percent; and West Town—32.3 percent.

Cubans are not a highly visible ethnic group: many have been successful in their adopted country and have been largely accepted as members of Anglo society. This view is shared by other Latinos, who consider Cubans to be at the top in terms of economic and social advantages (Walton and Salces, 1977). In effect, Cubans are seen by other Latinos as simply not sharing their own general economic and social problems of unemployment, education, and especially housing. Thus, even though some Cubans have achieved influence in the socio-political work of Chicago, the preceding discussion suggests that their success cannot be viewed as a Latino success, and we should center our discussion on the activities of Mexican and Puerto Rican voters.

LOCATION AND POLITICS

Thus far we have discussed Latinos in terms of their situation in several of the seventy-six designated community areas first sketched by Ernest Burgess and his students at the University of Chicago. These community areas, with some modifications (cf. Hunter, 1974) still reflect, at least symbolically, social units of some homogeneity in measures of income, ethnicity, and life-style. Neighborhood organizations often use the community area boundaries as the limits of their jurisdiction. But citywide services do not follow community boundaries, which are intersected by school catchment districts, police precincts, redevelopment areas, and sanitation districts. Most important, they are dissected by the fifty wards that are the basis of political representation and participation in Chicago. No single community area in which Latinos predominate falls wholly within one ward. This could, of course, be sheer happenstance, but Kornblum's (1974) vivid description of the history of the South Chicago Mexican community suggests that this division has been a practical application of the maxim "divide and conquer."

In his book Kornblum chronicled the history of the two Mexican neighborhoods in the area surrounding steel mills. The leaders of each neighborhood were able to combine their resources to support an independent Democratic candidate for alderman. The candidate lost, and the election was quickly followed by a redistricting, which placed the two Mexican neighborhoods in different wards. Although their united efforts could still be useful for citywide and higher office campaigns, their potential for control of the original ward and the ability to manipulate patronage to maximize and strengthen control were obliterated.

Only two wards, the First and the Thirty-first, had a goodly proportion of precincts with a majority of Spanish voters in 1975 (Neuman,
1976). Both are in the Mexican communities, where, as we have discussed, any political participation that threatens the established order of
authority may produce repercussions in addition to the loss of patronage
and services. This may explain why even these wards do not show a majority of Latinos on the rolls of registered voters (Table 2). Registration

Table 2. Distribution of Latinos (Registered Voters) in Selected Wards.

Ward No.	1	7	22	25	26	30	31	32	33
Percent Latino	14.8	10.5	20.0	19.8	26.3	12.7	38.7	19.8	22.7

figures for 1977 show that the highest proportion in any ward is less than
40 percent Latino (*Chicago Sun-Times,* Sept. 21, 1977).

But numbers are not the sole basis of power within the wards. Both the
First and Thirty-first wards have long been strongholds of Italian political influence, influence based both on fact—who inhabits the offices of
alderman and ward committeeman—and on rumor: the open speculation
on who is involved in Syndicate activities and what sort of "connections" may be supposed to affect power relations. Suttles (1968)
documented the sense with which Italians in the Near West Side (parts of
the First, Twenty-fifth, and Twenty-seventh wards) discussed their
group's hold on the political organization of that community. While
blacks, Mexicans, and Puerto Ricans might make encroachments on
their social space, it appeared that the Italians felt totally secure politically. Although the establishment of the University of Illinois Chicago Circle Campus decimated the Italian neighborhood, it is probable that at
least some of the "connections" that aided Italians then may be
operating still, actually or symbolically. To date no study has investi-
gated that situation.

In other neighborhoods, the design of wards and community areas
again serves to restrict rather than to increase the political potential of
community-based organizations. Map 1 shows the crazy quilt of dissected wards and community areas.

The Lake Shore communities in northern Chicago (Uptown, Lakeview, Lincoln Park, and the Near North Side) are still very much a combination of the "Gold Coast and the Slum," a phrase made famous by
Zorbaugh (1929). In the space of only a few blocks expensive condominiums and apartments yield to blocks of massive brick roominghouses and
hotels, dwarfing the few aged and peeling homes and duplexes scattered
along the streets. In recognition of the diversity in these areas, the Council for Community Service has developed dual profiles, with the eastern
halves showing up in the top and the western halves in the bottom quar-

tiles of the rating system. The racial and economic differences between the two sides of the community lead to a great deal of tension, as exemplified by efforts on the part of some of the eastern residents of Lakeview to make use of the name "Edgewater," thus placing social distance between themselves and the undesirable Latinos to the west.

The situation in Lakeview is characteristic of the problems within each Latino community. Besides the conflict of ethnic and income groups within the community, Lakeview is divided into four wards, wholly comprising the Forty-fourth, roughly one-half of the Forty-sixth, and minor segments of the Forty-seventh and Forty-third wards. The Forty-fourth Ward cuts across the community, thereby uniting within its bounds both upper-income whites and lower-income Latinos. Lakeview has a dual organization structure, one social, one political. Socially, community organizations that unite ethnics are embedded within an area that has diverse ethnic lines. The geography of the community retains symbolic importance but also prevents groups with differing ethnic allegiances to feel "in control" of the area. Politically, ward boundaries cut across these ethnic lines, resulting in Latinos being the minority in all wards of the community. Within this political structure, Latinos are represented somewhat uniquely. In the next section we shall investigate how the political position of Latinos reflects the infiltration of ethnic community organizations into ward politics.

LATINOS AND POLITICAL REPRESENTATION

The city of Chicago no longer has any elected Latino officials.[1] Mayor Jane Byrne removed Bilandic-appointed Latinos from their offices and has only recently begun a search for replacements. Her first Latino appointment, Dr. Hugo H. Muriel as head of the Chicago Public Health Commission, was widely criticized by both Latinos and the medical profession.

None of the previous appointments, and none of those presently being considered, can be said to have strong ties to the mostly working- or lower-class Latino communities in the city. Charges of tokenism are the usual response of community-based organizations to city hall's attempts to provide for Latino representation. Those Latinos who come to the notice of the Anglo power structure are typically highly educated Cubans and Puerto Ricans living in the upper-income neighborhoods of the city. Many of the Cubans are refugees and have come to Chicago as adults, with few close ties other than immediate family in the area.

Another common mark of the Latinos considered for appointments is their lack of contact with the daily workings of government. Many have sat on commissions and study groups; many are active in special-interest groups for issues such as bilingual education, favorable immigration laws, affirmative action, etc. They have provided favorable contacts for city hall within these special-interest groups, but do not reach the typical blue-collar Latino. Few of the publicly acknowledged Latino leaders have been involved in the hard and unglamorous work of precinct organization in the Latino wards, work that results in a sharing of the rank-and-file jobs for their supporters. In 1974 Latinos accounted for only 1.7 percent of the full-time city payroll (*Chicago Reporter,* 1974). The percentage has not changed significantly in the past six years.

Walton and Salces (1977) have described the political representation of Latinos as a two-tiered structure of community leaders and political brokers. This structure is the result of an inability to absorb ethnic community organizational manifestations into the existing political structure. It uses recognition via ethnic representatives to give the appearance rather than reality of influence.

The tight organization of each ward does not provide room for more leaders, only more followers. Community groups are an unneeded addition to neighborhood politics—from the ward organization's perspective. At best, they can deliver votes, but they can only be trusted to do this if the group's leaders are sound ward personnel. At worst, the groups present a level of citizen participation that the ward is not equipped to handle.

Chicago's political world centers on its fifty wards. The wards are composed of precincts, as many as fifty-five for a ward population that averages around 68,000. The rigid hierarchy of the ward places an ever-increasing number of voters under precinct worker, precinct captain, and ward committeeman. The mode of interaction at the lowest level is on a highly individualized plane. Individual voters are approached on a one-to-one basis, and individual needs—for a job, new garbage cans, a letter of recommendation, or perhaps aid in obtaining a building permit for household improvements—become the "coin of the realm" that "finance" the smooth running of the Democratic organization. Needless to say, precinct workers' first responsibility is not to constituents but to their immediate supervisors. As with any service-providing bureaucracy, the bottom line—where client and bureaucratic interest meet—is fraught with contradictions. The client, to whom the services are directed in theory, is apt to make claims for those services in amounts and kinds that the agency may be unable or unwilling to provide. The bureaucrat, who may well be personally concerned about his clients, has the responsibility of representing the bureaucracy and insuring its authority to determine the services and their delivery.

In some agencies, this responsibility is met by selecting certain types of clients, especially the "good client" who can make use of the services that the agency is prepared to deliver, who does not demand much more, and who does not threaten the social authority of the bureaucrat. It may be suggested that Latinos are not generally "good clients" for the Democratic organization.

The precinct workers and captains with Latino neighborhoods face a perplexing situation: how to deal with a minority group that has been self-described as culturally unique and unlike any other population in its social needs. The answer seems to have been neglect. Even though Latinos are strong supporters of the machine, city services do not appear to have been delivered to them. Numbers may provide a partial explanation for this situation. Their minority position in the wards makes Latino support a welcome but not completely necessary component in winning elections. It may also be that the ethnic organization of Latinos has engendered a defensive posture within the machine, resulting in the isolation of Latinos from the political mainstream.

The minority position of Latinos in ward populations is of strategic importance in maintaining established groups' control over each ward and the patronage attached to ward dominance. If Latinos could attain majority in their wards, would the established manner of voter/client interaction work to alleviate Latino concerns? To answer this, we may look to the past and to the response of the Democratic organization to the development of black majorities in the wards to the south and southwest of the Loop. Katznelson (1973) and Speer (1967) have documented some of the activities that arose out of the particular style of machine politics in Chicago and that helped to create a black political hierarchy, partly separated from the central Democratic structure.

Speer is especially helpful in describing what happened once blacks became a socially problematic population, at the point of the Great Migration after World War I. Until that time, blacks had made up a small and stable population in northern cities, with a separate and well-ordered social system. Chicago's black elite of the early 1920s was divided among those who sought institutional integration and those who followed Booker T. Washington's theories of race separation for autonomous power. (The division of Latino activists between these strategies is a prominent element in current political discussions.) As long as the black population remained a slowly expanding one, the divisiveness of its leaders was unfortunate but not critical. However, the massive numbers of southern blacks who came unprepared for urban life and unknown to local community authority became a political factor of consequence almost immediately. Unrestricted by united black leaders, white response was institutionalized racism: the establishment of dual service systems (separate churches, schools, and social service agencies) where feasible, and elsewhere the sanctioning of dual eligibility and benefit guidelines for shared services.

The political system of the Democratic organization appears to have followed a path incorporating methods of both total exclusion and differential inclusion based on a hierarchical division between central control and local representation.

Black wards became politically more important as the city's residential patterns became more segregated, due to neighborhood pressures to concentrate members of the Great Migration in areas with an already existing black population. These wards, formerly represented by whites, became the homes of black representatives. Black politicians had been active previously, of course, but their potential use of token representatives in the authority structure of the machine increased with the population growth and as the needs of the new black population created political problems of service delivery for the city. By giving up full local domination while maintaining centralized control, the white Democrats could better manage the client-bureaucracy relation; they gave the appearance of recognition and participation, thereby translating client questions of the adequacy of the system into practical questions of which black politician to back.

Yet by these maneuvers the Democratic organization also gave impetus to the development of black politics. The institutional inroads made by black political organizations developed into strongholds of partisan support, particularly helpful in training and establishing black leaders as worthy candidates for black voters. Is this the likely future of Latinos?

There are differences in the populations, the times, and the city. There are also some differences between the Democratic organization of the 1920s and that of the 1970s, which may be measured in terms of the organization's response to tests of its hegemony.

As noted above, Latinos are dispersed throughout the city, reducing their ability to achieve dominance in any ward. Similarly, the economic and social issues facing Latinos change in priority and degree of intensity as one moves from one community to the next. Prejudice, directed primarily toward Puerto Ricans, has not had the latent function of providing a group identity as "outside" of Anglo society. Thus unity based on simple exclusion is not likely to develop.

It is also possible that Latino immigrants of the 1970s, while having generally lower educational levels than present-day urban blacks, have come to the cities with greater sophistication regarding politics and urban society than the black migrants of the 1920s. Much of the immigration from Puerto Rico is from towns rather than villages, and many of the Mexican immigrants had previous experiences in other U.S. towns. Such sophistication can often turn to cynicism when confronted with the headway made by blacks and could certainly make the development of a following a problem for emerging Latino leaders. There is also the possibility that the political realities of Mexico and Puerto Rico shade the interpretations of Chicago politics made by Latinos. A predisposition to see and accept patronage and vote-buying as politics-as-usual may weaken Latinos' beliefs that change can be brought about through participation.

Thus, in terms of the groups themselves, we have quite dissimilar situations. Early black migrants appear to have had a much more homogeneous background than current Latino immigrants. They may also have been less politically informed and more able to be educated and led by politically aware blacks. Residential segregation, while disrupting the pre-1920 social order in black neighborhoods, at least created a critical density that gave rise to black-controlled wards.

Latinos, on the other hand, have numerous community organizations geared to issues of education, housing, employment, cultural events, among others. Can these organizations be turned into a political base that would provide a springboard for entry into the Democratic organization? Can the ethnic identity emphasized by the very presence of these organizations be of aid in Chicago, a city of ethnics?

RECENT ATTEMPTS AT REPRESENTATION

In 1975 four Latino candidates attempted to gain the local offices of ward alderman for the Twenty-second, Twenty-sixth, Thirty-first, and Forty-sixth wards. None of these candidates was sponsored by the machine: each ran as an independent Democrat. None of them won, but two candidates garnered 27 percent of the votes in their wards, a better performance than any of the eleven Latino candidates who have waged campaigns since 1963 (Salces, 1978). It should also be pointed out that in the 1975 elections, Latino voters favored Latino candidates, albeit only slightly.

That the Latino candidates lost their elections is hardly surprising given the well-ordered and time-proven tactics of the machine. But the behavior in these elections allows us to refine the work done by Wolfinger (1973) and recently revised by Salces. In his study of Chicago Latinos, Salces considered two points worth restating here. First, ethnic voters must not be seen simply as ethnic units existing in a vacuum. Their ethnicity should be viewed as having a specific relationship to ongoing political organizations within their localities. Second, the ethnic group must perceive itself as a political agent. Salces argues that the existence of a Spanish name on a ballot serves as a valid indicator for Latino voters that their group may be politically important. Thus, even though they lost, Latino candidates may have helped change the awareness of Latino voters, making them more receptive to future Latino candidates.

But the road to office cannot rely solely on ethnic identification for

Latinos, especially considering their minority status in all wards. Their chances will be affected by the behavior of the machine in their wards.

The Democratic organization has, since the beginning of the Daley era, given appearance of solidifying its white voter base and of extending its influence generally along lines found suitable for incorporating other whites (the strategy for managing black participation involved a parallel and subordinate organization). As it congealed under Daley, the machine maintained its mold of late 1940s demographic representativeness with Irish and Italians still strongly represented in the upper levels of authority. Poles and Latinos, the two largest groups of postwar migration, have been largely excluded from those upper reaches (although Poles have been more successful in gaining some authority than have Latinos).

The 1975 machine candidates in the Latino-contested wards were powerful political figures, fiercely entrenched in the system of patronage that forms a cornerstone of political power. (One candidate was the wife of an Irish alderman serving five years for mail fraud and conspiracy. Despite this blemish, the wife received nearly 70 percent of the Democratic vote and was able to assume her husband's vacant seat.) Three out of the four organization-backed contestants had received an average of more than 81 percent of the vote in their respective wards in the previous election. The fourth, a liberal newcomer, had received 60 percent in his first race (Salces, 1978).

The Latino voters in Chicago are by and large Democrats. In 1974 one estimate showed that 60 percent of the registered Spanish-surnamed voters were Democrats, 28 percent Republicans, and 11 percent independents (Salces, 1978). For those who participate, it seems that participation as a Democrat is preferable to the uncertainty of Republican efforts to wrest portions of power from their opponents. But in the 1975 elections, party and ethnicity were in opposition (Table 3).

Table 3. Selected 1975 Aldermanic Elections: Latino Voters and Votes for Latinos.

Ward	Latino Voters (%)	Vote Received by Latino (%)	Dominant Latino Group
22	16	18	Mexican
26	25	7	Puerto Rican
31	33	27	Puerto Rican
46	8	27	Mixed

The figures provide no strong basis for predicting how the Latino will vote when faced with the choice of voting for an ethnic independent or a machine candidate. In the Thirty-first and Forty-sixth wards, Salces found that Latino voters had voted ethnically, that is, for the Latino candidate. In the Twenty-second Ward, however, the Latino vote had stayed with the machine candidate. And in the Twenty-sixth Ward, some ethnic voting was perceived but in meager amounts.

The incumbents presented strong defenses against Latino threats. Despite their relatively short time on the scene, the aldermen of the Twenty-second and Forty-sixth wards kept Latino candidates to less than 30 percent of the vote. As was to be expected the Latino running against the machine-entrenched Twenty-sixth Ward incumbent received the lowest percentage of votes. In the Thirty-first Ward, the strong showing of the Latino candidate may have been partly assisted by the scandal involving the former alderman.

Salces found a weak negative correlation between the presence of Latino candidates and voter turnout. He attributes this to the psychological strain of choosing between party and ethnicity; the result is a nonvoter. One must add to that explanation possible actions taken by the machine to encourage low voter turnout. It seems possible that by neglecting to push voters in wards where there might be the chance of losing Democrats to ethnic ties, only party faithfuls will turn out. First-time candidates can hardly be expected to have the organization required to turn out reluctant voters in large numbers.

If this interpretation is correct, it suggests that the Democratic organization not only withholds political authority from Latinos but that Latino voters may be considered an unstable factor when offered the chance to vote for a Latino candidate.

The organization's reluctance to incorporate Latinos cannot be based on the most recent mayoral campaigns. When one compares citywide turnout with those areas having a majority of Latino registered voters, it is evident that Latinos show higher turnouts with larger proportions voting for the Democratic organization's chosen candidate. In 1975 there were fifty-six precincts with at least 50 percent Latino registered voters (Neuman, 1976). These wards were distributed as shown in Table 4.

Table 4. Precincts with 50 Percent or More Latino Registered Voters.

Ward	1	7	10	22	25	26	31	32
Precincts (No.)	13	6	2	4	5	2	20	4

Table 5 lists results from the 1975 mayoral primary, in which Daley was challenged by independent Democrat William Singer, and the 1977 special mayoral primary, in which then Acting-Mayor Bilandic sought the party's endorsement over Roman Pucinski. The table shows percent turnout and percent votes going to the candidates for the city as a whole,

Table 5. Comparison of Turnout and Voter Choice: 1975, 1977.

Election	City	Latino Wards	Latino Precincts
1975 Mayoral Primary			
Turnout	57	61	63
Daley	53	60	62
Singer	27	22	21
1977 Special Primary			
Turnout	47	54	56
Bilandic	49	57	58
Pucinski	31	27	24

NOTE. All data are given as percentages.

for "Latino" wards (using the list made available by the Chicago Board of Elections that shows all wards with what the board considered "large" concentrations of Latinos—see Table 2), and for those precincts with at least 50 percent Latino registered voters.

Considering the weaknesses of using only two elections, having to deal with geographic units in describing individual behaviors, and slight (though perceptible) variations, we may not have much evidence to develop any hard and fast rules about Latino political behavior. But a few cautious remarks might be hazarded. Given the larger turnout in Latino wards and precincts than in the city as a whole, it seems possible that the Democratic organization may have subjected these areas to heavy campaigning in citywide elections. The absence of Latino candidates may have reduced any party-ethnicity tensions, allowing for greater use of the ballot in these elections. It is also possible that for aldermanic elections, areas with higher proportions of Latino voters are seen as risky, and thus voters are not so strongly encouraged (especially if a non-machine Latino is in the race).

COMMUNITY OR WARD?

In "The Political Organization of Chicago's Latino Communities," Walton and Salces (1977) discovered over 200 Latino organizations operating in the widely dispersed Latino communities. They were involved in all aspects of community life, from cultural and social events to active planning for political change. But for the most part, these organizations have been isolated from the actions of the Democratic organization. The network of community organizations has given rise to new Latino leaders as spokespersons for their communities, but with no legitimized position within the machine. Those Latinos who work for the Democratic party may sometimes be caught in the middle when party and community conflict. The Latino street-level worker, while having the support of the organization during citywide elections, must admit the disadvantages of his position in these moments: that is, that the Democratic organization, not he, is the source of power, and thus, in order to maintain his connection to that power, community interests must take second place.

Latino interests are primarily oriented to local community issues, rather than citywide reforms, as suits their spatial distribution in the city and their varying immediate problems. When Latino political action is discussed, it is usually discussed in terms of one or two activist organizations that have developed power bases in their communities, but that are seen as strangers in other Latino communities. The present structure of Latino political involvement is intertwined with local social organizational ties and focused on local rather than metropolitan needs. It must be remembered, too, that the term "Latino" encompasses several distinct ethnic groups. It describes more a sense of developing identity within Anglo culture rather than an existing population.

The twelve major Latino communities are divided among twenty-four wards (see Map 1). Only two wards (the Forty-third and Forty-fourth) lie wholly within the boundaries of two of these communities. In the following discussion we will exclude the Fortieth, Forty-ninth, and Fiftieth wards, small portions of which lie within the community of Uptown, and

Table 6. Distribution of Latino Wards by "Deliverability."

Wards in 1975 Primary					
Mainline		*Deliverable*	*Controlled*	*Independent*
7[a]	31[a]	11	1[a]	8
12	32[a]		14	43
22[a]	33[a]		25[a]	
24	42		26[a]	
27	44			
28	46			
30	48			
Wards in 1977 Primary					
Mainline		*Deliverable*	*Controlled*	*Independent*
7[a]	30[a]	11	1[a]	8
12	32[a]		25[a]	43
14	33[a]		27	
22[a]	42		31[a]	
24	44			
26[a]	46			
28	48			

[a]Wards with large proportions of Latinos as designated by Chicago Board of Elections.

look at the remaining twenty-one wards in terms of Kemp and Lineberry's categorization of wards as "mainline party," "deliverable," "controlled," and "independent" (see Chapter 1 herein). In the 1975 mayoral election, these wards were distributed as shown in Table 6.

Noting the distribution of wards with large numbers of Latinos, one must conclude that most Latino voters live either in wards where the machine works or in wards where the machine works *very well.*

One may also look at the distribution of other ethnic groups within these wards. Using Zikmund's (see Chapter 2 herein) categories of ethnic geographic spread, we see that Latinos will have to form alliances with every other major ethnic group in the city if they hope to develop power within the ward system (see Table 7).

Table 7. Distribution of Latino Wards by Area Voter Blocs.

Machine Core	White Ethnics	Black	Reform North Shore	Polish Northwest	South Side Ethnics
1[a], 11, 25[a], 27 31[a]	26[a], 42	7[a], 8, 24, 28	43, 44, 46, 48	30[a], 32[a], 33[a]	12, 14, 22[a]

[a]Wards with large proportions of Latino voters.

The steps that Latinos must take, then, to enable them to develop a power within the Democratic organization will include the following: (1) the initiation of action that will bond community identity and organization to ongoing political organization, (2) developing influence in those wards where Latino voters are already concentrated (unfortunately coincident with strongly controlled machine wards), and (3) establishing alliances with the diverse ethnic and racial groups residing with them in these wards. It appears that it will be an uphill battle.

CONCLUSIONS: THE 1980s

The findings of the 1980 census will substantiate claims by blacks and Latinos that they comprise new majorities in the neighborhoods surrounding the Chicago Loop. These majorities will play a large part in the redistricting of wards scheduled for 1981. Latinos are acknowledged to be the fastest-growing group in the public school system, comprising 17.2 percent of total enrollments in 1979 (*Chicago Sun-Times,* Jan. 1980). The percentage drops to 13.9 percent when considering only high school enrollments; Latinos have a high dropout rate, reflecting both problems with the educational system's ability to work with Latinos, and the economic realities of many Latino families that pressure fifteen- and sixteen-year olds to find work to help support the younger children.

The election of Jane Byrne showed that the automatic voting of Richard Daley's era can sometimes be disrupted if voters' personal interests are affected. However, Latinos did not follow the trend toward independence from the Democratic organization that gave victory to Byrne (Table 8); ironically their loyalty to the organization may have placed them in a politically worse position than previously.

Table 8. 1979 Mayoral Primary Results (Democratic) in Latino Wards.

		Wards								
Candidate	Citywide	1	7	22	25	26	30	31	32	33
Byrne	51	31	65	49	31	39	52	40	47	47
Bilandic	48	69	35	51	69	61	48	60	53	53

SOURCE. *Chicago Sun-Times*, Apr. 1979. These represent partial and unofficial counts of the votes, but are substantially the same as the final counts.
NOTE. Data are given as percent of total vote.

Bilandic averaged 55.4 percent of the vote in Latino wards. It should be remembered that these wards are all considered strongholds of the Democratic organization, with few registered independent Democrats, and with well-run precinct operations. The new mayor has been working to obtain the loyalty of these wards but may still feel unsure of her support among Latino voters.

The entire 1979 mayoral campaign was disastrous for Latinos in terms of gaining influence in city hall and support from the general public. Public opinion in Chicago does not favor disruptive political action, and in the media coverage of the campaign Latinos made headlines only when they staged sit-ins and harassed candidate Byrne. When Byrne reneged on a meeting with Latino community people, the group held a demonstration at her campaign headquarters, coercing promises from her that she soon denied by inaction. After Byrne's primary victory, an attempt to name a Latina, Mary Gonzales, to her transition team of advisors ended badly for Latinos' public image, as Gonzales refused to sit with the team. Gonzales charged that she had never been invited to join the team before her name was used by Byrne to indicate Latino support for her candidacy (*Chicago Tribune,* Mar. 1979). Insiders commented that Gonzales was pressured by Latinos to avoid connection with the candidate's team in a poorly contrived attempt to develop a Latino "power-bloc." As a result, no Latino served on Byrne's transition team. When the election was won, Elena Martinez, Byrne's Latina campaign organizer, was dismissed rather than rewarded with one of the high-paying jobs at the mayor's disposal, an action quite in line with Byrne's reputation for demanding successful results and her willingness to cut unproductive relationships.

During her first year in office, Byrne helped Carmen Velasquez, a member of the Chicago School Board, and later dumped her in a wholesale replacement of that board. Her only Latino appointment during the year was Dr. Hugo H. Muriel, an old family friend and a specialist in endocrinology, as head of the Public Health Commission. Dr. Muriel's abilities to manage his post were widely questioned: his medical background did not include public health expertise, and he had no community contacts with Latinos. Dr. Muriel subsequently shored up his position by naming Dr. Jose Gonzales as medical director of the Mental Health Division of Public Health, a highly qualified, bilingual psychiatrist formerly connected with Cook County Hospital in Chicago. This appointment was easily accepted by both Latinos and the medical community and went some way toward developing a kindlier disposition toward Dr. Muriel.

A week after Dr. Muriel's appointment, Latinos occupied the mayor's offices, demanding action on patronage jobs, neighborhood development funds, and better police work with juvenile gangs (*Chicago Sun-Times,* Apr. 1979). The mayor responded with a presentation to a local community group, promising a future request for federal target money for one Latino neighborhood. One year later, none of the mayor's promises had been fulfilled.

With lack of positive action from city hall, Latinos might have been expected to voice their disapproval and displeasure at the polls in the 1980 presidential primary, an election in which the mayor pushed her own political popularity into the forefront via her public shift of support from Jimmy Carter to Edward Kennedy and by her backing of Alderman Edward Burke in his race against Richard Daley for Cook County state's attorney. This was the race that saw the son of the deceased mayor and party leader run as an independent Democrat after the mayor pressured the county Democratic committee to support his opponent.

As voting history accumulates, Latinos are showing themselves to be a very conservative voting group, with a tendency to favor the incumbent when possible, and to follow the guidance of the Democratic organization if no Latino candidate is in the race. In the 1980 election, these two tendencies were in opposition, with the result that Kennedy won in only one Latino ward, the Twenty-fifth, that always deliverable ward headed by Alderman Vito Marzullo. However, in all but one of the Latino wards, Kennedy did better than elsewhere in the city.

In the state's attorney race, Latinos showed that they were willing to follow the mayor's lead and supported, if meagerly, Burke. In the Latino wards Burke averaged a higher proportion of the vote than he garnered elsewhere: he won five of the nine wards and broke even in a sixth. It seems that Latinos are attempting to follow as best they can the vagaries of the Democratic organization. Unfortunately, they, and the machine, backed three losers: Bilandic, Kennedy, and Burke (Table 9).

Table 9. 1980 Primary Results (Democratic) in Latino Wards.

Candidate	Citywide	Wards								
		1	7	22	25	26	30	31	32	33
President										
Carter	62.0	57.7	60.6	54.4	38.4	59.7	62.1	49.5	73.6	49.2
Kennedy	32.0	35.1	34.1	36.9	55.2	35.2	30.5	43.6	31.4	44.6
State's Attorney										
Daley	60.0	41.7	67.6	64.1	42.0	51.5	42.9	48.9	41.4	39.2
Burke	40.0	58.3	32.4	35.9	58.0	48.5	57.1	51.1	58.9	60.8

SOURCE. *Chicago Sun-Times,* Mar. 1979. These represent partial and unofficial counts of the votes, but are substantially the same as the final counts.
NOTE. Data are given as percent of total vote.

The radically inclined political activists in the Latino communities, with their focus on demonstrations and sit-ins, have probably hurt the efforts of the organization Latinos in selling Latino voters to the machine as solid party supporters. As a result, Latinos may find themselves in the position now held by Chicago's Polish citizens. Ironically, most of the Latino communities were formerly Polish and Slavic neighborhoods. And like their predecessors in those wards, Latinos may see themselves shunted aside in the power plays still managed largely by Irish politicians. Both Latinos and Poles are large in number, but unsuccessful in attaining the political representation their numbers would be expected to warrant. If Chicago has something of a "silent majority"—underrepresented and unacknowledged except at election times—the languages of that majority are Polish and Spanish.

Latinos are trapped by current terminology in the role of minorities. Their case illustrates the "dysfunctions" of such a label. Having determined that this large and diverse population is different from the white population, by reason of their distinction as "minorities," social scientists and government officials have expected Latinos to fit into the model of social disadvantages, racial discrimination, and potential for violent social upheaval that described the black situation of the mid-1960s when minorities were "discovered." But "minority" cannot be defined solely as a group with racial and cultural characteristics different from a more numerous group. The only meaningful application of the term minority involves the description of unequal social relations within a society. The ludicrous use of minority status is seen in the self-designation of all kinds of groups who wish to justify their cause: both smokers and nonsmokers refer to themselves as "minorites" whose "rights are being violated," depending upon how many sympathizers happen to be within earshot.

Latino history in Chicago does not fit one consistent model and certainly does not parallel that of Chicago's blacks. Latino history is bound up with the history of the growth of the city itself from hinterland trade center to heavy industrial capital and now to a growing service-centered city. Latinos have worked in all of those areas; they have not been excluded systematically from jobs or neighborhoods. It must not be overlooked that there is prejudice against many Latinos, particularly those with strong Indian and black ancestry. But the similarities between Latinos and the white ethnics of the city deter the acceptance of the impersonalized and uniform "distancing" experienced by blacks.

Latinos are mostly Catholic, as is most of Chicago. There are visible and stable families with traditional male dominance. There is no neighborhood rush to move when Latinos buy or rent in a new area. The only genuinely negative public notice taken of Latinos is the fierce and drug-connected gang activity in areas like West Town and Humboldt Park. Perhaps, if Chicago did not already have a black population, Latinos would have received the brunt of racism, as was the case in the Southwest. There, Latinos may be said to hold "minority" status, even though they are numerically in the majority. For in the Southwest, social and economic patterns developed dependent upon the subjugation of Latinos as underpaid farm workers, unorganized factory workers, and strikebreakers in the mines of Colorado.

Socially and economically, Latinos are between white ethnics and blacks. As census tables show, Latinos do not suffer as severely as blacks from unemployment and poor housing, but they do not do as well as their white neighbors. Social scientists who hold to the model of minority behavior and insist upon applying it to Latinos must wait for a major shift in our present situation before Latinos will display the expected behavior: if there should be a severe economic disruption that forces widespread unemployment both among the less skilled and in the service industries, where many Latinos are employed, only then will the level of frustration build to a sufficient degree to approximate behavior of a "minority."

The particular case of Latinos in various regions of the United States exemplifies how our commonplace definitions of "ethnicity" and "minority" are as impermanent as the social relations that produce them. Given their particular history in Chicago, the ethnicities that comprise the Latino population can be called minorities only if Poles, Italians, and even the Irish can also share the label. At the same time the Chicago

Mexican family, moving to Texas or New Mexico, may suddenly experience the role of social minority.

Political action has also been muddied by this misuse of the minority tag. There is glamour in large numbers: Latino political aspirants can easily be overwhelmed by the thought of heading a movement thousands strong. The realities demand, however, that the community and ethnic differences among Latinos be understood when building such movements. And it is more likely that success will be achieved at the community level, in coalitions with other ethnics, rather than through a citywide homogeneously Latino group. Likewise, those holding political power cannot expect to silence Latino demands by negotiating only with one or another group: a token appointment of a southside Mexican will not go very far in appeasing a northside Puerto Rican who needs a bilingual emergency room nurse. Yet the symbolic use of a uniform Latino population can be effective as a negotiating tool. As long as Latinos themselves recognize the dissimilarities of their people, the massed numbers will be beneficial in pressuring for those programs that are purportedly for "minority" improvement.

The 1980s will show whether Latinos can develop a dual approach to greater political power, hinging on a sliding social identity. At one level it will serve them well to encourage recognition as "ethnics" rather than "minorities" in their communities, to be better able to foster coalitions with white ethnics. On another level, when negotiating with citywide, state, and federal agencies, the identification as "minority" will be a strong incentive for reaching solutions, since fears of discrimination charges and the availability of minority-targeted funds coerce positive action. A major barrier to the development of these strategies is the possibility of an economic crisis. As in the 1930s, Latinos' weak citizenship position may once again provide a simplistic remedy for unemployment: the mass deportation of thousands with "irregular" papers. In the long run, to safeguard their advances in Chicago, Latinos may well need to turn their attention to Washington.

NOTE

1. Since this was written, Ray Castro was elected committeeman in the Seventh Ward.

REFERENCES

Burgess, Ernest W., ed., 1920, 1930. Census data of the City of Chicago. Uncatalogued publications of City of Chicago, Northwestern University Library, Evanston.

Chicago Reporter. 1974.
Cicago Sun-Times. Sept. 21, 1977; Apr. 1979; Jan. 1980; Mar. 1980.
Chicago Tribune. Mar. 1979.
Hunter, Albert J. 1974. *Symbolic Communities.* Chicago: University of Chicago Press.
Jones, A. E. 1928. "Conditions Surrounding Mexicans in Chicago." M.A. thesis. Chicago: University of Chicago.
Katznelson, Ira. 1973. *Black Men, White Cities.* Chicago: University of Chicago Press.
Kerr, L. A. 1975. "Chicano Settlements in Chicago: A Brief History." *Journal of Ethnic Studies,* 2 (Winter): 22–32.
Kornblum, William. 1974. *Blue Collar Community.* Chicago: University of Chicago Press.
Neuman, D. 1976. "Notes for a Study of Latino Voting Behavior." Manuscript. Northwestern University, Evanston.
Padilla, E. 1947. "Puerto Rican Immigrants in New York and Chicago: A Study in Comparative Assimilation." M.A. thesis. Chicago: University of Chicago.
Salces, Luis. 1978. "Spanish-Americans' Search for Political Representation in Chicago." Manuscript. Northwestern University, Evanston.
Sinclair, Upton. 1906. *The Jungle.* New York: Jungle Publishing Co.
Speer, Allan H. 1967. *Black Chicago.* Chicago: University of Chicago Press.
Suttles, Gerald D. 1968. *The Social Order of the Slum.* Chicago: University of Chicago Press.
Taylor, P. S. 1932. *Mexican Labor in the United States: Chicago and the Calumet Region.* Berkeley: University of California Press.
Walton, John, and Luis Salces. 1977. "The Political Organization of Chicago's Latino Communities." Red Cover Report. Evanston: Northwestern University Center for Urban Affairs.
Wolfinger, Raymond. 1973. *The Politics of Progress.* New Haven, Conn.: Yale University Press.
Zorbaugh, Harvey W. 1929. *The Gold Coast and the Slum.* Chicago: University of Chicago Press.

KENNETH R. MLADENKA

The Urban Bureaucracy and the Chicago Political Machine: Who Gets What and the Limits to Political Control

IT HAS LONG BEEN ASSUMED THAT urban political machines trade services for votes (Wilson, 1960: 53). Machines manipulate "specific, material inducements" to maintain power (Banfield and Wilson, 1963: 115). Voters are tied to the machine through the provision of a variety of material rewards (Gosnell, 1937). Machine aldermen are primarily concerned with the level and quality of urban services distributed to their constituents (Meyerson and Banfield, 1955: 66, 258; Rakove, 1975: 117–31). According to this perspective, urban services are political resources that can be manipulated, redistributed, and withdrawn in the scramble for electoral advantage. Loyal wards are rewarded with superior services. Major service decisions are made by the machine, handed down to the bureaucracy, and implemented in accordance with a scheme that seeks to wring maximal political advantage from the distribution of finite service resources.

However, recent research reveals that decisions about the distribution of resources in large cities are made by professional administrators who rely upon technical-rational rather than political criteria to guide choices (Levy et al., 1974; Lineberry, 1977; Jones et al., 1978; Mladenka, 1978; Mladenka and Hill, 1978). Although the use of bureaucratic rules may have distributional consequences, resource allocation is little affected by electoral outcomes, income levels, or the racial composition of neighborhoods. The complexity of municipal government requires the services of career specialists who bring professional values to bear during the resolution of distributional issues. The pattern of service distribution can best be understood in terms of the need of public bureaucracies to simplify reality and avoid conflict.

In order to test these competing hypotheses in Chicago, data were gathered on the distribution of several municipal services, including parks and recreation, fire protection, refuse collection, and education. Several strategies for the collection of data were used. First, data were collected on the distribution of resources across the fifty wards in the city for each of the four services analyzed.[1] These indicators of the variation in resource allocation were then supplemented with an analysis of a variety of written materials, including departmental records, city codes and ordinances, budgets, capital improvement plans, and proceedings of the city council. In addition, departmental operations were observed. Numerous agency personnel and key bureaucrats were interviewed. Finally, a research assistant interviewed ward aldermen to explore the role of ward politicians in the service distribution process.[2]

The first step in analyzing the role of the political machine in resource distribution was to interview thirty-one of the forty-eight aldermen in the city (two seats were vacant). Several of these interviews reinforced the image of the urban machine as a small band of professional politicians in tight control of service decisions. One alderman observed that "I produce the votes so when I talk I get results." Another noted that "people vote services. I can deliver the vote because I provide my ward with services." Still another alderman maintained that "if you want something you have to use influence. If I need something from the bureaucracy I just tell them there are six voters in that house; . . . get it fixed." These aldermen are disdainful of the notion that the bureaucracy may control the service distribution process and that professional managers rely upon technical-rational criteria to resolve distributional issues. Instead, they are confident of their ability to manipulate the administrative apparatus to secure superior services. Their power stems from their ability to deliver the vote, and they can count on the vote because they provide their constituents with tangible, material rewards.

This perspective is tempered by the responses of another group of Chicago aldermen, who suspect that the exercise of power with regard to service distribution is considerably more complex. These aldermen agree that bureaucrats often rely upon technical-rational criteria for distributing resources. Several mentioned that the library department allocates resources to neighborhood branches on the basis of reader levels, while police officers are assigned on the basis of crime rates and calls for service. One alderman observed that his constituents wanted a higher level of police patrol, but he knew that the crime rate in his ward would not justify the assignment of additional personnel.

The interviews produced mixed findings. Some aldermen perceive themselves as ward bosses, supremely confident of their power and secure in the knowledge that their relationship with the machine can be readily translated into tangible rewards for their constituents. Who gets what is simply a question of who has influence. Other aldermen believe that it is the bureaucracy that defines the rules that govern distributional choices. They lack the resources necessary to challenge administrative outcomes effectively. They play little role in shaping and monitoring distributional policy either for their ward or for the city as a whole. Technical-rational rather than political considerations are often employed to justify bureaucratic choices about the division of service resources.

THE DISTRIBUTION OF PARKS AND RECREATION

To assess the distributional pattern for park and recreational services, data on all city parks in both 1967 and 1977 were gathered. In addition to acreage, variables for each of the several hundred parks include number and type of recreational facilities, programs, and activities. Each park was identified by ward, and the relationships between the income, racial, and electoral characteristics of wards and park acreage and facilities were explored through correlation analysis.[3] The "all facilities" variable was formed by summing the total number of facilities at each park. This indicator assigned the same weight to each facility and was insensitive to the variation in major recreational facilities. The "selected facilities" variable was limited to major recreational items—swimming pools, athletic fields, golf courses, day camps, playgrounds, and gymnasiums. In addition, individual correlations between ward characteristics and key recreational facilities were also examined.

The analysis revealed that park acreage was equally distributed in the city in 1967. Black and other low-income wards did not receive less acreage than wealthier wards. A different pattern emerged when the other relationships were examined. Parks located in black wards tended to receive fewer facilities. Although the associations were moderate (correlations of -0.30 and -0.20 between black and "all facilities" and "selected facilities"), the pattern was consistent. This relationship was even more evident when the associations between the measures of wealth and number of facilities were examined. The correlation between family income of wards and "all facilities" was 0.52, the association between income and "selected facilities" was 0.43, and the correlation between income and athletic fields was 0.42.

To determine if and why the distributional pattern changed from 1967 to 1977, a procedure identical to the one employed in analyzing the 1967 data was followed. An examination of the results again revealed an essentially equal distribution of acreage for the 576 parks in the city. Further examination revealed that while parks located in black wards still tended to receive fewer facilities than parks in white wards, this tendency was considerably less pronounced than it was a decade earlier. In 1967 the correlation between the proportion of the ward population that was black and "all facilities" was -0.30, while the association between percent black and "selected facilities" was -0.20. By 1977 the correlation between percent black and all park facilities had declined to –0.13, while the association of percent black and selected recreational facilities was –0.01. A similar pattern is noted for the relationship between ward income and the other indicators of recreational resources. The correlation between ward income and selected ward recreational facilities declined from 0.43 in 1967 to 0.18 in 1977.

The data do not support the notion that the political machine rewards electorally loyal wards. In fact, the correlations between the Daley vote for mayor in the 1963 and 1967 elections and the distribution of recreational facilities in 1967 were consistently negative. As support for the political machine increased across wards, resource levels decreased. The correlations between the Daley vote in 1963 and the "all facilities" and "selected facilities" variables for 1967 were –0.44 and –0.38, while the associations between the Daley vote in 1967 and these same measures of recreational resources were –0.38 and –0.32. A somewhat different pattern emerged when the distributional results for 1977 were examined. The allocation of total and selected recreational facilities tended to be equally distributed on the basis of electoral support, the distribution of swimming pools and gymnasiums favored loyal wards, and park acreage and golf courses were negatively correlated with the vote for the machine. Although the relationship between electoral support and resource allocation changed during the past decade, there is little evidence to suggest that supportive wards were rewarded with preferential service treatment. The analysis also revealed that the geographical distribution of park sites did not vary on the basis of electoral loyalty to the machine.[4]

What factors are responsible for the pattern of service distribution? The evidence argues that past decisions, population movements, and black demands and protests are important determinants for the allocation of parks in Chicago. Many of the large parks in the system were acquired and developed in the last century. Much of the total parkland in the city is accounted for by a handful of giant sites. Decisions made many decades ago about where to locate these huge parks and the subsequent movement of the central city population toward, around, and away from them offer the most convincing explanation of the present distribution of park acreage. In the past, decisions as to the location of parks were influenced by the recreational opportunities afforded by the Chicago lake front and by the need to serve a central city population that was more geographically concentrated than it is today. Now, because of these decisions, in conjunction with population shifts and the limited supply of land available and suitable for further park development, political and administrative authorities are severely restricted in reallocating recreational sites.

These factors do not, however, account for the apparent shift in resource allocation that took place between 1967 and 1977. Why are recreational facilities more evenly distributed today than they were a decade ago? The data from interviews strongly suggest that local officials responded to black demands and protests by providing black neighborhoods with a greater share of available resources. Black wards primarily gained swimming pools, athletic fields, and playgrounds, while wealthier wards received fewer of these facilities. Distributional policy was apparently more sensitive to group demands and protests than to patterns of electoral support.

THE DISTRIBUTION OF FIRE PROTECTION RESOURCES

The distributional pattern for fire protection was assessed by examining data on the allocation of fire department resources in both 1965 and 1978. Variables include the number of stations per ward, the number of engine and ladder companies assigned to each station, age and condition of stations, and age of equipment. The analysis did not support the hypothesis that wealthier wards were favored in terms of resource allocation in 1965. The correlation between income and number of stations was −0.36, while the association between welfare and number of stations was 0.30. Examination of scatterplots for the principal pairs of variables revealed a nonlinear relationship between the proportion of the ward population that was black and number of stations. When wards were categorized on the basis of race, it was found that predominantly black wards (80.1–100 percent black) had a considerably greater number of fire stations in 1965 than predominantly white wards (0–10 percent black). Black wards received 2.8 stations per ward, while white wards were allocated only 2 stations. The mixed wards (10.1–40 percent black), however, emerged as the clear winners, receiving twice as many stations per ward as white wards and an average of one more station than black wards. Similarly, white wards were allocated an average of only 2.8 engine and ladder companies per ward, black wards were assigned 3.6 such companies, and mixed wards received 5.4. The geographical distribution of fire stations also favored black and poor wards.[5]

Some significant changes in resource distribution took place between 1965 and 1978, when forty-one fire stations in the city were closed and twenty-four new stations were constructed. The fifty wards were classified on the basis of race, and each station in 1978 was assigned to the appropriate category. The results of this exercise revealed that, although black wards continued to receive a slightly greater number of stations and trucks than white wards, the differences were considerably less pronounced than they were in 1975. In fact, the evidence suggested a basically equal level of resources in predominantly white and black wards.

However, mixed wards again emerged as the winner in the distributional process. These wards received one and a half more stations and two more engine and ladder trucks per ward than white wards.

What factors determined the pattern of resource allocation for fire protection services in 1965 and 1978? Again, the electoral explanation of resource allocation must be rejected, for it turns out that distributional policy within the Chicago Fire Department was largely a function of historical developments, population shifts, a series of unique events, and the triumph of professional values. Although dramatic population shifts occurred after 1930, the fire station network was largely complete by that time. Only 9 percent of the stations in the city in 1965 had been constructed between 1950 and 1965, and only one out of four had been built after 1930. Not only was the early development of the fire protection system heavily influenced by the need to accommodate a geographically concentrated population, but it was also affected by prevailing fire-fighting technologies. Not until 1923 was horse-drawn equipment completely phased out of the system and replaced by motorized vehicles. Reliance on the horse required that fire stations be located at relatively short distances from each other. As modern equipment replaced animals, these motorized vehicles were housed in stations designed to reflect the limitations of turn-of-the-century technology. The outcome of these developments was a heavy concentration of fire stations in inner-city wards. The two Chicago stockyard fires of 1910 and 1934 also profoundly influenced distributional decision-making. These fires and the probability of more left a deep and lasting imprint on the distributional pattern. In 1965 there were still six fire stations within a half mile of the abandoned stockyards, eight within a mile, and seventeen within two miles.

The distributional pattern that existed in 1965 can be attributed in large part to a failure to adapt to technological changes, to only a limited reshaping of the system in response to the geographic dispersal of the inner-city population, and to a preoccupation with the old Chicago stockyards. Although racially mixed wards contained more fire stations in 1965, the evidence does not support the hypothesis that they were rewarded with preferential treatment in return for consistent electoral support. Instead, these wards received higher resource levels because they included within their boundaries both the inner city and the old stockyards.

The distributional changes that occurred between 1965 and 1978 can be largely attributed to the recommendations made by a private management consulting firm. Professional administrators were sensitive to the obsolescence of the system and hired the National Loss Control Service Corporation to document inadequacies and offer specific recommendations. In a series of reports issued in 1964, 1968, and 1971, the firm criticized the excessive protection provided the inner city and the inadequate protection for outlying sections of the city. Using guidelines established by the National Board of Fire Underwriters, the firm conducted several hundred tests in various commercial, industrial, and residential areas of the city to determine an "optimum distribution of resources." The reallocation that occurred in the city between 1965 and 1978 can be attributed to the specific suggestions contained in the management reports. The service distribution process in the Chicago Fire Department during the 1960s and 1970s was dominated not by machine politicians bent on maximizing electoral advantage but by reliance on technical-rational criteria. The aggregate analysis, examination of written documents, and interviews with both bureaucrats and ward aldermen reinforce the conclusion that redistribution was little affected by the urban machine.

THE DISTRIBUTION OF EDUCATIONAL RESOURCES

Education is the third major service to be analyzed. Data were gathered on all 599 public schools in the city (491 elementary, 40 middle, and 68 high schools) for the year 1974–75. Variables for each school included racial composition of the student body, age of the physical plant, number of teachers, counselors, and librarians, staffing costs per pupil, teacher experience, teacher qualifications, number of foreign languages offered, and number of special education programs. Correlational analysis was employed to examine the relationships between the minority composition of the student body (percent black, Mexican-American, Puerto Rican) and educational resources for elementary and high schools.

The results for elementary schools were mixed. Teacher/pupil ratios were equally distributed, while the associations between percent minority students and both age of school and staffing costs per pupil were weak (correlation of –0.10 between percent minority and staffing costs). Minority schools were favored in terms of number of special education programs; white schools received both the most experienced and best educated teachers (correlation of –0.54 between percent minority students and teachers with the M.A. plus advanced work). The 491 elementary schools in the system were then classified into four categories on the basis of the minority composition of the student body, and the average values for the various indicators of educational resources were determined for each category of schools. Predominantly white schools tended to receive the highest resource levels. Although minority schools (50.1–80 percent minority) ranked first on teacher/pupil ratios, white schools spent most on staffing and were assigned the most experienced and best educated teachers. White schools spent an average of $703 per student for staffing, as opposed to $688 in 50.1–80 percent minority schools and

$671 in 80.1–100 percent minority schools. In white schools 74 percent of the teachers had six or more years experience, and 35 percent had an M.A. or an M.A. plus advanced work, while the corresponding percentages for teacher experience and education in heavily minority schools were only 56 percent and 22 percent, respectively.

For high schools, the pattern of resource allocation again favored white students. Although teacher/pupil ratios were slightly lower in minority schools (–0.10), minority schools had lower staffing expenditures (–0.20), less experienced teachers (correlation of –0.80 between minority students and teachers with thirteen or more years experience), and fewer teachers with advanced degrees. White schools spent $48 more per student than black schools, and 54 percent of the teachers in white schools had an M.A. compared with only 32 percent in black schools.

What factors account for the variations in the distribution of educational resources? Again, a political explanation for service distribution must be rejected. Teacher/pupil ratios in the Chicago public school system are determined by bureaucrats who rely upon a complex formula to ensure that these ratios are identical across schools. Variations in the distribution of staffing costs, teacher experience, and teacher training are also a function of bureaucratic rules. Assignment of teachers is highly decentralized. Transfer requests within the Chicago public school system are granted largely on the basis of seniority. White schools have the most experienced faculty because, when given the choice, teachers prefer to work in white schools. Transfer policy also determines the distribution of staffing costs and teacher qualifications. More experienced teachers also tend to be the best educated, and teacher salaries are determined by experience and education.

THE DISTRIBUTION OF REFUSE COLLECTION SERVICES

The primary measure of the distribution of resources for refuse collection was the total number of refuse trucks assigned to each ward on a weekly basis. These data were gathered for each of the fifty wards, and the relationships between ward characteristics and the number of assigned vehicles were explored through correlation analysis. An examination of the data revealed that black and other low-income wards were assigned fewer trucks than wealthy wards. The correlation between the proportion of the ward population that was black and the number of vehicles was –0.32, while the association between ward income and trucks was 0.51. Is the relationship among race, income, and number of trucks spurious? The evidence suggests that it is. When the effects of the level of home ownership were held constant, the correlation between percent black and number of trucks declines from –0.32 to –0.07, while the association between welfare and trucks dropped from –0.53 to –0.18. When the racial variable was controlled, the correlation between home owner- ship and trucks remained a strong 0.84; when the welfare variable was controlled, the association between home ownership and the dependent variable was 0.79; and when the effects of the income variable were held constant, the correlation between ownership and number of vehicles was 0.82.

A large number of interviews with administrators at both the bureau and ward levels provides strong support for the finding that resources for refuse collection are allocated on the basis of the level of home owner- ship in a ward. In addition, the pattern is affected by the distance to be traveled between pickups and the amount of refuse generated per ward. It should be noted, however, that these policies do not operate to the ex- clusive advantage of white, wealthy wards. For example, ten of the twen- ty-six predominantly white wards have below the citywide average num- ber of vehicles, while two of the three wards that are 40.1–80 percent black and three of the twelve wards 80.1–100 percent black have above the city average. Similar variation characterizes the pattern of resource distribution when wards are classified on the basis of income. Six of the fourteen low-income wards have more than the citywide average number of trucks, while eleven of the twenty-four middle-income and three of the twelve upper-income wards are assigned a below average number. These differences in the number of assigned vehicles can be largely accounted for by the variation in the ward distribution of home ownership.

Resources for refuse collection are distributed on the basis of owner- occupied housing because a city ordinance prohibits collection from multi-family dwellings containing five or more apartments. An examina- tion of city codes revealed that the ordinance limiting refuse collection was in operation as early as 1911. That ordinance has survived in basical- ly unaltered form until the present and continues to guide the distribu- tion of refuse collection services. Why was the ordinance adopted? Dur- ing the nineteenth and part of the twentieth century, coal was the major fuel source. The use of coal enormously complicated refuse collection. Large tenement buildings generated tons of coal cinders. Collection problems were particularly severe during the winter months when huge cinder heaps froze and picks were required to break them apart before loading. It was not until 1940 that motorized vehicles replaced the horse- drawn garbage wagon in Chicago. Rather than increase manpower levels to deal with the problems associated with the use of coal, the city council opted for exluding large multi-family structures from collection. Gas and oil have long since replaced coal as heating fuels. Nonetheless, residents of low-income tenements as well as occupants of apartments, high-rise buildings, townhouses, and condominiums continue to bear the costs of refuse collection themselves.

Whether Chicago citizens are entitled to have garbage picked up by city government is determined not by their loyal support of the political machine but by the type of housing they occupy. Distributional outcomes are the legacy of policies made many decades ago and designed to address conditions that no longer exist.

CONCLUSION

Table 1 summarizes the results of these studies. The analysis of resource distribution in Chicago provides little support for the hypothesis that urban services are used by the political machine to reward loyal supporters and to punish enemies. There is no evidence that the pattern of service distribution in the city is a consequence of rational political calculations about who should win and who should lose in the struggle over finite resources. Instead, distributional outcomes are largely a function of past decisions, population shifts, technological changes, and reliance upon technical-rational criteria and professional values. The allocation of park facilities in 1977 provides the only exception to this pattern. Even in that instance distributional policy was more sensitive to black demands and protests than to the vote. What Levy et al. (1974) discovered for Oakland, what Lineberry (1977) found for San Antonio, what Jones et al. (1978) reported for Detroit, and what Mladenka and Hill (1978) discovered for Houston apply to Chicago as well. Distributional decision-making is routinized and largely devoid of explicit political content. Although Nivola (1978) offers a different explanation of the determinants of the distributional pattern in Boston, he also found that bureaucrats control distributional outcomes.

However, it would be misleading to conclude that all urban services are distributed on the basis of organizational routines. Several factors distinguish the service bureaucracies analyzed in this study. First, these urban bureaucracies lack well-defined constituencies and clientele groups. Second, the resource measures considered in this article (parks and fire stations) limit the opportunities for discretionary behavior in distributional decision-making. Finally, these bureaucracies differ from the classic street-level organization. The services delivered at the neighborhood level by "street-level bureaucrats" (policemen, welfare workers, or housing inspectors) are unlikely to be governed by organizational rules that ensure predictable behavior. The severe limitations on the ability of administrators to control the behavior of these bureaucrats has been well documented (Wilson, 1968; Lipsky, 1976). In fact, Nivola (1978: 70) analyzed the distribution of services within a street-level organization and concluded that housing inspection outcomes in Boston were a consequence of "technical difficulties, patterns of bureaucratic discre-

Table 1. Summary of Zero-Order Correlations between Ward Characteristics and Service Distribution Variables.

Demographic and Electoral Variables for Wards	All Park Facilities, 1967	Selected Park Facilities, 1967	All Park Facilities, 1977	Selected Park Facilities, 1977	Distance to Largest Parks, 1977	No. of Fire Stations, 1965	Distance to Fire Stations, 1965	No. of Fire Stations, 1978	Distance to Fire Stations, 1978	No. of Refuse Collection Vehicles, 1977
Percent black	-0.30	-0.20	-0.13	-0.01	-0.27	0.12	-0.23	-0.05	-0.19	-0.32
Percent Spanish	-0.19	-0.18	0.12	-0.15	-0.10	0.23	-0.23	0.30	-0.04	0.05
Family Income	0.52	0.43	0.35	0.18	0.48	-0.36	0.56	-0.16	0.44	0.51
Percent welfare	-0.37	-0.29	-0.18	-0.03	-0.32	0.30	-0.44	0.07	-0.39	-0.53
Percent home ownership	0.54	0.52	0.50	0.41	0.61	-0.23	0.71	-0.24	0.56	0.85
Daley vote										
1963	-0.44	-0.38				0.31	-0.56			
1967	-0.38	-0.32				0.40	-0.52			
1971			-0.03	0.09	0			0.01	-0.10	0.29
1975			-0.01	0.14	0.03			-0.01	-0.05	0.32

SOURCE. See note 1 for list of sources.
NOTE. The strength of several of these relationships declines when controls are introduced.

tion, and problems of control within the housing inspection department itself.''

Although the determinants of distributional outcomes vary across types of bureaucracies, it is significant that distributional patterns in both reformed and machine cities are little affected by voter choices or elected officials. Organizational rules and unanticipated events and developments provide a better explanation of who gets what than any combination of distinctly political and electoral variables.

NOTES

1. Aggregate data on Chicago parks and recreation were obtained from the *Table of Parks and Park Facilities* (1967, 1977), while data on fire protection resources were gathered from *Comprehensive Survey of Fire Department Engine and Ladder Company Distribution* (1964); *Chicago Fire Department Operations Study* (1968); *Fire Department Management and Operations Study* (1971); and *Chicago Fire Department Directory* (1970). Additional data were obtained from unpublished records from the office of the Chicago Fire Department Commisioner. Indicators of educational resources were taken from the Chicago Board of Education's *Selected School Characteristics: 1974–75.* The measures of resources for refuse collection were gathered from unpublished records located in the office of the general superintendent, Bureau of Sanitation, Department of Streets and Sanitation. These data were verified by consulting the records maintained by the ward superintendents, Bureau of Sanitation.

2. I thank Steve Brooks, who conducted the interviews with the aldermen.

3. The various analyses for each of the services studied are available from the author upon request.

4. Accessibility to park sites was measured by calculating the average of the linear distance from seven points in each ward to various parks. Separate computations were made for four categories of parks: 1–5 acres, 5.1–25 acres, over 25 acres, and any park of at least 1 acre. The results for 1977 did not support the hypothesis that electorally supportive wards were favored in terms of accessibility to parks. The correlations between the Daley vote in 1975 and distance to the smallest and largest parks were only 0.03. These correlations were not significant at the 0.05 level.

5. The geographical distribution of fire stations was determined by calculating the average of the linear distance from seven points in each ward to the nearest station. Black and poor wards were closer than wealthier wards to the nearest fire stations in 1965. The correlation between percent welfare and distance was –0.44, while the association between income and distance was 0.56.

REFERENCES

Banfield, Edward C., and James Q. Wilson. 1963. *City Politics.* Cambridge, Mass.: Harvard University Press and the M.I.T. Press.

Chicago Fire Department Directory. 1970. City of Chicago.

Chicago Fire Department Operations Study. 1968. City of Chicago.

Comprehensive Survey of Fire Department Engine and Ladder Company Distribution. 1964. City of Chicago.

Fire Department Management and Operations Study. 1971. City of Chicago.
Gosnell, Harold F. 1937. *Machine Politics: Chicago Model.* Chicago: University of Chicago Press.
Jones, Bryan D., Saadia R. Greenberg, Clifford Kaufman, and Joseph Drew. 1978. "Service Delivery Rules and the Distribution of Local Government Services: Three Detroit Bureaucracies." *Journal of Politics,* 40 (May): 332-68.
Levy, Frank S., Arnold J. Meltsner, and Aaron Wildavsky. 1974. *Urban Outcomes.* Berkeley: University of California Press.
Lineberry, Robert L. 1977. *Equality and Urban Policy.* Beverly Hills, Calif.: Sage.
Lipsky, Michael. 1976. "Toward a Theory of Street Level Bureaucracy." In Willis D. Hawley and Michael Lipsky, eds., *Theoretical Perspectives on Urban Politics,* pp. 196-213. Englewood Cliffs, N.J.: Prentice Hall.
Meyerson, Martin, and Edward C. Banfield. 1955. *Politics, Planning and the Public Interest.* Glencoe, Ill.: Free Press.
Mladenka, Kenneth R. 1978. "Organizational Rules, Service Equality, and Distributional Decisions in Urban Politics." *Social Science Quarterly,* 59 (June): 192-201.
———, and Kim Q. Hill. 1978. "The Distribution of Urban Police Services." *Journal of Politics,* 40 (Feb.): 112-33.
Nivola, Pietro S. 1978. "Distributing a Municipal Service: A Case Study of Housing Inspection." *Journal of Politics,* 40 (Feb.): 59-81.
Rakove, Milton L. 1975. *Don't Make No Waves, Don't Back No Losers.* Bloomington: Indiana University Press.
Selected School Characteristics: 1974-1975. 1975. Chicago Board of Education.
Table of Parks and Park Facilities. 1967, 1977. Chicago Park District.
Wilson, James Q. 1960. *Negro Politics.* New York: Free Press.
———. 1968. *Varieties of Police Behavior.* Cambridge, Mass.: Harvard University Press.

DONALD H. HAIDER

Capital Budgeting and Planning
in the Post-Daley Era

IT HAS LONG BEEN HELD that one of the principal advantages old large cities have in competing for economic activity is their in-place capital structure. Newer growth cities, so the argument goes, will have to pay a tremendous price to develop an infrastructure that will meet the needs of an expanding population as measured against the services provided in older cities. Whether inherited capital stock gives old larger cities like Chicago an economic advantage depends on its condition and the extent to which adequate resources are being allocated for maintenance. How Chicago chooses to balance preservation and replacement of existing stock with plans for major new construction may well determine the city's overall financial viability in the years ahead. Few resource allocation decisions in the post-Daley era are more critical to the future of the city than those involving capital plant maintenance.

The capitalizing of operating expenditures contributed to New York City's financial crisis. Once conventional markets had closed the city off from the sale of long-term bonds, New York halted capital projects and substantially reduced expenditures for capital maintenance programs. Even though it has received federal loan guarantees, the city's capital expenditures have not yet returned to pre-crisis levels, or anything approaching the more than $1 billion annual capital modernization and repair schedule estimated to be required over the next several decades. As David Grossman indicates (1979: xvi), the city is not "falling down," but "its infrastructure is deteriorating and needs a significantly increased rate of investment in maintenance and replacement if serious problems are to be avoided in coming decades."

Even more than New York, Cleveland serves as the prime example of the cumulative costs that stem from neglect and advanced deterioration. Political stalemate kept taxes and utility rates low, while little attention was paid to the long-term consequences of capital stock deterioration. Today 30 percent of Cleveland's 163 bridges—for which it has full maintenance responsibility—are in "intolerable or unsatisfactory condition"; $250 to $500 million are needed for water system replacement; and another $300 to $400 million are required for immediate sewer repairs. Like New York, Cleveland has no independent access to long-term capital markets, faces economic and financial decline, and relies substantially on higher government levels for funding improvements, especially in transit and sewage treatment (Peterson et al., 1979a: xv).

In contrast to New York and Cleveland, Cincinnati faced up to its capital maintenance problems. Its five-year capital investment program based on a systematic needs assessment and a comprehensive local plan required taxes and user fees to be raised for the express purpose of upgrading the city's capital plant. The Urban Institute has noted that Cincinnati "was among the first in the nation to systematically direct its capital planning toward preservation, maintenance, and improvement of existing facilities, accepting the necessity for cutting back on new capital projects if it was to operate within its budgeting limitations" (Peterson et al., 1979b: xv).

Dallas, a relatively newer city and located in the so-called Sunbelt, may serve as a benchmark for measuring deterioration in older cities. Due to rapid economic growth, Dallas's strong tax base enables it to meet current needs, to limit dependency on debt, and to maintain a strong financial position. Dallas also has been able to channel much of its federal aid into its capital budget, whereas many Snowbelt cities generally use such aid to close operating budget deficits (Wilson, 1980).

CHICAGO'S SITUATION

Chicago is NOT New York or Cleveland. It does not suffer from as advanced a case of deferred maintenance and capital stock deterioration as either of them. It enjoys access to financial markets and is taking significant steps toward upgrading its transit stock. Nor is Chicago a Cincinnati, fully facing up to its capital stock problems and giving priority to preservation and maintenance of existing facilities. And Chicago cannot be compared to Dallas. It does not enjoy the luxury of being able to divert unrestricted or semi-unrestricted federal aid to long-term capital as opposed to operating purposes.

Chicago faces a major turning point in the early 1980s. It has a unique opportunity to get on top of its capital maintenance problems. It also faces potential problems because it has failed to develop a capital budget and capital priority process. The city has a sizable cumulative deficit from prior years, has nearly exhausted the use of new home rule taxes, and could weaken its economic competitive position through additional large property tax increases. The urgency of this priority stems not simply from an overview of the city's capital and other financial needs. It is also due to the assurance made by city officials to New York bond rating agencies, which were aimed at stemming further slippage of the city's credit rating that had been lowered twice in 1979 from an AA position (high quality investment) to A− (between favorable investment attributes to medium grade) (City of Chicago, 1980).

Chicago was one of the first major cities to have a general plan for its development. Prepared by Daniel Burnham and financed by local businessmen, the plan called for—and the mayor responded by appointing—a large advisory commission to study and promote its proposals. The advisory body, known as the Chicago Plan Commission, was highly successful in helping the development of the city's physical assets. The commission was later reduced in size, subsumed into city government, and, with statutory aid, its scope broadened to include the review of proposals by any public body or agency for development within the city. The commission's authority was further bolstered under the Lake Michigan and Chicago Lakefront Protection Ordinance (1973) and the Planned Unit Development Ordinance (1974), which gave it public hearing and approval rights.

In contrast to the part-time, largely advisory nature of the Plan Commission, the city's Department of Planning, City and Community Development, and its commissioner are responsible for supervising and coordinating the formulation and execution of physical improvement projects and programs affecting the present and future development of the city. The commissioner is also responsible for maintaining and updating the city's comprehensive plan to guide and direct growth as well as change within the city. The growth of this department reflects the deepening federal involvement in cities: the expansion of slum clearance to include commercial redevelopment as well as housing (1954); the merger of urban renewal and social programs (1966); the consolidation of physical development, planning, and housing rehabilitation programs (1974); and the leveraging of private sector financing for economic development and for neighborhood revitalization (1978). The Planning Department became the principal city agency for physical and social planning, for land use, urban renewal, and housing rehabilitation. Through its commissioner it also became involved in zoning, historic landmarks, economic development, transportation planning, and buiding within the city.

In the fall of 1978 the Planning Department released its twentieth annual Five-Year Capital Improvements report, which noted that this annual statement was a "product of a planning and programming process inspired and created by Mayor Richard J. Daley at the time the Department of City Planning was established on January 1, 1957" (Commissioner of Planning, 1978). In fact, two decades earlier Daley had consolidated a great deal of executive power into two government agencies. Planning was given power over capital allocation decisions, and a budget office and its director—transferred from the city council's Finance Committee—brought budgeting into the mayor's own office.

The capital improvements program was to be an iterative plan reflecting a five-year scheduling of projects by city, state, and federal agencies. It called for all city operating departments and other government agencies serving the city to submit lists of proposed projects to the Planning Department for review and resubmission to the Plan Commission for conformity with the city's comprehensive plan. After these had been reviewed by the department and the city's capital improvements program committee (comprising representatives of each participating agency), the five-year program would be released but without formal approval either by the department or the commission. Instead, statutory authority and municipal code requirements stipulated that individual and detailed project descriptions be resubmitted for final review by both entities prior to approval and construction. In addition, the city's municipal code requires that the Chicago Plan Commission report at least once a year to the mayor and the city council on conformity of the citywide capital improvements program to the general plan of Chicago (City of Chicago).

The capital improvements program comprised an updated report along with schedules for some 2,000 projects costing $7 to $9 billion; more than 30 percent of the projects were to be carried out by the city itself. The sources of the city's financial contribution, other than the federal or state governments, were variously listed as local tax funds, revenue and general obligation bonds, motor fuel tax funds, and others to be determined later. The resulting program reflected more a pictorial "wish list" than a capital plan. Funding remained obscure, priorities unspecified, approval indefinite, and integration into a financial plan nonexistent. Moreover, not all capital improvements were to be found in the document, and not everything in the listed program constituted capital improvements. Indeed, by the late 1970s the reports tended to be produced more for show (municipal analysts, economic development, business promotion) than for internal decision-making or guidance.

Chicago's planning and capital allocation process suffers from internal fragmentation. Each of the major infrastructure-related departments—Public Works, Water and Sewers, Streets and Sanitation—comprises several bureaus, and each has an assortment of capital maintenance responsibilities: design, planning, engineering, building management, construction, equipment services, and the like. Each guards its mission and individual overhead staff and competes vigorously for maintenance funds from several resources—annual budgets, bond funds, motor fuel tax monies, and various federal funds. They also compete for the mayor's attention, urged on by the city's fifty wards and their committeemen to meet service imperatives and electoral needs.

Tight budgets and a reluctance to increase property taxes during the 1970s had the effect that only certain capital maintenance needs were attended to—those that could be generated by the infusion of federal grants for capital purposes. Building and material costs, driven upward by inflation, necessitated the scaling down of scheduled repairs and quickly depleted general obligation bond funds. Road and bridge replacement fell victim to lengthy city-state negotiations and unfulfilled promises of state assistance. For example, the city geared up its planning, engineering, and design staff for the proposed multi-billion dollar Crosstown Expressway, but even its scaled-down versions failed to gain state approval.

Interdepartmental competition was exacerbated by competition among professional staffs. Both Public Works and Planning had their own architects, urban designers, and transportation planners; capital planning was handled by the Planning Department and was rarely seen by budget personnel or the comptroller's office. Each infrastructure department also had its own engineers, so that there was very little coordination between engineers and planners, or between these professionals and those charged with financial tasks.

Fragmentation at city hall paralleled that among the six other Chicago area units of local government, each of which is separately incorporated under state law and has its own independent tax levy—the Board of Education, Park District, Community College District, Cook County, the Forest Preserve of Cook County, and the Metropolitan Sanitary District of greater Chicago. All levy taxes upon property located in the city and build and operate public facilities. To these must be added other public bodies, such as the Chicago Transit Authority, the Regional Transportation Authority, the Public Building Commission of Chicago, Cook County Hospital as well as the Chicago Housing Authority, Public Library, and various regional planning units.

Coordination, planning, setting priorities, and capital allocation among these government units have become increasingly complex and haphazard. Although any capital project within the city requires review and approval by the Planning Department and the Plan Commission, each agency tends to follow its own missions and institutional/professional imperatives (e.g., health, education, recreation, etc.) without much concern for shared facilities, alternative uses, historic preservation, community input, or operating costs. It has not been uncommon for bond funds to be used for health facilities, parks, or libraries without sufficient operating funds to staff or to service those facilities completely.

Further fragmentation of capital maintenance responsibility occurred under the Public Building Commission, an independent municipal corporation created in 1956 and empowered to construct, acquire, and rehabilitate public buildings for use by various government agencies, including the city and county as well as the parks, Board of Education, library, and junior colleges. Chicago was a pioneer in lease-rental revenue bonds, which permit building construction and rehabilitation to be financed through fixed rentals. These are supported by individual government property tax levies, excluded from statutory rate limits, and protected by the provision that lease rental payments receive first claim on property tax revenues. Using this method of financing, the commission renovated Navy Pier and city hall, constructed the Daley Center, and built numerous library branches, schools, and fire houses. Indeed, it has functioned as a model of intergovernmental cooperation among seven government units, although not as a mechanism for capital coordination and planning across taxing jurisdictions. This is not its purpose.

A NATIONAL PROBLEM

The scope and magnitude of the capital infrastructure problem of older regions are undergoing substantial review by federal departments and congressional committees. Sufficient examples exist to suggest that the problems of deferred urban maintenance are severe in most large urban areas, and growing worse. High interest rates, inflation, the prospect of reduced federal assistance, and pressing financial problems may all force state and local governments to defer once again capital construction, maintenance, and renovation. Chicago's particular situation, then, may be most appropriately viewed in the context of national trends and forces that have produced a widespread capital infrastructure problem. At the same time attention must be paid to those factors intrinsic to Chicago in both the pre- and post-Daley periods.

First, general political and financial constraints have prohibited adequate levels of capital maintenance. Many cities are confronted with state constitutional debt limits and growing voter resistance to general obligation bond issues. Sluggish growth and even decline of the property tax bases reduced the amount of general obligation debt cities could float. Also, the need to balance operating budgets often came at the expense of capital maintenance and repairs. Inflation drove up expenditures faster than revenues, while periodic recessions often resulted in increased service demands and revenue shortfalls. Following New York's collapse, most older cities paid an added risk premium for borrowing, which increased costs and limited their access to markets.

Second, the types of functions supported by borrowing changed as did the form of securities being sold. The financing of long-term borrowing shifted from full faith and credit obligations, or general obligation bonds, to limited liability obligations, generally known as revenue bonds. The proportion of revenue bonds to total state-local bond sales increased from 30 percent in 1960 to more than 70 percent by 1979. These changes—in conjunction with court decisions, legislative measures, and new purposes for tax-exempt financing—focused greater attention on special districts and authorities, enterprise funds (user fees), and lease-revenue bonds. Frequently these devices were simply aimed at circumventing statutory authority (levy or debt limits), but they had the effect of balkanizing a single local unit's responsibility for overall capital maintenance.

Demographic changes and the assertion of new federal priorities affected the purposes of tax-exempt borrowing. This resulted in a shift away from traditional focuses such as schools, sewers, transportation, and water to housing, hospitals, solid waste disposal, and waste water treatment. Governments also began playing new roles as financial intermediaries for relending within the public sector or for supplying funds to the private sector. For example, the city of Chicago in 1979 not only had nearly $100 million in principal outstanding on Chicago Public Building Commission bonds secured by leases with the city, but also $200 million in mortgage (housing) revenue bonds and millions of dollars for industrial revenue bonds. Thus, much of Chicago's long-term borrowing shifted from general obligation bonds or general government purposes to revenue bonds, and from traditional purposes to housing and industrial aid.

Third, the decline in state and local borrowing for traditional capital infrastructure purposes is directly related to the infusion of massive amounts of federal aid for capital uses. Table 1 shows the sources of state and local financing of capital investment and indicates that federal aid as a percentage of total financing has increased nearly fourfold over the past twenty-two years. In larger cities the ratio of federal aid to local and state aid is considerably greater. The share contributed by the federal government increased dramatically for primary and secondary highways (from 50–50 to 75–25), airport development (from 75–15 to, in some cases, 90–10), mass transit (to 80–20), and waste water systems (to 75–25), among others.

Table 1. Financing of State and Local Capital Expenditures.

Sources for Funds	1955	1970	1977
Long-term bonds	56.0%	51.0%	43.3%
Federal aid	8.5%	22.0%	32.1%
Other local sources	35.5%	27.0%	24.6%
Total	100.0%	100.0%	100.0%

SOURCE. Peterson, 1978:57.

In addition to functional sorts of aid (e.g., highways or airports), the federal government infused general unrestricted aid into cities: $4.5 billion in annual general revenue-sharing entitlements to 39,000 local governments; $4 billion in Community Development Block Grants (CDBG) for cities; $400 million in Urban Development Action Grants (UDAG); and during the 1975–76 recession, $6 billion in antirecession public works funds for immediate spend-out in 1976 and 1977.

Federal intervention took a great deal of pressure off old larger cities. At the same time relaxation of local responsibility for capital stock condition generated dependency on higher government levels—and an expectation of shared responsibility for a function. For example, sufficient evidence exists to conclude from the design and implementation of the 1976–77 local public works programs that they provided strong incentives for local officials to postpone commitment of their own resources to construction in anticipation of possible federal funding. Most large local governments have problems in getting projects started, so that an immediate infusion of funds results either in chaos or direct substitution.

Federal aid proved to be a double-edged sword, providing much needed revenue on the one hand, but conditions for its use on the other. Federal aid and regulations governing use directed capital allocation into certain functions (e.g., pollution control), to certain areas (e.g., CDBG eligible areas), for multiple purposes (e.g., job creation and economic development), and for specific time periods (e.g., antirecession spending or for six months to one year). Moreover, federal aid for capital purposes generally seeks to stimulate local effort as opposed to substituting for planned expenditures. It is not supposed to assist in repairs and maintenance but rather reflects a bias toward new construction. Federal highway funds, for example, could not be used for maintenance purposes before 1976. Since then they have been for the sole purpose of road reconstruction. Sewer repairs also are no longer eligible for funding under the basic public works programs. The Economic Development Administration does provide some limited funding for urban capital infrastructure work, but only if it is related to economic development purposes.

These forces and trends have contributed to a breakdown of municipal capital planning and maintenance systems. Years ago these functions constituted the very heart of municipal purposes. Local public officials operating under retrenchment conditions have readily succumbed to the temptation of cutting spending either where it has least impact on the current generation of taxpayers or where service levels are least perceptible, namely below ground. Bridges, sewers, water mains, solid waste incinerators, and road beds, until they fail, disintegrate, or collapse, rarely generate the same level of constituent concern as do reductions in current levels of services that cities deliver.

Finally, a state-of-the-art problem exists in capital budgeting. Handbooks, manuals, and instructional guidebooks do not address the needs of a highly fragmented intergovernmental system and the modern complexities of public finance (White, 1980: 43). Capital budgets can be narrow in scope or so broad that they tie into planning, budgeting, financial forecasting, and integrated management information systems. Capital budgets and processes suffer from definitional problems, are fraught with accounting perils, neglect operating and maintenance costs, and typically do not account for participation requirements mandated by higher government levels. In short, capital budgeting for large local governments has entered a lost world of public-sector finance and budgeting at a time when growth management has attained a national priority. Chicago is not alone in seeking ways and methods to manage its public investments.

CAPITAL STOCK IN CHICAGO

The most important requirement for capital management is information. Chicago lacks a comprehensive and consistent inventory of its physical plant, including leased facilities. It also lacks reliable and updated measures of its capital stock condition and need. Existing financial statements provide few clues to these questions. Moreover, Chicago, like most governmental and nonbusiness entities, does not depreciate its general fixed assets (and many government accountants would argue that they should not), so that the value of the city's fixed assets is unclear. Depreciation of assets is recorded only in the Water Fund (an enterprise fund operated in a manner similar to a private business enterprise) and in the working capital accounts for major equipment.

A professional judgment on the overall condition of the city's capital stock would be inappropriate here, since there is neither a comprehensive inventory system nor a technically based assessment of condition and need. What follows is, therefore, a partial inventory of capital stock based on very rough estimates of need and estimated replacement costs. The cost figures are intended neither to alarm nor to argue that maintenance should be given a higher municipal priority than new development. It should not give comfort to the "small is beautiful" school or lead to the conclusion that the city is pursuing what one federal budget director characterized as the "if it ain't broke, don't fix it" approach. Rather, a list of replacement costs and of prospective new developments raises questions of balancing needs, financing, and priorities so that preoccupation with current problems does not drive out concern for long-term consequences.

The city's sewer system, for example, consists of 4,200 miles of sewer line and 215,000 catch basins. Many miles of sewer lines are single-ring brick, largely unserviceable, exceed 100 years of age, and are obsolete. Replacement costs run to an estimated $1 to $3 million per mile. Water main leakage is considerable and results in loss of water, lowered pressure, and interrupted flows. Estimated replacement costs are $750,000 or more per mile. Three of the city's four incinerators have been permanently closed due to obsolescence and Environmental Protection Agency regulations, increasing costs for waste disposal, and landfill fees. Acceptable sites are becoming increasingly expensive and remote. The Environmental Protection Agency is restricting future use of open landfills, which means that alternatives must be developed soon. Millions of dollars will have to be allocated for new incinerators, dumping stations, and for whatever new solid-waste disposal technology emerges. The 1,000 or so blocks of vaulted sidewalks built after the Great Chicago Fire are in various stages of decay, with excavation and repair running as high as $1 million per block; in some cases, replacement costs exceed the value of surrounding development. The city has long been shortchanged in federal-state aid for bridge reconstruction—it has fifty-two movable and thirty-six fixed waterway bridges—with the cost of the new Columbus Drive Bridge alone amounting to $32 million. The city has nearly 3,700 miles of streets, in various stages of disrepair. Reconstruction of a four-lane street runs $2.5 million per mile.

Actual and proposed capital construction projects range from hundreds of millions to billions of dollars. The 7.2 mile O'Hare Rapid Transit Extension carries a cost of $177 million; a new main library, $50–$80 million; a total O'Hare development package, including terminals, intra-airport person movement system, existing facility relocation, runways, and new road structures, exceeds $1 billion. North Loop and South Loop developments carry multi-million dollar price tags. Branch libraries, fire stations, and senior citizen centers run $1 to $4 million each. Add to the list commuter railroad extensions, city college buildings, Navy Pier redevelopment, Phase II city hall renovation, and the aggregate capital costs are staggering.

The concern here is less about the magnitude of the problem than about the need for plans and strategies. The preponderance of high-priced expenditures is likely to be supported, partially or totally, by federal funds. The City-State Transportation Agreement holds the prospect of providing more than $2 billion in federal-state funds for a combination of new transit extensions, highway resurfacing, and operating and capital funding for the Chicago Transit Authority. Year VI CDBG funding, much of which will continue to be used for capital improvements in designated eligible areas, will again exceed $120 million annually. These programs provide immediate resources that may not come the city's way again. For example, use of designated interstate highway funds for other transit uses ceases in 1990, and federal aid to state and local governments has already begun to decline in constant dollar terms.

User fees are among the fastest growing local government revenue sources. In response to property tax limits, local governments are learning how to employ pricing models for providing an array of services, shifting capital and other costs to a variety of users, ranging from private developers to recreationalists. In Chicago both water and sewer charges provide resources for meeting these systems' needs.

Once Chicago's rates are adjusted upward to meet rising costs, and cash flows are generated to service new revenue bonds, major water repair and replacement programs can begin again. The newly established sewer enterprise fund, if used exclusively for sewers—as was the legislative intent and stated purpose—may soon record a revenue collection history to support a series of sewer revenue bonds for an ongoing replacement program.

The city's tax base remains relatively strong. Last year Chicago led the nation's cities in central city commercial construction investments. Future construction plans announced thus far should result in several million square feet in new commercial space by the mid-1980s. In other words, although the city's debt burden has increased and deficits of earlier years have not been fully liquidated, the city should be able to float additional general obligation debts for capital construction alongside the aforementioned revenue bond financing.

MANAGEMENT IN THE POST-DALEY ERA

Recent notoriety and revisionists notwithstanding, Chicago was a well run and managed city during the 1970s. Credit analysts and the financial community alike—to apply one standard of municipal performance— generally gave Chicago high marks compared to other larger cities. Annual budget increases fell into the 5 to 6 percent range set against higher inflation levels; direct debt remained low, and overall debt (overlapping units), moderate; the city's own outstanding general obligation debt was well synchronized for early retirement. The city's need for additional revenue sources coincided with large new infusions by state and federal governments: Illinois income tax (1971), general revenue sharing (1973), and federal antirecession assistance programs (1975–78). The city reduced its heavy dependence on property taxes and diversified its revenue base to the extent permitted by its home rule powers. However, standards of management performance change. Perhaps the single most scholarly, indepth probe of any American city, *Governing New York City,* asked in 1965: "What other large American city is as democratically and as well governed?'' (Sayre and Kaufman, 1965: xlvii). It is doubtful that scholars would have posed the same rhetorical question a decade later. The post-Daley era coincides with the period following the New York City debacle. Long-standing informal ways of conducting a city's business can no longer meet the tests of the market place and the Proposition 13 environment.

Chicago is experiencing four major transitions simultaneously—demographic, economic, financial, and political. In contrast to other older cities, which experienced these transitions earlier or sequentially, Chicago is confronting their full force simultaneously. Although casually related, each transition is seemingly propelled by its own dynamics, tied to regional, national, and even international forces of change.

Briefly and simply stated, the four transitions interact to make the management difficulties of the post-Daley era quite distinctive from the problems, trade-offs, and choices that faced city leaders between 1955 and 1974. Demographic changes are among the most conspicuous, powerful, and compelling of the four. Not only is the 1980 census likely to register the city's single largest decennial population loss, but it is likely to reflect a population loss in the entire SMSA. Black and Hispanic populations will probably outnumber the white population. The city's population is growing older, public schools have greater minority enrollments, and per capita income is falling behind national or metropolitan growth.

The city's economy and economic base are also experiencing a profound transition, a reflection of national, regional, and state trends. Eastern states and cities felt the full impact of the 1973–75 national recession, but the Midwest has experienced the largest regional downswing thus far in the 1979–80 recession. For example, four industrial groups—iron and steel, fabricated metals, electrical machinery, and nonelectrical machinery—constitute over 50 percent of the manufacturing employment in Illinois and a higher segment within the Chicago SMSA. These industries have been among the hardest hit by the most recent recession.

Manufacturing employment in the city and county continue to shrink, job loss mounts, and the passing from the manufacturing age to the service industry age has taken its toll as measured by unemployment and the mismatch between available jobs and skills. Cities are not in a particularly good position—legally, politically, or economically—to plan and execute their own employment recycling and unloading problems successfully. The consequences of these transitions are interactive. A declining economic base impairs the capacity of the city to maintain existing service levels, and eroding service levels and rising tax rates accentuate economic decline.

The city's financial transition, and that of the Board of Education, began in 1979 with revelation of cumulative deficits, the need to raise $140 million in additional revenues, refinancing by banks, and the appointment of a financial control board for the Board of Education. The city, having nearly exhausted new home rule taxes, will require state approval for additional sales taxes or an income tax. Further property tax increases entail great political and economic risks. Federal aid already has slowed and will not likely resume growth levels experienced in the 1960s or 1970s. Illinois is financially solvent, but a governor bent on maintaining the state's economic competitiveness and opposed to new statewide taxes is unlikely to be very receptive to pleas for special aid from Chicago.

The city's political transformation (amply covered elsewhere in this volume) is the fourth and perhaps the most important transition that is occurring. Further party slippage is likely in the years ahead, exacerbated by reapportionment—affecting both ward boundaries and representation to Washington and Springfield—as well as by minority pressures throughout the city's political system. Greater independence, volatility, and personal followings can be expected in the years ahead. With patronage constrained by the courts and the city's finances, and the city's work force facing choices of unionization or civil service security, mayoral resources for influencing political outcomes will continue to decline. In short, Chicago's mayoralty in the 1980s is an office and a position in obvious trouble.

The coincidence of these demographic, economic, financial, and political trends is forcing a reevaluation of how to effect change and to make that change work to the benefit of the city. Aging stock, declines in the population and the economic base, declining numbers among the middle class, and loss of job-producing industry point to the necessity for management. This overwhelming need for leadership and management comes at a time when a mayor's political imperative is consolidation of power and assembling large bits and pieces of various constituencies in order to govern. The hard trade-offs and management/resource allocation decisions the mayor must make, if the city is to respond rather than simply react to forces of change, are politically risk-laden. Management needs in the post-Daley era are, therefore, quantitatively and qualitatively quite different from those that served the city so well in an earlier period.

THE NEED FOR PLANNING AND A CAPITAL ALLOCATION SYSTEM

Municipal credit raters and credit analysts alike have expressed growing concern that municipal credit risks are being increasingly used to determine how well a city is managing its capital infrastructure. In many

large cities those responsible for capital planning have not adjusted to the
highly complicated, intergovernmental system of relationships, fragmented authority and responsibility, and complex methods of finance.
Old larger cities like Chicago have muddled through, caught between financial strain and optimistic assumptions about future federal largesse.
Chicago needs plans and strategies for dealing with its capital renewal
process and can ill afford to operate as it has in the past. Equally important, the decisions Chicago's leaders make in the early 1980s—from
transportation modes to capital maintenance–replacement schedules—
may set the stage for how well the city will respond to emerging and future changes.

The city's capital plant is aging. Renewal can stem escalating maintenance costs and improve services. Although a wide range of funding
sources and development strategies exists, there will always be more projects than funds to support them. The complexity of intergovernmental
relations and new public-private development ventures necessitate the
development of long-term plans flexible enough to respond to short-term
needs and opportunities. Set against the prospect of slower growth in
federal funding and limited access to capital markets, Chicago will need
to design and implement a capital budget and capital planning process in
the context of an overall comprehensive plan for the city.

First, the city requires a comprehensive *needs assessment,* function by
function, that specifies condition of stock, future needs and priorities,
and estimates of current and future funding sources. The needs assessment becomes the basis for designing a *long-range plan*—ten to twenty
years into the future. The needs assessment should be technically based
in terms of age and condition of facilities, demographic changes, user
estimates, and costs of operation and maintenance. The resulting plan
should give particular attention to minimizing system costs or deal with
trade-offs between maintenance versus replacement in those cases where
capital stock replacement may reduce maintenance costs and improve efficiency. The plans should meet feasibility standards in terms of available
resources, actual and potential. They should also meet feasibility criteria
of administrative approval by higher governmental levels and regulations
(environmental, citizen participation, relocation assistance, etc.). Capa-
bilities of the construction industry (e.g., capacity) should also be
considered.

The long-range plan can be disaggregated by system components, priorities, and resource availability into a *short-range program* with three- to
five-year schedules. This program would define project scheduling and
financing—once again compatible with existing and foreseeable resource
availability—and be closely coordinated across departments (e.g., sewer,
water, and road resurfacing are synchronized in a specific area). From

the short-range plan comes the *annual capital budget,* a one-year snap-shot of the ongoing capital programs of the city, which both cuts across functional lines and becomes integrated into the city's annual budget process. The capital budget then plays a pivotal role in the transition be-tween the annual budget process of resources consumable in a single year and longer term resource commitments.

The capital budget is an absolutely essential instrument for financial planning and for developing an overall multi-year financial plan for the city. It is the link between current expenditures and future costs. Projects involving multi-year costs from design, approval, acquisition, or bidding to construction have long-term implications for budget decisions, tax levies, and debt management. A process that includes the systematic re-view and scheduling of capital projects also forces the integration of skills, techniques, and information across government, whether it be cost benefit analysis, revenue forecasting, or close adherence to land use and demographic trends. The experience of New York and other cities with capital budgets suggests that a budget and plan mean little unless they are totally integrated into a city's operations. Chicago's own capital im-provements program is a standing testimony to planning without an agreed-upon process and rules to bind agencies and departments.

To be institutionalized, the process must be continuous, particularly at the interdepartmental levels that draw upon planning, engineering, fi-nancial, and operating perspectives. A continuous process also allows for a more open process, one in which advisory committees and community organizations can participate, and during which the Chicago Plan Com-mission and city council committees can be consulted and lend their approval. Such an iterative process for building consensus and for nar-rowing options has its costs in terms of time and money, but it is essential for building public support for government action. In fact, the necessari-ly lengthy nature of the capital process, if it is to be a successful device for allocating scarce resources, is itself the strongest argument for imple-menting that process as soon as possible. The process should also be technically defensible and documentable—answering questions about how and why decisions are made. Once decisions are arrived at, the pro-cess also must accommodate a system for implementation through con-trols, scheduling, and tracking overall progress.

CONCLUSION

This chapter deals with what may appear to be a narrow perspective on the post-Daley era. It is not intended to be a thorough review of the city's financial problems or prospects, but focuses on the city's capital plant. The city needs a capital budget, plan, and process. It also needs a comprehensive plan, a long-term financial plan, new zoning and building codes, and perhaps even a new city charter. A journey of one thousand miles is said to begin with the first step, and, in an exhortative way, the purpose here is simply to suggest what one of those first steps might be.

REFERENCES

City of Chicago. 1980. General Obligation Tax Anticipation Notes Series of January 1980. Official Statement issued Feb. 1, 1980.
————. Municipal Code, section 3.21–43.
Commissioner of Planning, City and Community Development. 1978. Report of the Chicago Plan Commission. Oct. 12.
Grossman, David A. 1979. *The Future of New York City's Capital Plant.* Washington, D.C.: The Urban Institute.
Peterson, George. 1978. "Capital Spending and Capital Obsolescence," in R. Bahl et al., *The Fiscal Outlook for Cities.* Syracuse, N.Y.: Syracuse University Press.
———— et al. 1979a. *The Future of Cleveland's Capital Plant.* Washington, D.C.: The Urban Institute.
————. 1979b. *The Future of Cincinnati's Capital Plant.* Washington, D.C.: The Urban Institute.
Sayre, W. S., and H. Kaufman. 1965. *Governing New York City.* New York: Norton.
White, Michael J. 1980. "Capital Budgeting," in John Peterson and Catherine Spain, eds., *Essays in Public Finance and Financial Management.* Chatham, N.J.: Chatham House.
Wilson, Peter. 1980. *The Future of Dallas's Capital Plant.* Washington, D.C.: The Urban Institute.

LAWRENCE N. HANSEN

Suburban Politics and the Decline of the One-City Party

ILLINOIS VOTERS WENT TO THE POLLS on November 7, 1978, to elect a U.S. senator, governor, secretary of state, attorney general, treasurer, and comptroller. As usual, the candidates of the Democratic party outdistanced their Republican opponents by enormous margins in the city of Chicago; the Democrats received between 57 and 84 percent of the city vote in their respective races. Despite this advantage, the election's outcome and the Democratic ticket's fate were determined in the traditionally Republican precincts of the city's suburbs, not, as in many past elections, by Chicago's overwhelmingly Democratic and once numerically superior electorate. Three Democrats—the candidates for secretary of state, treasurer, and comptroller—were elected; Democratic candidates for U.S. senator, governor, and attorney general were defeated.

The 1978 elections dramatized once again the political importance of the Chicago suburbs—a region composed of the thirty townships of Cook County and the surrounding counties of DuPage, Kane, Lake, McHenry, and Will (Map 1). In the last decade, this geographic crescent has spawned a political giant whose behavior is as unpredictable as it is decisive. As a result, orthodox assumptions about the distribution of political power in Illinois and election campaign strategies are no longer relevant. Senior party leaders, both Democratic and Republican, have utterly failed to grasp and adjust to the new demographic and political imperatives thrust upon them by this awakening giant.

Just how badly Democratic leaders had misjudged the situation was made clear a year before the 1978 elections, when the twenty-four members of the state Democratic party central committee huddled in Springfield and Chicago to endorse a slate of candidates. In light of the new demographic realities, the seventeen committeemen from outside Chicago generally advocated a ticket reflecting the party's geographic and human diversity. Rather than a slate dominated by Chicagoans, they sought one

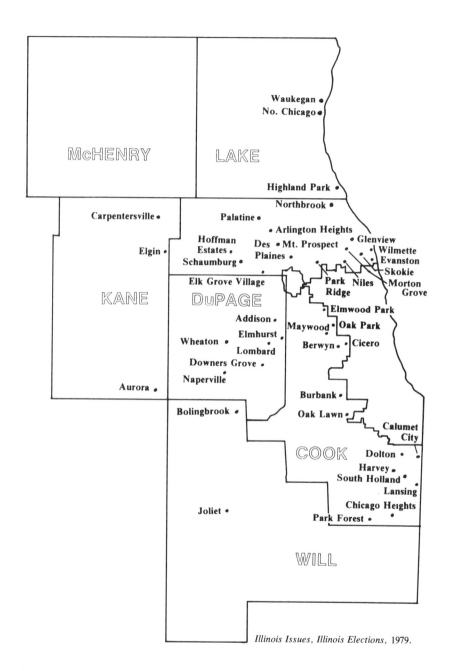

Illinois Issues, Illinois Elections, 1979.

Map 1. Chicago Metropolitan Area.

that would have broad public appeal through the purposeful inclusion of women, minorities, independents, downstaters, and suburbanites.

In the end, the selection of candidates was indelicately dictated by Chicago's committeemen, and the consequences proved costly: a severely divided party; primary challenges; weakened party leadership; a 1978 slate of candidates given little prospect for success; and the revival of old and deeply rooted tensions between Chicago Democrats, on the one hand, and suburban and downstate Democrats, on the other. Suburban and downstate Democrats felt betrayed. There were expressions of gloom and outrage. Without reform, the *Southern Illinoisan* (Nov. 15, 1977) predicted, "Downstate and suburban Democrats will have to continue to settle for the crumbs left on the table—as in the Daley days—by Chicago Democrats." The *Chicago Tribune* (Nov. 12, 1977) viewed the party's slatemaking process as a "compromise between attracting voters and appeasing a few powerful committeemen from Chicago's machine wards. The result was a ticket so heavily weighted for Chicago against downstate—and for politicians against voters—that it is likely to sink without a trace outside the Chicago area." One downstate member of the Democratic central committee summed up the anger and frustration of his suburban and downstate colleagues in a widely distributed letter, part of which reads: "The Chicago boys are obviously a lot more interested in sanitation than they are in the Governorship. But it has always been thus. The State's Attorney's office has always had priority over the Presidency. Ward Committeemen are more important than the State Treasurer. The County Assessor is more important than all statewide elections and all elections involving the Democratic Party outside of Cook County. We are basically a one-city Party" (Mahoney, 1977).

Fashionable as the mythology may be, the Democratic party is not and never has been a "one-city Party." Nor, in fact, is the party the private domain of Chicago Democrats, although they frequently behave as if it were. The simple truth is that Chicago's political influence over the remainder of Illinois is on the decline—a sharp and irreversible decline. The heavy-handedness of Chicago Democrats in fashioning the party's 1978 slate and the resulting divisiveness suggested it; the election returns on November 7 confirmed it.

A look at some of the voter statistics should have prepared the Democratic leadership. On election eve, 58 percent of the registered voters within the Chicago metropolitan region—the city and the suburbs—comprised suburbanites. Chicago had over a half million fewer eligible voters than the suburbs, a dramatically new reality. While the percentage of voters turning out on November 7 was larger in the city than in the suburbs, 237,000 more suburbanites than Chicagoans voted, and that, too, was an inescapable reality.

In just one decade, Chicago lost 310,000 registered voters. During this same period the suburbs gained a quarter million new registrants. In 1968 the city had accounted for almost one-third of the state's registered voters, but by November 1978 its share had dropped to less than 25 percent.

These numbers markedly altered traditional strategic formulations. To win statewide in 1978, a Democratic candidate had to roll up a plurality in Chicago in excess of 70 percent of the vote and garner no less than 40 percent of the suburban vote. This explains in part why three of the Democratic candidates won and three lost.

The election results, as represented in Table 1, fully reveal the discrimi-

Table 1. 1978 General Election: Chicago/Suburban Results (in thousands).

Political Office		Chicago		Cook County Townships		Six-County Suburbs	
U.S. senator							
Seith	(D)	503	58.4%	217	33.4%	372	34.1%
Percy	(R)	358	41.6%	434	66.6%	720	65.9%
Governor							
Bakalis	(D)	497	60.0%	177	27.0%	284	26.1%
Thompson	(R)	331	40.0%	480	73.0%	804	73.9%
Attorney general							
Troy	(D)	455	56.8%	135	20.6%	217	20.3%
Scott	(R)	346	43.2%	517	79.4%	850	79.7%
Secretary of state							
Dixon	(D)	684	84.4%	452	69.1%	761	69.3%
Sharp	(R)	126	15.6%	202	30.9%	337	30.7%
Comptroller							
Burris	(D)	587	77.0%	271	43.4%	431	41.3%
Castle	(R)	176	23.0%	354	56.6%	613	58.7%
Treasurer							
Cosentino	(D)	581	77.1%	295	46.9%	451	43.0%
Skelton	(R)	173	22.9%	334	53.1%	598	57.0%

SOURCE. State Board of Elections (1978).

nating and independent nature of today's suburban voters. They are not mortgaged to either political party or wedded to their candidates. Their votes are cast for those perceived as most fit for public office. While party affiliation is undoubtedly an influence, it clearly is a less dominant determinant of voter preferences in the suburbs than in Chicago. Some analysts estimate that close to 50 percent of voters in Illinois split their ballots in 1978, casting votes for both Republican and Democratic candidates. One half million more suburbanites, for example, cast votes for Alan Dixon, the Democratic candidate for secretary of state, than for Richard Troy, the party's candidate for attorney general. On the other hand, James Thompson, the incumbent Republican governor, received more than twice as many suburban votes as did Sharon Sharp, the Republican candidate for secretary of state. A relatively new phenomenon in Illinois politics, split-ticket voting is more profuse in the suburbs than anywhere else in the state.

The growing political importance of the suburbs in relation to Chicago is not without its ironies. So massive was Democrat Dixon's 1978 suburban plurality that he would have won his race without the benefit of a single Chicago vote. Similarly, but less surprising, Thompson and William Scott, the Republican candidate for attorney general, so overwhelmed their Democratic opponents in the suburbs that the Chicago vote could not conceivably have affected the final results.

In 1970 Richard Scammon and Ben Wattenberg (1970: 293) observed that the future "battle for the hearts and minds of the electorate will probably be most acute and most significant in the suburbs." Chicago's suburban crescent is the newest political battlefeld, a region where, despite historic Republican biases, candidates are now made or broken almost without reference to party labels. Running well in Chicago and in downstate Illinois is still important; doing so in the suburbs is absolutely imperative. Stumbling badly in the suburbs, as 1978 proved, is certain to doom even the most promising political candidates. To avoid stumbling, they must keep the following in mind:

1. More people lived in the suburbs of Chicago in 1979 than in the city.

2. Population projections for the remainder of this century point to larger losses for the city and continued growth in the suburbs.

3. Major elements of the old Democratic coalition—white ethnics, Catholics, Jews, and union members—once concentrated in Chicago and other large industrial cities, have been generously dispersed throughout the suburbs.

4. There are more registered voters in the suburbs today than in Chicago.

5. Suburban participation in Democratic party primary elections has grown enormously while participation has generally declined in Chicago.

6. More suburbanites than Chicagoans vote in general elections today.

Ten or fifteen years ago, none of these conditions existed; at that time few people would even have dared predict them. This chapter traces these developments and suggests some of their implications for the future of Illinois politics. Clearly, a major shift in political power from Chicago to the suburbs will occur, and with it a new type of voter may emerge, one whose emancipation from the rigid orthodoxies of the past may portend the end of political parties as we now know them.

DEMOGRAPHY AS DESTINY

Where people live, work, and educate their children are among the demographic circumstances that influence attitudes about a whole range of subjects, including politics. And because such attitudes invariably influence elections, it can be said, at least in an electoral sense, that "demography is destiny"—a phrase coined in 1970 by Scammon and Wattenberg.

Those who move from inner cities to suburbs in earnest search of improved housing, new jobs, safer streets, and better schools view the world differently, particularly if they succeed in achieving a larger measure of contentment. Such movements of people alter their politics. Neither political party, however, has adapted imaginatively to the new demographics. The infusion of humanity into the suburbs has not profited the Republican party to the degree once expected. Nor have the Democrats, pleased with scattered suburban victories, ever taken full advantage of the promising opportunities for growth.

Yet remarkable changes are occurring within the parties themselves and in the power relationship between Chicago and the suburbs. By the end of the twentieth century, an enormous shift in population and political power from Chicago to the suburbs will have taken place. One result will be a transformed Democratic party, whose outlook and appeal will be more consistently statewide in nature. Chicago's domination of the party will end, as will its ability to orchestrate events, like slatemaking, to serve its own parochial and internal political needs.

Chicago's domination of Cook County politics stems from its population advantage in relation to the county's thirty suburban townships. In 1930 a mere 15 percent of the county's population lived in the townships: 600,000 people in the townships, 3.5 million people in Chicago. During the next two decades, a demographic equilibrium of sorts was maintained between the city and the townships. While the number of people living in the townships had increased 10 percent by 1950, Chicago's population also jumped by a quarter million.

In the 1950s, however, a demographic metamorphosis began. The outmigration of people from Chicago to the suburbs gained momentum in the 1960s, accelerated in the 1970s, and will continue into the 1980s and 1990s. By 1970, as Table 2 reveals, Chicago was losing people faster than

Table 2. Population Factors.

Chicago and the Six Counties	Year	Population	Gain/Loss
Chicago	1950	3,620,962	
	1960	3,550,404	− 70,558
	1970	3,369,357	− 181,047
Suburban Cook County	1950	887,830	
	1960	1,579,321	+ 691,491
	1970	2,123,012	+ 543,691
Du Page County	1950	154,599	
	1960	313,459	+ 158,860
	1970	491,882	+ 178,423
Kane County	1950	150,388	
	1960	208,246	+ 57,858
	1970	251,005	+ 42,759
Lake County	1950	179,097	
	1960	293,656	+ 114,559
	1970	382,638	+ 88,982
McHenry County	1950	50,656	
	1960	84,210	+ 33,554
	1970	111,555	+ 27,345
Will County	1950	134,336	
	1960	191,617	+ 57,281
	1970	249,498	+ 57,881

SOURCE. Bureau of the Census (1960, 1970).

it could replace them. The suburban region—the townships of Cook and the five surrounding counties—absorbed two million people during that twenty-year period, accommodating an aggregate population that exceeded the city's by a quarter million.

In Illinois, as in other large industrial states, the rural-to-urban-to-suburban hegira was coming full circle. Nationally, in 1930, 54 million people lived in areas denominated as urban, 51 million in rural areas; by 1950, 96 million lived in urban areas, 54 million in rural areas; and by 1960, 125 million lived in urban areas compared to 54 million in rural areas (Scammon and Wattenberg, 1970: 67–68). The population gap between the cities and the rural areas widened substantially in these years because of the census bureau's redefinition in 1940 of urban areas, which for the first time recognized the social phenomenon known as the suburbs.

By the 1960s suburban growth was generally eclipsing the growth of central cities everywhere, and in Illinois, as Table 2 illustrates, it was spectacular. Chicago's share of Cook County's population in 1970 stood at 60 percent—a decline of 25 percent since 1930. New communities—

like Schaumburg, Hanover Park, Glendale Heights, and Wood Dale—
seemed to spring up overnight and in the 1960s experienced 100 percent
population increases. The movement of people in the 1950s and 1960s from city to suburb,
of course, was not peculiar to the Chicago metropolitan region; it was a
national phenomenon. The suburbanization of America had been hap-
pening for fifty years (White House Conference, 1978). In 1930 only 35
percent of the population within metropolitan areas lived in suburbs; by
1973, 56 percent were suburbanites (ACIR, 1977). The decline of central
city populations, however, is a more contemporary development. Between 1950 and 1960 only 38 percent of the nation's cities with populations of 200,000 or more declined in population; between 1960 and 1970,
73 percent experienced population decreases. And between 1970 and
1974 central cities lost an estimated 1.1 million people, while nationwide
the suburbs gained 6.2 million residents (Peterson, 1974).

The political implications of these population shifts became manifest
as the national electorate assumed an increasingly suburban character.
The correlation between overall suburban population increases and the
growth in the suburban electorate, as suggested in Table 3, was clear and
unmistakable (Bureau of the Census, Mar. 1978).

Table 3. Voters by Place of Residence: 1968 and 1976.

	Percent of Electorate	
Residence	1968	1976
Central cities	29.6	28.1
Suburbs	35.6	39.8
Small cities, towns, and farms	34.8	32.1

The 1968 data lead Scammon and Wattenberg (1970: 294) to conclude
that "suburbia will indeed be the major psephological [the study of elec-
tions] battleground in the years to come but will probably be the major
battleground only because so many Americans will be living there." And
then, as if to alert Richard Daley and his heirs, they issued a warning:
"Anyone who automatically deeds that turf to Republicans does so at his
peril."

The demographic trends that commenced in the early 1950s are expected to continue. Most population projections, like those in Table 4,
show that by the year 2000 Chicago and suburban Cook County will
have achieved population parity. The entire suburban region, on the
other hand, will have approximately twice as many people as the city
(NIPC, 1976), an anticipated gain of four to five million residents between 1930 and 2000.

Table 4. Projected Population: 1970–2000 (in thousands).

Chicago and Six Counties	1970	1980	1990	2000
Chicago	3,369.4	3,030.0	3,027.0	3,011.0
Suburban totals	3,608.3	4,405.1	5,178.1	5,914.4
Suburban Cook County	2,124.5	2,476.3	2,733.0	3,000.1
Du Page County	490.8	651.3	829.4	987.1
Kane County	251.0	303.5	376.7	433.6
Lake County	382.6	470.4	593.9	700.1
McHenry County	111.6	147.2	185.5	240.5
Will County	247.8	356.4	459.6	553.0

SOURCE. Northeastern Illinois Planning Commission (1976).

DISPERSING THE DEMOCRATIC COALITION

Franklin D. Roosevelt fashioned a Democratic coalition composed largely of union members, white ethnics, Catholics, Jews, blacks, liberals, and intellectuals. In its most vibrant form, the coalition prospered for three decades in large American cities—New York, Chicago, Detroit, and Boston. In Chicago remnants of the coalition persist, but the suburban migration has appreciably altered its composition. Today it is decidedly more black, less Catholic, less white ethnic, and less labor-based than during the Roosevelt-Truman-Kennedy era.

The Democratic party's rising fortunes in the suburbs can be traced *partially* to the exodus from Chicago since the 1950s of large elements of the old Democratic coalition. In 1950 more than one-third of Chicago's white foreign stock—614,000 people—were Polish, Italian, and Irish. By 1970, according to Table 5, this population, much of it Catholic and Democratic, was almost halved. Many of these 265,000 people migrated to the suburbs, and their grown children stayed there.

During this same period, thousands of Chicago's Jewish residents—

Table 5. Chicago White Foreign Stock.

Country of Origin	1950	1960	1970	Population Loss, 1950–70
Poland	315,504	258,657	191,955	123,549
Italy	171,549	134,963	97,642	73,907
Ireland	126,946	85,120	59,218	67,728
USSR	139,509	96,626	64,179	75,301

SOURCE. Department of Development and Planning (1976).
NOTE. Foreign stock includes foreign-born and the native-born children of parents who are either born in the same foreign country or in different foreign countries. This narrow definition deflates the number of people of Polish, Italian, and Irish origins. It has been estimated, for example, that as many as 600,000 people of Polish extraction may live in Chicago.

many of German, eastern European, and Russian descent—moved from Lawndale, Rodgers Park, and other city neighborhoods to the suburbs. In 1951, by one estimate, 95 percent of the Jews in the Chicago area lived in the city. By 1973, 52 percent of them lived in the suburbs (Askin, 1977). While 112,000 city residents claimed Yiddish as their mother tongue in 1940, only 52,000 did so in 1970. In terms of numbers, of course, Jews represent one of the smaller population subgroups in the metropolitan region; they account for less than 4 percent of the region's 6,974,000 people. But it is a subgroup that historically has had a strong attachment to the Democratic party, and what it lacked in size it has amply compensated for through a high degree of political participation.

Blacks—an important component of the old Democratic coalition—comprised an infinitesimal percentage of the suburban population in 1970 (Department of Development and Planning, 1975); current population trends suggest that blacks are now also moving from Chicago to the suburbs in measurable numbers. Dempsey J. Travis, a black Chicago real estate expert, predicts that by the year 2000 twenty-six suburban communities in Cook County will be 95 percent black. And beyond Cook County, blacks will constitute 50 percent of the population in two communities in both Kane and Will counties and in three communities in Lake County. Only McHenry County at the end of the century will remain virtually all white (*Chicago Tribune,* Oct. 31, 1977). These estimates generally comport with national trends. While blacks constitute only 6 percent of the nation's suburban population, the number of blacks living in the suburbs increased 34 percent between 1970 and 1977 (Bureau of the Census, 1978). Whether or not these trends hold up, the presence of a growing black electorate in the suburbs will further alter the prevailing political environment.

Though there are no precise data, in 1979 more Catholics and labor union members may have been living in the suburbs than in Chicago. Officials of the Chicago Archdiocese are inexplicably reluctant to disclose precise data, but it is generally accepted that in the early 1960s, 40 percent of Chicago's population was Catholic. But more important, 40 percent of the population in those suburban areas comprising the Archdiocese—suburban Cook and Lake counties—was probably also Catholic. By 1970, according to the Archdiocese's Office of Research and Planning, 60 percent of the Catholics in the Cook-Lake region resided in Chicago. When one factors in the large number of Catholics who reside in Will, DuPage, and Kane counties—areas outside the Chicago Archdiocese—it is probable that suburban Catholics are now as numerous as Chicago Catholics.

The political significance of this Catholic migration, according to Ralph Whitehead (1977: 110), is that "the Catholic share of the Chicago vote is 54 percent and falling. For the suburbs, the percentage is roughly

51 points and rising. Here are the makings of political change.'' While they do not vote monolithically anymore than Jews or union members, Catholics, as a group, identify more strongly with Democrats than do either Protestants or the electorate in general. This finding is borne out by Gallup surveys of group presidential voting patterns over a twenty-eight-year period (Gallup Opinion Index, 1976). Although it may be foolish in these times, as Whitehead suggests, to speak of a Catholic vote ''as if all or most . . . spoke with a single voice on a steady list of public issues,'' there are hundreds of thousands of Catholic voters ''whose choices are somehow affected by their religious loyalties.''

In addition to white ethnics, Catholics, Jews, and some blacks, the suburbs have experienced an enormous infusion of union members in the last twenty years. The geographic distribution of union members is directly related to the location of job opportunities. Chicago lost 12.1 percent of the jobs located within its corporate boundaries between 1960 and 1970, while employment opportunities in the suburbs increased by 62 percent. More recently, Pierre De Vise, a University of Illinois urbanologist, estimated that the city lost an additional 200,000 jobs between 1970 and 1976, 60 percent of which, according to the Real Estate Research Corporation, were in the manufacturing sector (*Christian Science Monitor,* May 29, 1979). Schaumburg, which had only two manufacturing firms in 1966, had sixty-six in 1977. While Chicago was losing 1,600 plants during this period, Elk Grove Village expanded from 111 to 405 firms, Woodstock from three to forty-six (*Chicago Daily News,* May 1977).

Representatives of the AFL-CIO and the UAW agree, though precise data are not available, that there are probably more union members living in the suburbs today than in Chicago. The Sixth Congressional District, located just west of Chicago, is generally believed to embrace more union members than any of the other twenty-three congressional districts in Illinois. Whatever the explanation for Chicago's diminishing organized labor base, this much seems clear: With the exception of steel, an increasing number of the city's heavy industrial plants have moved or are moving to the suburbs. The General Motors transmission plant in suburban LaGrange, to cite just one example, is the state's largest UAW employer.

With the exception of blacks, then, large parts of the old and once conspicuously Chicago-based Democratic coalition have been transplanted to the suburbs.

SUBURBIA: THE EMERGING POLITICAL GIANT

Whether measured in terms of voter registration levels or in terms of participation in primary and general elections, the suburban role in Illi-

nois politics has been expanding, largely at Chicago's expense. The implications are staggering.

VOTER REGISTRATION

When Richard Daley ran for a fifth term as mayor in 1975, he must
have been troubled by the realization that 30 percent fewer Chicagoans
were registered to vote than in 1955, the first year he ran for that office.
As the registration figures in Table 6 show, this erosion began in the mid-

Table 6. Chicago General Election Registration Figures.

Year	No. Registered	Year	No. Registered
1952	2,170,795	1968	1,722,618
1956	1,993,691	1972	1,714,641
1960	1,935,974	1976	1,607,406
1964	1,853,895	1978	1,413,253

SOURCE. Chicago Board of Election Commissioners.

1950s—when the city-to-suburbs exodus was gathering steam—and it
continues.

Between the time Adlai Stevenson sought the presidency in 1952 and
Jimmy Carter was elected in 1976, Chicago lost more than one-half million registered voters, and, as Table 7 indicates, the suburbs were the
principal beneficiary, gaining 225,000 new voters between 1968 and 1978
alone. Depending on whether or not it is a presidential election year, the
current registration in the suburbs over Chicago ranges between 500,000
and 600,000 voters.

Table 7. Voter Registration in General Elections: 1968–78 (in thousands).

Chicago and the Six Counties	1968	1970	1972	1974	1976	1978
Chicago	1,723	1,548	1,715	1,494	1,607	1,413
Suburban Cook County	1,139	1,058	1,426	1,285	1,223	1,117
Du Page County	190	208	248	270	320	294
Kane County	104	105	106	114	130	160
Lake County	150	145	165	186	208	211
McHenry County	51	52	63	65	77	76
Will County	109	115	132	134	159	143
Total of six-county suburban area	1,743	1,683	2,140	2,054	2,117	2,001
Suburban margin	20	135	425	560	510	588

SOURCE. Secretary of State.

PRIMARY ELECTIONS

Chicago's primary election turnouts have at least equaled, if not exceeded, the Democratic party's vote in the remainder of the state. In 1968, for example, Chicago's share of the statewide Democratic primary vote was 60.5 percent. The suburban region, in contrast, cast only 80,000 Democratic ballots that year, or 9.6 percent of the statewide vote. Of the metropolitan vote, Chicago's share was 86 percent, the suburban share, 14 percent.

Participation in Democratic primaries since 1968 has gradually increased in the suburbs and generally declined in Chicago (Table 8). Spir-

Table 8. Democratic Primary Vote in the Metropolitan Region: 1968–78 (in thousands).

Chicago and the Six Counties	Vote and Percent of Total Vote					
	1968	1970	1972	1974	1976	1978
Chicago	504	471	745	571	761	497
	86%	82%	68%	69%	67%	80%
Six Counties						
Cook County suburbs	51	73	246	181	239	89
	9%	13%	22%	22%	21%	14%
Du Page County	7	12	42	24	43	10
	1%	2%	4%	3%	4%	1.6%
Kane County	5	4	15	11	17	5
	0.08%	0.06%	1.4%	1.3%	1.5%	0.08%
Lake County	8	5	27	16	35	10
	1.4%	0.08%	2.5%	2%	3%	1.6%
McHenry County	3	3	7	6	10	2
	0.05%	0.05%	0.06%	0.07%	0.08%	0.03%
Will County	6	8	19	16	27	8
	1%	1.4%	1.7%	2%	2.4%	1.3%
Total suburban vote	80	105	356	254	371	124
	14%	18%	32%	31%	33%	20%
Total metropolitan vote	584	576	1,101	825	1,132	621

SOURCE. Secretary of State.

ited and highly publicized primary contests for the governorship in 1972 (Simon vs. Walker) and 1976 (Walker vs. Howlett), a judicial decision permitting Republican and Democratic crossovers in primary elections, and suburban population growth have contributed to this turnabout.

Though Chicago provided nearly 55 percent of the Democratic primary vote in 1978, its percentage of the statewide total has tapered off in every other primary election since 1968—from 60.5 percent that year to 45.6 percent in 1976.

More startling is the fact that the number of voters requesting Democratic ballots in the five suburban ring counties increased 340 percent between 1968 and 1976—jumping from 30,000 to 132,000 voters. And in suburban Cook County, there was a 368 percent increase; 51,000 people voted a Democratic ballot in 1968, 239,000 in 1976. It is significant, too, that in the 1972, 1974, and 1976 primary elections a substantially greater number of voters in suburban Cook County cast Democratic rather than Republican ballots—a distinction that formerly in the metropolitan region was exclusively Chicago's. Thus in 1976, between 38 and 57 percent of the primary ballots requested in each of the five ring counties were

Table 9. Chicago, Suburban, and Downstate Votes for Major Democratic Party Candidates: 1964–78 (in thousands).

Year	Candidate, Office	Statewide Vote	Vote and Percent of Total Vote		
			Chicago	Suburbs	Downstate
1964	Otto Kerner Governor	2,418	1,002 41.4%	511 21.1%	905 37.4%
1966	Adlai Stevenson Treasurer	1,890	782 41.3%	428 22.6%	680 35.9%
1968	Michael Howlett Auditor	2,215	894 40.3%	526 23.7%	796 35.9%
1970	Adlai Stevenson U.S. Senator	2,065	818 39.5%	547 26.4%	699 33.8%
1972	Daniel Walker Governor	2,371	779 32.8%	657 27.7%	935 39.4%
1974	Adlai Stevenson U.S. Senator	1,811	618 34.0%	490 27.0%	704 38.8%
	Alan Dixon Treasurer	1,796	579 32.2%	503 28.0%	714 39.7%
1976	Alan Dixon Secretary of State	2,906	892 30.6%	946 32.5%	1,068 36.7%
	Michael Bakalis Comptroller	2,298	800 34.8%	660 28.7%	838 36.4%
1978	Jerry Cosentino Treasurer	1,549	581 38%	451 29%	516 33%
	Alan Dixon Secratary of State	2,315	684 30%	761 33%	870 38%

SOURCE. Secretary of State.

Democratic, an interesting figure even if we grant that the Walker-Howlett battle brought some Republicans over to the Democratic primary.

GENERAL ELECTIONS

The suburban vote in general elections, when viewed as a percentage of either the total state or the total metropolitan vote, has also rapidly increased in recent years. Until the late 1950s, Chicago normally provided 40 to 45 percent of the statewide vote, but by 1978 its share had slipped to 27 percent. The suburban vote, by contrast, has grown substantially and now accounts for 35 percent of the statewide vote. The days when political candidates, especially Democrats, would virtually disregard the suburbs and hope to be swept into office on the crest of Chicago's massive Democratic pluralities alone are over. Otto Kerner, who received only 21 percent of his statewide vote from the suburbs in his successful 1964 gubernatorial campaign, would lose today if he won less than 40 percent of the suburban vote. A comparison of the sources of votes for winning Democratic candidates between 1964 and 1978 amply illustrates the growing importance of the suburbs to candidates of both parties (Table 9). It shows quite clearly that while Kerner received almost twice as many votes in Chicago as in the suburban region in 1964, just fourteen years later Dixon not only defeated his Republican opponent in the suburbs, but won 77,000 more votes there than in Chicago.

This phenomenon can be viewed from another perspective. When

Table 10. Suburban Democratic Vote as a Percentage of the Chicago-Suburban Democratic Vote.

Year	Candidate, Office	Suburban Percentage
1964	William Clark Attorney General	35
1970	Adlai Stevenson U.S. Senator	40
1974	Adlai Stevenson U.S. Senator	44
1976	Michael Bakalis Comptroller	45
1976	Alan Dixon Secretary of State	51
1978	Alan Dixon Secretary of State	53

SOURCE. Secretary of State.

measured against the total vote cast in the Chicago metropolitan region, there has been a significant progression in the suburban vote for winning Democratic candidates since 1964 (Table 10).

An examination of presidential election returns over a forty-four-year period further reveals that Chicago's percentage of the quadrennial vote has dropped off 15 points. In 1932 Chicago provided 41 percent of the presidential vote in Illinois, the suburbs a mere 14 percent. This margin was of such magnitude that it invariably sent quivers of foreboding or joyful anticipation through presidential candidates—depending, of course, on whether they were Republicans or Democrats. By 1976, 35 percent of the presidential vote was cast by suburbanites and 25 percent by Chicagoans. In formulating a campaign strategy for Illinois, Carter and his advisors mistakenly believed that victory was assured if Chicago were won by a margin sufficient to offset predictable Republican pluralities in the suburbs and downstate. Although Carter received 67.5 percent of the city's vote, 400,000 more votes were cast in the suburbs, where Carter did not campaign, than in Chicago. The result was that President Gerald Ford walked out of the metropolitan region with an 18,000-vote margin and Illinois tucked securely into his pocket.

In summary, more people and more registered voters now live in the suburbs than in Chicago; participation in Democratic primary elections is generally on the rise in the suburbs and declining in the city; and the suburban vote in statewide general elections eclipses the city vote in size. Because of these developments, the suburban region has emerged as a distinctive geopolitical entity, rivaling both Chicago and downstate Illinois in influence.

SUBURBAN VOTING BEHAVIOR

For generations, the Republican party has lorded over the suburbs; that control has rarely been interrupted, never relinquished. But the hegemony historically enjoyed by Republicans has been cracked, principally because of a suburban electorate that is more discriminating and less tolerant of single-party rule than in the past. This is not to suggest that suburban Republicans are in full retreat or have lost control. The Republicans' once intractable stranglehold on the suburbs has been loosened, and the result has been a string of Democratic successes no one could have reasonably predicted a decade ago.

THE SUBURBAN DEMOCRAT

Otto Kerner, seeking reelection as governor in 1964, salvaged a majority in only one of Cook County's thirty suburban townships. Six years

later in his first campaign for the U.S. Senate, Adlai Stevenson led fourteen townships into the Democratic column, nineteen in his 1974 reelection campaign. For forty years the Republican party customarily delivered 60 percent, on the average, of the suburban Cook County vote for
its candidates. In 1976 the extent to which this base had eroded became
manifest when Alan Dixon, seeking election as secretary of state, defeated his Republican opponent in twenty-eight of the county's thirty
townships. Two years later, Dixon handily won all the townships.

Though less dramatic, a similar progression has been unfolding in the
five surrounding counties. In 1966, a demonstrably Republican year,
Adlai Stevenson, running for state treasurer, barely survived; as a Democrat, he lost the ring counties by predictable margins. But four years
later, as a candidate for the U.S. Senate, he was victorious in Will County and in 1974 in both Will and Lake counties. Stevenson's 1974 running
mate, Alan Dixon, added Kane County to his victory column, as well as
Will and Lake counties. And then in 1976, in what was an unprecedented
achievement for a Democrat, Dixon defeated his Republican opponent in
all five suburban counties, only to repeat that feat two years later.

To some political observers, these events are aberrations from which
no defensible generalizations about the future of the suburbs can be
drawn. The fact that Republican heavy hitters—James Thompson,
Charles Percy, and Willian Scott—run exceptionally well in Chicago,
they argue, is no basis for concluding that the city is going Republican.
However, the Republican experience in Chicago and the Democratic experience in the suburbs are clearly distinguishable. They are distinguishable because Democratic inroads have been more pervasive and at all
levels in the suburbs, while Republican successes in traditionally Democratic provinces have been few and short-lived.

Ten years ago, Democrats controlled only two countywide offices in
the ring counties, both in Will County. As of this writing, Democrats are
serving in nine offices in the suburban counties: two county clerks, two
sheriffs, one state's attorney, one treasurer, one coroner, one auditor,
and one regional superintendent of educational services. Of the elected
county offices in the suburban counties, 30 percent are now held by
Democrats. Similarly, there was virtually no Democratic representation
on suburban county boards a decade ago. Except in DuPage County, significant gains have been made in the suburban counties, and in Will
County the board of supervisors is controlled by Democrats. The Republicans have enjoyed no comparable successes in Cook County, Chicago,
or other Democratic strongholds.

The election of a DuPage County Democrat, William Redmond, as
Speaker of the Illinois House of Representatives in 1975 symbolized a
new era in the shifting relationship between suburban Democrats and the

Illinois legislature. In the late 1960s there were sixteen legislative districts in the suburban region, and, because of the system of cumulative voting, one in three representatives from each district was a Democrat. In those years not one suburban Democrat served in the state Senate. However, by the mid-1970s suburban Democrats had gained five additional seats in the House, for a total of twenty-two, and three seats in the Senate. The election of two Democratic House members in two three-member suburban districts showed that Democrats were slowly neutralizing the institutional advantages enjoyed by suburban Republicans. Again, no such inroads have been made by Republicans in identifiably Democratic areas.

Other examples of the Democratic party's growing acceptance in the suburbs can be cited. One entirely suburban congressional district (the Tenth) and another that bridges the city and suburbs (the Third) are represented by suburban Democrats. An increasing number of suburban township governments—Thornton, Niles, Bremen, and Aurora, among others—are today controlled by Democrats. Aurora and Waukegan, two of the suburban region's largest cities, have elected Democratic mayors.

These gains are not the result of any calculated strategy or organizational acumen on the part of the Democratic party. Today's suburban voters are too mercurial and freewheeling to enter into a lasting contract with either party. Party identification, ideology, and political personalities are three factors that in varying degrees influence voter behavior. In Chicago, party identification affects voter choices more than either of the other two factors. In the suburbs, however, the importance of party identification is gradually receding in favor of political personalities whose acceptance, whether the individual candidate is a Republican or a Democrat, depends increasingly on the espousal of centrist rather than overtly conservative or liberal views and values.

THE SUBURBAN INDEPENDENT

"I am not certain," Senator Adlai Stevenson has written (Nov. 3, 1978), that "the old parties with all their baggage can produce the leaders and ideas. . . . The public is dissatisfied with the existing order of things and rightly so. New parties have appeared at such times, rarely to succeed at the polls, but with lasting effects on the nation's politics." While a new political party is unlikely to evolve soon, discontent with the two major parties is so widespread that a Gallup poll conducted in late 1978 found that 41 percent of Americans believe there is a need for a new "center party." Dissatisfaction is especially acute among younger voters, the college-educated, and independents (Gallup, 1978).

Defections from the two parties have been rising steadily for a decade. Harris organization polls in 1978 showed that 43 percent of the American voters think of themselves as Democrats, 22 percent as Republicans, and 29 percent as independents. The data reveal, too, that independent sentiment is most pronounced in the Midwest—and in the suburbs of large cities (Harris, Feb. 23 and Aug. 3, 1978).

Suburban election results show that city Democrats who migrate to the suburbs do not become Republicans instantaneously, though for many years that was commonly accepted. As Scammon and Wattenberg (1970: 294) noted ten years ago, "There is no evidence that Democratic-oriented voters switch parties simply because they move from cities or become more affluent. The old affluent are traditionally Republican; the new suburbanite is neither so affluent nor so Republican." But the new suburbanite is not decidedly Democratic, either. Though the trend was less obvious in the 1960s, the typical suburbanite today is as likely to be an independent voter as either a Democratic or a Republican. These voters, who may comprise as much as 50 percent of the suburban electorate, may lean to one party or the other, but they are not behavioral Republicans or Democrats, i.e., those who vote for 90 percent of a party's candidates 90 percent of the time.

A 1977 survey revealed that 27 percent of the suburb's voters were behavioral Republicans, 22 percent behavioral Democrats, and 49 percent ticket-splitters (Teeter, 1977). In other words, more than 70 percent of the suburban electorate was not doctrinairely Republican, and therein

Table 11. Incidence of Ticket-Splitting: Comparing Statewide Democratic Candidates with Highest (H) and Lowest (L) Votes.

Year	Candidates	Vote	Vote Difference
1964	(H) William Clark	2,530,921	112,577
	(L) Otto Kerner	2,418,394	
1968	(H) Paul Powell	2,278,868	212,884
	(L) Francis Lorenz	2,065,984	
1970	(H) Adlai Stevenson	2,065,054	292,845
	(L) Alan Dixon	1,772,209	
1972	(H) Dan Walker	2,371,303	758,200
	(L) Tom Lyons	1,613,103	
1974	(H) Adlai Stevenson	1,811,496	15,352
	(L) Alan Dixon	1,796,144	
1976	(H) Alan Dixon	2,906,311	1,296,053
	(L) Michael Howlett	1,610,258	
1978	(H) Alan Dixon	2,315,000	1,265,000
	(L) Dick Troy	1,050,000	

SOURCE. Secretary of State.

lies the key to the Democratic party's recent and spectacular break-throughs in the traditionally Republican suburbs.

What do we know about ticket-splitters? First, the incidence of ticket-splitting is much greater now than fifteen years ago. In 1964, for example, only 39 percent of Lake County's voters split their ballots: within a decade the number increased 41 points. This decline of traditional partisanship is more salient when one considers that in 1968 the spread between the greatest and the least number of votes received by statewide Democratic candidates was just over 10 percent. By 1978 some Democratic candidates were receiving twice as many votes as others within their own party (Table 11).

Second, ticket-splitters are more numerous in the suburban region than anywhere else in Illinois, and, although they cut into both political parties about equally, more ticket-splitters identify with Democrats than Republicans.

And third, in terms of proportions of subgroups, ticket-splitters are more representative of the total registered voting population than either Republicans or Democrats. As of 1977, they were 47 percent Protestant, 37 percent Catholic; 43 percent college-educated, 42 percent high school–educated; 34 percent earned more than $20,000 and 43 percent less than $15,000; 65 percent were in nonunion households, 33 percent in union households (Teeter, 1977).

An analysis of a representative cross-section of Illinois voters shows that among those who come from union households, almost 87 percent are behavioral Democrats and ticket-splitters. And of the voters who are Catholic, 85 percent are Democrats and ticket-splitters. Therefore, only 13 percent of the voters from union households and only 15 percent of those who are Catholic have a strong attachment to the Republican party. These statewide ratios are undoubtedly reflective within a few points of the preferences of union household and Catholic voters living in the suburban region.

Ticket-splitters represent a large and volatile bloc of voters in the suburbs. If the balance of political power in Illinois lies in the suburbs, it is equally true that the exercise of that power is being determined less by Republicans and Democrats than by the 49 percent of the electorate that is fiercely independent, discriminating in its preferences, and blindly loyal to no party. This development explains why Democrats like Adlai Stevenson and Alan Dixon have performed well in the suburbs. It also helps explain why in recent years candidates with conspicuous ties to the Chicago Democratic organization have run demonstrably worse.

The Rooseveltian coalition no longer exists. But the pieces are still around, and under the right conditions, as Democrats have recently proven in the suburbs, the elements can occasionally be summoned, reassembled, and appealed to successfully. A permanent and relatively stable Democratic coalition may emerge in the suburbs someday, but, given current attitudes toward political parties, Republican and Democratic organizations will have to contend with a restless and unpredictable electorate. The likelihood is that winning combinations of suburban voters will continue to lack permanency.

GUESSING THE UNSEEN FROM THE SEEN

Although our present knowledge of suburban politics is modest, it is probably sufficient to enable us, as Henry James observed, "to guess the unseen from the seen, to trace the implications of things, to judge the whole piece by the pattern." In the post-Daley era, the politics of the Chicago metroplitan region will be shaped by four conditions.

First, while the region's population is expected to stabilize, the migration of people from Chicago to the suburbs, which had become an inexorable movement just two decades ago, will continue into the twenty-first century.

Second, organized political parties, as we know them, will change appreciably as they compete with one another to accommodate an electorate that feels liberated from old party loyalties and the more predictable voting habits of their forebears.

Third, the political consciousness of the suburban region will grow markedly and reach its maturity in the next twenty-five years. In the process, it will graduate from a relatively inferior position of political authority vis-à-vis Chicago to a position of superiority.

And finally, if history is any guide, the Chicago Democratic organization, though beset with serious and continuing internal problems, will employ all its power and genius to neutralize the emergent power of the suburbs and to postpone, as long as possible, the further decline of the "one-city party."

Richard Daley neither understood the demographic and political changes unfolding on the edges of his city nor tried to avail himself of the political opportunities those changes might yield. His unshakeable conviction that the Democratic party was essentially a "one-city party" ranks among his most serious political misjudgments. There was no room for the suburbs in Daley's political formulations and, therefore, suburban Democratic and independent voters were accorded little recognition. This avoidable neglect may have stemmed from Daley's fear that eventually a competitive center of Democratic power might emerge in the suburbs. His fear was not without substance.

Chicago's current Democratic party leadership, still heavily concentrated in the hands of white ward committeemen, finds itself uncomfortably skewered on the horns of a dilemma. Like Daley, the leaders wish to preserve Chicago's and their preeminent authority in state party affairs and in the governance of Cook County, but demographic forces within and outside of Chicago threaten to disrupt the existing order forever. The city's white committeemen are caught in a vice—wedged between the suburbs, on the one hand, and, on the other, a growing black constituency within the city, a population that is finally flexing its political muscle in demonstrable and unpredictable ways.

Blacks constituted 34 percent of Chicago's population in 1970. Based on present trends, sociologist Philip M. Hauser estimates that this percentage will grow to 51 points by 1990 and to 75 points by the year 2000 (*Chicago Tribune,* Mar. 12, 1978). The consequence will be more black government in Chicago—more black aldermen, ward committeemen, state legislators—and eventually a black mayor.

If Chicago Democrats have ignored the suburbs for decades, they have also successfully repressed the rising political expectations of the black community. But blacks, like suburbanites, are neither so predictable nor manageable as in former times; and neither can nor should be ignored. Jane Byrne's defeat of incumbent Michael Bilandic in the 1979 mayoral primary election is a portent of future developments. Of the city's fifty wards, sixteen are predominantly black, and Byrne beat Bilandic in fifteen of them.

In light of these conditions—the escalating political power of blacks within Chicago and of outlying suburbs—the strategic options available to the city's white Democratic party establishment appear limited. However, whatever strategies are finally adopted will probably be insufficient to postpone certain inevitabilities.

Inevitably, the state legislature and the congressional delegation will be represented more heavily by suburbanites than Chicagoans.

Inevitably, control of Cook County's government will be more equally divided between the city and the townships. While Democrats will continue to control the board of commissioners and major county offices, traditional Democratic-Republican tensions will be overshadowed by a struggle between an entrenched, predominantly white, principally suburban-based Democratic party establishment, on the one hand, and the burgeoning black and Latino Democratic forces of Chicago, on the other.

Inevitably, the methods by which the state Democratic party is governed will change, and with reform the principal nexus of authority in party affairs will shift from Chicago to the suburbs and downstate Illinois.

Inevitably, control of the Cook County Democratic party will be more equally shared by Chicago and township interests. The suburbs, in fact, may enjoy an edge because political participation will be consistently greater there than in the city, where voter registration and election turn-outs by blacks and Latinos will continue to lag behind suburban whites.

STRATEGIC OPTIONS

The strategic options available to Chicago's ruling Democrat can be grouped into four general categories: acquiescence, accommodation, de-lay, and cooptation. The first and second options are the least realistic and, thus, require little discussion. Faced with an eroding power base, the last thing city Democrats will do is relax and permit the new demo-graphics to circumscribe their authority. It is simply not in the nature of the Chicago Democratic organization to acquiesce or accommodate itself to anything—without first engaging in a good and spirited fight.

In the short term, what is more likely will be efforts to retard the growth, if not the exercise, of suburban political power. For example, Republican proposals to increase the numbers of in-precinct voter regis-tration days in suburban Cook County have been dismissed by Chicago Democrats on the grounds of cost (*Chicago Tribune,* Oct. 10, 1977). Similarly, a 1977 proposal in the state legislature to liberalize voting hours to enable commuters—mostly suburbanites—to participate more easily in elections was subtly sidetracked because of drafting problems, a circumstance greeted with relief by some Chicago Democrats (*Chicago Tribune,* Nov. 12, 1977).

More recently, legislation designed to constrain participation by inde-pendent voters in party primary elections was considered by the General Assembly. This measure would require that voters wishing to change their party declaration between primary elections re-register twenty-eight days before the next elections. If enacted, re-registration would impact more on the suburbs where ticket-splitters and independents abound than on city voters. As the *Chicago Tribune* (May 20, 1979) warned, "Party loyalists, of course wouldn't have to worry about re-registering. They could turn out in force, while the registration handicap could be counted on to keep a great many independents from voting—or at least from voting in the race they'd prefer." This latest attempt to retard sub-urban political power is bottled up in a legislative committee.

Long-run strategies for curbing the suburbs—especially in Cook County—involve preemption. Some of Daley's heirs may attempt to rep-licate the Chicago political machine in the suburbs. Several prominent city Democrats have already moved to the suburbs and taken over exist-ing township Democratic organizations—others are contemplating such a maneuver. It is too early to determine whether the suburban environ-ment will be congenial to these intrusions or whether old-fashioned patronage, as an organizing and disciplining tool, can be effective. There are two obvious impediments, neither of which may be insurmountable: the scarcity and financial unattractiveness of patronage jobs and an ingrained resistance by suburbanites to political dictation.

Furthermore, a large number of Democratic township committeemen are on public payrolls—payrolls controlled by Chicago Democrats, and this lever will be more fully employed to augment the latter's designs on the suburbs. The city's agenda will include state legislative and congressional redistricting proposals that, if adopted in 1981, will expand the frontiers of Chicago's democracy at the expense of suburban Republicans, Democrats, and independents.

Eventually, these seemingly unrelated activities may result in an alliance between predominantly white Democratic ward organizations on the city's periphery and predominantly white Democratic township organizations in suburban Cook County—township organizations controlled by former Chicagoans. This convenient marriage of interests would enable Daley's heirs to contend with the two principal threats to their power base: Chicago's burgeoning black population and the suburbs' numerically superior and free-thinking electorate.

GOVERNING COOK COUNTY

The Cook County Board of Commissioners comprises sixteen members, ten from Chicago who immutably are Democrats and six from the townships who invariably are Republicans. Historically, this arrangement has permitted city Democrats, who frequently are also ward committeemen, to control the board, the board presidency, the chairmanship of the Finance Committee, and most countywide elected offices. The Republican role in this arrangement is appreciably larger than the part played by suburban Democrats. No suburban Democrat has ever been elected to the Cook County Board of Commissioners; none has ever been slated by the party as a candidate for a major county office—clerk, sheriff, assessor, or treasurer.

In the 1980s Chicago Democrats will finally recognize that the party's monopoly of county government will end unless suburban Democrats are made full partners in this enterprise. The partnership will require that suburbanites be slated regularly for county office and that they be accorded a larger voice in the governance of the Cook County Democratic organization. By the year 2000, if not before, the county's township population will equal Chicago's. Accompanying those shifts will be pressure periodically to review and reapportion membership on the county board between Chicago and the townships. Eventually, Chicago's present four-commissioner advantage will disappear. Unless city Democrats adjust, they will end up either sharing control of county government with Republicans on a more equal footing or surrendering control to them. These eventualities can only be avoided if suburban Democrats are granted a significantly larger role in governing the party and the county.

Cook County Board President George Dunne, who is also chairman of the Cook County Democratic organization, has suggested, to almost everyone's surprise, that the current system of electing the city's ten commissioners and the townships' six commissioners on an at-large basis within those areas be abandoned (*Chicago Tribune,* Dec. 5, 1978). He recommends instead that commissioners be elected from sixteen districts. In addition to enhancing accountability, Dunne knows, though he has not said so publicly, that such districts would probably insure the election of two or three suburban Democrats to the county board in 1982, thus neutralizing the gains Republicans expect as a result of the 1980 census. Moreover, this arrangement would allow for greater representation on the county board by Chicago's blacks, who, while constituting 25 percent of the county's population, hold only two of the sixteen seats on the board.

Adjustments cannot be postponed indefinitely; time and numbers are working against Chicago. The trend is clear, and it is irreversible. Between 1968 and 1978, Chicago's registration advantage over the townships of Cook County was halved. This index of political participation will come into greater balance in the 1980s, and that balance, with or without the active involvement of Chicago, will markedly alter the politics of Cook County.

THE REPUBLICAN RESPONSE

Can the suburban Democratic "menace" be contained? Will Democratic gains precipitate a Republican counteroffensive?

A Republican renaissance in the ring counties—DuPage, Kane, Lake, McHenry, and Will—is possible, but the current critical battleground is Cook County, where the Republican party appears to be in a state of severe, perhaps irreversible decay. The Republicans' refusal in 1976 and 1978 to slate judicial candidates in Chicago, thus insuring the uncontested election of Democratic candidates, is but one indication that the party has abandoned its loyal opposition role.

Although Republicans have managed to elect countywide officeholders in Cook County in only nine of the last twenty-five elections, Republicans had a rare opportunity in 1978, so it was widely believed, to punish the Democrats. Two Democratic incumbents—Sheriff Richard Elrod and County Clerk Stanley Kusper—were viewed as hopelessly vulnerable, especially in the suburbs. Some suburban Democratic leaders publicly urged that they be replaced, preferably with suburbanites (*Chicago Sun-Times,* Oct. 6, 1977). Elrod and Kusper, they argued, were a potentially dangerous drag on the entire ticket. Both were reslated, however, and in typical fashion the Republicans named an undistinguished ticket that was ridiculed and then humiliated in the primary when the party's endorsed candidate for sheriff was defeated by challenger Donald Mulach. As a result, former Republican Governor Richard Ogilvie, himself a former Cook County sheriff, tacitly supported Democrat Elrod against Republican Mulach in the general election. On election day, Elrod and Kusper easily won reelection, the latter leading the ticket countywide.

Perhaps no event illustrated the plight of county Republicans better than the debate that began in late 1978 over pay raises for the Cook County Board of Commissioners. Prompted by the Carter administration's call for wage and price restraint, George Dunne, the Democratic Cook County board chairman, opposed and then vetoed a 10 percent salary increase. In the subsequent efforts to override Dunne, the board's suburban Republican members did not line up, as might be expected, on the side of restraint and economy, but joined city Democrats against Dunne. Here was a chance for Republicans to ally themselves with the public on an issue that had aroused profound passion. Instead of capitalizing on the public's anger, the Republicans not only defied the public, but the philosophical foundations of their own party.

These episodes suggest that the Republican party, which now commands significantly less voter loyalty statewide than either Democrats or independents, may regress further as a significant political force. Though the situation is most acute in Cook County, deterioration has set in throughout the suburban region, where until recently 46 percent of the behavioral Republicans in Illinois lived.

In early 1978 suburban Republicans announced the establishment of the Northeastern Illinois Republican Council. The council's objectives are to coordinate party building in suburbia, to improve representation for suburbanites at all levels of government, and to create a more clearly defined suburban identity (*Chicago Sun-Times,* Jan. 19, 1978). How successful this effort will be is difficult to assess. However, a full Republican recovery in the suburbs will require more than a new organization, hobbled as the party is by its unwillingness or inability to identify with the electorate's essential center. That center is socially, economically, numerically, and ideologically more diverse than the Republican party, which in the suburbs tends to be dominated by right-of-center ideologues. In the competition for the center, the Democratic party is probably better equipped by tradition and temperament to accommodate diversity and to identify with the needs and aspirations of most suburban voters.

If a Republican counteroffensive is in the making, there is little evidence of it. The immediate expectation is that the party's narrowing appeal will invite further setbacks and that the atrophy will be more pronounced in local suburban elections rather than statewide, where candidates, like the Thompsons and Percys, tend to rise or fall in spite of, not because of, their Republican affiliations.

CONCLUSION

These scenarios may represent the shape of things yet to come. But there are few certainties in politics. Changing values and economic conditions, for instance, can intrude unexpectedly and invalidate the soundest predictions. Consider the following:

In the late 1970s the number of families headed by women without husbands was growing at a more rapid rate in the suburbs than in either central cities or nonmetropolitan areas.

Suburban men today are as likely to be nonwhite-collar workers as their central city counterparts. Only 47 percent of suburban men compared with 44 percent of those in central cities are white-collar workers.

Fifty percent of suburban women are part of the civilian work force; only 48 percent of city women are.

Despite the suburbs' "family-oriented" image, 43 percent of suburban families have no children under the age of eighteen living at home (Census Bureau, 1979).

None of these realities comport with traditional portrayals of the stereotypical suburbanite. The average suburbanite is, in fact, a markedly different creature today than a decade ago, and his changing nature is beginning to affect profoundly the texture of suburban politics. Those who recognize these differences, discarding the assumptions and stereotypes of the past, will prosper politically in the suburbs; those who do not will wither. At this point, only two things are clear: the race is on, and it is too early to predict the outcome.

REFERENCES

Advisory Commission on Intergovernmental Relations. 1977. *Trends in Metropolitan America*. Washington, D.C.: Government Printing Office.

Askin, S. 1977. "Chicago Exodus to the Suburbs." *The Chicago Reporter* (Sept.).

Bureau of the Census. 1960. *Census of Population, 1960*. Vol. 1, *Characteristics of the Population*. Washington, D.C.: Government Printing Office.

———. 1970. *Census of Population, 1970. General Social and Economic Characteristics*. Washington, D.C.: Government Printing Office.

———. Mar. 1978. *Current Population Reports, Population Characteristics, Voting, and Registration in the Election of November 1976*. Washington, D.C.: Government Printing Office.

———. 1978. *Social and Economic Characteristics of the Metropolitan and Non-metropolitan Population: 1977 and 1970.* Washington, D.C.: Government Printing Office.

———. 1979. *Illustrative Projections of State Populations by Age, Race, and Sex: 1975 to 2000.* Washington, D.C.: Government Printing Office.

Chicago Daily News. May 1977. "Chicago and Its Suburbs . . . the Future" (special edition); and Dec. 31, 1977.

Chicago Sun-Times. Oct. 6, 1977; Jan. 19, 1978.

Chicago Tribune. Oct. 10, 1977; Oct. 31, 1977; Nov. 12, 1977; Mar. 12, 1978; Dec. 5, 1978; May 20, 1979.

Christian Science Monitor. May 29, 1979.

Department of Development and Planning. May 1975. *Chicago's Black Population: Selected Statistics.*

———. 1976. *The People of Chicago: Who We Are and Who We Have Been.*

Gallup Opinion Index. Dec. 1976. "Political, Social and Economic Trends." Princeton, N.J.: The American Institute of Public Opinion.

Gallup, George. Nov. 13, 1978. "Many Americans Favor Creation of a 'Center Party.' " The Gallup Poll.

Harris, Louis. Feb. 23, 1978. "Party Adherence." The Harris Poll.

———. Aug. 3, 1978. "Party Adherence." The Harris Poll.

Mahoney, F. X. Dec. 12, 1977. Letter to John Matijevich.

Northeastern Illinois Planning Commission. Aug. 19, 1976. Revised Population Forecasts. Chicago.

Peterson, G. E. 1974. "Finance" in William Gorham and Nathan Glazer, eds., *The Urban Predicament.* Washington, D.C.: The Urban Institute.

Scammon, Richard M., and B. J. Wattenberg. 1970. *The Real Majority.* New York: Coward-McCann.

Secretary of State, State of Illinois Official Vote.

Southern Illinoisan. Nov. 15, 1977.

State Board of Elections. 1976, 1978. State of Illinois Official Vote.

Stevenson, Adlai E. Nov. 3, 1978. Untitled Speech for the Center for the Study of the Presidency. Springfield, Ill.

Teeter, R. Aug. 1977. Illinois Statewide Study, Republican State Central Committee Report. Market Opinion Research of Detroit.

Whitehead, R. 1977. "The Machine Shops the Suburbs." *Chicago Magazine* (Oct.).

White House Conference on Balanced National Growth & Economic Development. 1978. The Geography of Growth (conference working paper).

SAMUEL K. GOVE

State Impact: The Daley Legacy

THE IMPACT OF THE LATE MAYOR RICHARD J. DALEY went well beyond Chicago and Cook County. He also wielded considerable influence in state political and governmental circles. The purpose of this chapter is to try to determine how Daley was able to exert influence in so many areas and what was the extent of that influence. Two specific questions underlie these considerations: Was Daley's impact personal or organizational? Can the present Democratic organization and its new leaders continue to have the same influence in state circles?

The mayor's influence outside Cook County was multifaceted. He had considerable power in slating candidates for statewide office at primary and general elections and controlled the state Democratic central committee. In the legislature Daley's organization supporters occupied a significant number of seats. He was influential in the selection of his party's leaders in the legislature, and, when Democrats held the governorship or other statewide executive offices, he had their ear. If an officeholder was in his camp, he also gained patronage.

Unfortunately, the mayor did not leave any personal papers, so it is difficult to document the era and to pinpoint precisely his impact on state events. A closer look may, however, offer some insights into the past and some clues about future Chicago Democratic influence.

STATE GOVERNMENT

For many years in downstate primaries and statewide general elections, the opposition for downstate Democrats and statewide Republicans was often Daley, even though his name was not on the ballot. In these elections he was pictured as an ogre who dominated the state or as an octopus whose tentacles were wrapped around the statehouse. While this made good campaign copy, it was somewhat exaggerated. The mayor did have considerable influence in Springfield, especially in the legislature. He did not, however, control state government. Rather, he made deals, particularly with Republican governors, to get done what he considered essential. Over twenty years ago, this relationship was described as follows: "The combination of a determined Republican Governor exercising effective control over downstate Republicans and a determined Democratic Mayor exercising effective control over Chicago Democrats is more likely to produce any desired result than is any other combination of public or private interests" (Steiner and Gove, 1960: 198).

One of the problems in trying to assess the late mayor's influence in state government is the confusing relations between the city and the state. Legally, the city is a subunit of the state. Prior to the grant of home rule power under the 1970 state constitution, Chicago had only that power and authority specifically delegated by state statute. While this was the legal arrangement, the political arrangement was quite different. Certainly in the ordinary citizen's mind, as well as in many practical ways, the city was the superior unit—especially with Richard J. Daley as mayor and party leader. The realities of this relationship meant that a Chicago Democratic organization member could be promoted from the state legislature to the Chicago City Council or the Cook County Board. As examples of legislators who followed this route, one might cite Matt Ropa and Vito Marzullo. In a somewhat lighter vein, it is interesting to note that the state's tourism division capitalized on this public image of state-city relations by advertising in Chicago that somewhere off in the distance "is a place called Illinois." The clear implication was that the city was not part of the state.

Compounding the real and imagined problems in the state-city relationship is Chicago area's sheer preponderance in numbers of inhabitants. In 1975 there were 3,126,000 people in the city plus another 3,857,000 in Cook and the collar counties. At the same time there were only 4,131,000 people in all the other ninety–six downstate counties. In other words, Chicago and its suburbs accounted for 63 percent of the total state population in 1970. The diversity of the city's inhabitants is another factor here. In 1970, 32.7 percent of those living in Chicago were black (and 7.3 percent were Spanish-speaking), while in the remainder of the state blacks made up only 3.4 percent of the population. This large minority population in the city clearly has quite different perceptions from the rest of the state's residents about the needs and priorities that ought to be addressed in Springfield.

A further example of this unusual state-city relationship may be seen in what happened when the Associated Press (AP) tried to identify the ten most powerful people in Illinois. In July 1977 the AP assembled a panel of knowledgeable men and women to participate in the selection process for this list. Among the difficulties encountered by the panel was that relatively few individuals wield statewide power unless they occupy or are planning to run for a statewide office. As one panelist said, "One of the problems is that Illinois is not a natural community. It is a very sharply divided state. Therefore, very few people really have statewide influence. . . . That is one reason Illinois is so difficult to govern, because it is so sharply divided, with half the people living in the metropolitan area and the other half downstate.'' Another panelist commented, ''Chicago and Illinois are two separate countries . . . two states within the same state. . . . The power is in Chicago.''

The results of the task force's efforts are interesting, not only for the list produced but also for what it may presage for the future. If Daley had lived, undoubtedly he would have topped the list. As it was, a Chicago banker very close to the Chicago Democratic organization was first. Eight of the ten people picked were from the metropolitan area. Secretary of State Alan Dixon was the only downstate political leader. Two newcomers, Governor James Thompson and Mayor Michael Bilandic, were also included, doubtless because of the offices they held, not because of any personal power held at that time.

One way to pursue the question of how Daley managed to gain such widespread power—and what a successor must do to follow in those footsteps—is to study the mayor's relationship with the three branches of state government: the legislature, the executive, and the judiciary.

STATE LEGISLATURE

Mayor Daley's impact on state legislative actions was especially marked after the legislative reapportionments of the 1950s and 1960s, which gave Chicago and Cook County more representation. Mythology even had it that the mayor had complete control of the legislature. Although myth, it should be remembered that Daley had considerable experience in Springfield, having been a member of the General Assembly for ten years—in the House from 1936 to 1938 and in the Senate from 1939 to 1946; during the latter period he served as vice-chairman of the Illinois Legislative Council. He had also had considerable legislative contact while serving as Governor Adlai Stevenson's director of Revenue.[1]

The mayor's influence may be seen at both the leadership and programmatic levels of the legislature.

Legislative Leadership

Except for the period following the unusual 1964 at-large House election, when many Democrats across the nation were swept into office on Lyndon Johnson's coattails, members of the Chicago Democratic organization rarely dominated the Illinois legislature in terms of numbers. Nonetheless, party members throughout the years have held many leadership posts, both formal and informal. An organization spokesman, Cecil Partee, served as president of the Senate from 1972 to 1976, the first president to be elected under the provisions of the new constitution. In the House, Gerald Shea served as majority leader under Speaker William Redmond in 1975–79.

The selection of Representative William Redmond as Speaker in 1975 illustrates some of the realities the Chicago organization faces in controlling the legislature, even with a clear Democratic majority. Redmond, representing a DuPage County district, was Daley's candidate for Speaker, but it took ninety-three ballots to elect him. In the usual procedure for selecting the legislative leadership in Illinois the party or parties caucus prior to the opening day of the session. There are frequently contests, but it is expected that all party members will vote for the party's winning candidate for speaker, or president, or minority leader. This system broke down in this instance when a group of seventeen dissidents in the Democratic party, led by Representative Clyde Choate, refused to vote for the caucus winner, Redmond. Thus the necessity for the long ninety-three-ballot fight. Crossover Republicans finally delivered the necessary votes. After his election, Redmond quickly selected organization man Shea as his floor leader. Redmond took for himself the role of presiding officer, leaving the policy and strategy moves mostly up to Shea.

A similar conflict in the Senate in 1977 (after Daley's death) illustrates what may lie ahead. Because of divisions in their ranks, the Democrats had doubled the number of House ballots needed to elect a president (186). Before Thomas Hynes was finally elected, two blocs of Democratic holdouts had gained prominence. One, a group of chiefly downstate liberal independents, was known as the "Crazy 8" (although by 1977 there were nine in the group). The other group was made up of black senators led by Harold Washington, at that time a candidate for nomination in the Chicago mayoral special primary. That the second group existed at all was a surprise. If Daley had still been alive, it would have been inconceivable for blacks as a group to challenge the organization candidate openly. On the other hand, if Daley had lived, there would not have been a special primary. The fight for the Senate leadership was the first visible political event that can be attributed to Daley's departure. But whether it foreshadows similar events is debatable. The leadership fight may have occurred more because of Washington's primary challenge to the organization's mayoralty candidate, Michael Bilandic, than because of inroads into the unity of the organization.[2]

Legislative Program

Prior to the adoption of the new constitution in 1970, Chicago's primary legislative concerns in Springfield centered on financial issues, and the most famous of these was doubtless the state income tax. Daley was a strong proponent of such a measure and was able to provide a sufficient number of organization votes that the tax was passed but not so many that Chicago could be blamed for it; that honor was reserved for the governor, Richard Ogilvie.

Except in certain areas, the city itself has had no great need for legislation since it gained home rule powers. In fact, much of the activity by Chicago legislators is defensive—they are trying to stop any infringement on the city's power. Thus the Chicago legislative contingent is concerned with only limited matters, i.e., tax legislation affecting the city, legislation (and money) for the city's schools, the sanitary district, and the Chicago Transit Authority (now under the Regional Transit Authority). (The latter are units of government that do not fall under the home rule grant of powers.) The state money that Chicago public schools receive, for instance, is dependent on a statewide equalization formula instituted in 1973. The city's success is, therefore, closely linked with what happens to school districts throughout the state. Despite this formula, however, there has always been tacit agreement that Chicago's share would be fairly large, a situation that has not changed since Daley's death.

Following Daley's death, the Chicago contingent continued to use logrolling tactics as they had in the past. The controversial Crosstown Expressway was approved after the new Republican governor had a meeting of the minds with the new Democratic mayor, a situation reminiscent of Daley's earlier successes with governors of the opposite party.

Overall the 1977 legislative session was different from earlier sessions. But then, each session seems to be unique, each with its special personalities, leadership styles, and governors. In 1977 the new governor may have caused the most change. Republican James Thompson, with a whopping 1.4 million plurality, replaced maverick Democrat Dan Walker.[3] In contrast to Walker's combative stance against the legislature, Thompson's style was cooperative. In his state of the state address he even said that "the war is over" between the governor and the General Assembly. He had gotten to know the senators well while he presided over them for the extended period before they elected their president.[4] Moreover, the leadership in the House in 1977 was not too effective, but this may have been more a result of personalities than of the post-Daley era.[5]

Indications of what may lie ahead may be found in several legislative areas. One area of particular interest is a state public employee collective-bargaining law, on which the Chicago organization successfully maintained its negative stance for many years. Daley opposed such legislation because it could have disrupted his favorable relations with the public employee unions in Chicago.[6] (The opposition has never been too open, not wanting to give the impression that the organization is anti-union—

which it definitely is not). The scenario followed in 1977 was similar to that of previous sessions. Several bills from the AFL-CIO, teachers, and other union groups were introduced in the legislature. As in the past, none passed, and the organization prevailed.

All of this changed when Jane Byrne was elected and came out for public employee collective-bargaining, especially for firemen. She mentioned this position in her inaugural address and almost immediately found herself in very deep trouble. Both the firemen and the city transit workers went out on strike, something that was totally unheard of in Daley's time. Despite her inaugural comments, Byrne did not actively campaign for public employee collective-bargaining legislation in Springfield, and once again no such legislation was passed at either the 1979 or 1980 sessions. In fact, the mayor had little positive impact on these early legislative sessions.

Moreover, Byrne hurt relations with some of her own Chicago legislative delegation when she supported (with organization agreement) Alderman Edward Burke for state's attorney over state Senator Richard M. Daley, the late mayor's son. Daley rather easily won the nomination in the March 1980 primary.

Another indication of Byrne's somewhat precarious relations with the legislature was the serious consideration of legislation permitting the recall of the mayor in the 1980 spring session.

Chicago's future relationship with the General Assembly is unclear. There is no reason to think it will change greatly as long as the Chicago organization can continue to control the election of organization candidates to the Senate and the House. Since Daley's death, the only major deviation from past practices has been the 1977 Senate leadership fight. But that may well have been due to the peculiar set of circumstances surrounding the special mayoral primary. It is clear that the strong loyalty among members of the Chicago delegation to Daley has not carried over to Byrne. Nonetheless, it must be mentioned that Byrne did reach into the Chicago legislative delegation for her contact person in Washington and Springfield, choosing well-respected Representative Michael Brady (although he has already left office, as have many other officials). In addition, she chose another well-respected representative, Eugene Barnes, to head the Chicago Transit Authority. He still holds the position.

THE EXECUTIVE

Generally Daley got along with governors of both parties. When he was elected mayor in 1955, William G. Stratton, a Republican, was in the governor's chair. These leaders of opposite parties were able to work out arrangements that benefited both, with the most notable example being the special bonding authority for the lakefront convention center, McCormick Place. Stratton's successor was Democrat Otto Kerner, who held the governorship from 1960 to 1968. Kerner came from the Chicago organization, and, although he tried to indicate his independence from it, he was only partially successful. Daley did fairly well in achieving his goals during these years. Kerner resigned just before his term was over to accept an appointment to a federal judgeship, leaving his lieutenant governor, Samuel Shapiro, to fill out the year. The next governor was Republican Richard B. Ogilvie, an activist governor, who held the office for one term. Here again the Democratic mayor–Republican governor arrangement worked quite well for both sides. During the Ogilvie administration, with Daley's collaboration, the state's first income tax (with one-twelfth set aside for cities and counties) was adopted. In addition, the Regional Transportation Authority, covering the Chicago metropolitan area, was established. A strong exception to Daley's usually friendly relations with the men who resided in the governor's mansion in Springfield was the personal public animosity between the mayor and Ogilvie's successor, Dan Walker. Walker's desire to strengthen the downstate Democratic organization, even at the expense of Chicago—as, for instance in the case of the Chicago Transit Authority—sharply curtailed the mayor's opportunities. Walker was to be the last governor with whom Daley had to deal.

Following Daley's death, relations between the Illinois governor and the Chicago mayor did not differ greatly from those in the past. Thompson and Bilandic were friendly. Bilandic attended Thompson's inauguration in January, and the governor came to the mayor's wedding in July. While Thompson did support the Republican candidate for mayor against Bilandic in 1977, he did not do so vigorously. In fact, he announced the settlement of the long-standing controversy on the Crosstown Expressway in May, late in the campaign.

Byrne is a highly political person and a staunch admirer of Daley—but her behavior is contrary to his style. Her one effort to act like the late mayor in Springfield was disastrous. Late in the 1979 legislative session, she and Thompson—with little legislative involvement—put together a transportation package that was unveiled late in the session. One part of the package dealt with the on-again, off-again Crosstown Expressway–Franklin Street subway project, which both Daley and Bilandic had supported. The package failed, but Byrne blamed the Democratic leadership—not the Republicans. She vent her wrath particularly on the majority leader, Michael Madigan, a Chicago ward committeeman, who had delivered his ward for her with a heavy vote in the April election, taking some legal patronage away from him.

Working with a Republican governor on a legislative compromise was a typical Daley move; in contrast to Byrne's experience, however, Daley generally got the compromise adopted. Byrne did have better results working with state officials on reaching a solution for the financial crisis in the Chicago school system, but in this instance the state clearly had the upper hand.

Another of Byrne's attempts to work with the governor also misfired, when she supported Thompson's opposition to removing the entire sales tax on food and drugs and favored a compromise that called for removing only one cent from the tax. She thus angered several organization Democrats in the legislature.

STATE JUDICIARY

One area in which it is difficult to pinpoint political influence is in the judicial process of the state courts. The election of supreme court judges from districts after nomination in primaries does permit open participation by political parties, but information and background on judicial decisions from the bench with political overtones are another matter. All that can be analyzed is the written opinions (and dissents, if any) and, if there is a divided court, the voting of the judges.

Election of judges is often criticized as bringing politics into the judicial process, and, in fact, most of those elected as judges in Chicago were organization people. Several attempts have been made to adopt merit selection plans by constitutional amendment, but these were opposed by Daley supporters both in the legislature and at the 1969–70 constitutional convention. Efforts for a merit selection amendment continue, but the Democratic organization in Cook County maintains its negative stance.

Only one election for the state supreme court has been held since Daley's death. The 1976 primary for two vacancies from Cook County was a disaster for the organization, with two of its candidates (including Daley's close associate, Joseph Power) defeated. Another significant defeat occurred in 1980, when independent Seymour Simon upset organization candidate Francis Lorenz.

The Illinois Supreme Court has had a four to three Democratic majority since the late 1960s. Very seldom, however, do votes on a decision follow party lines; instead they seem to follow ideological or other lines. This is not too surprising, because the principle of *stare decisis* (legal precedents) is used as the basis for decisions. Only when a case involves an election or when other political matters come up do political overtones occasionally arise. For example, in a decision handed down in 1976 in a case involving the selection of national convention delegates, the court ruled against the Democratic state central committee (*Touhy* v. *State Board of Elections*). Two of the judges who had risen through the Chicago Democratic organization filed dissents. The political impact of this decision is not clear, but it did mean that Illinois was not in compliance with national Democratic party standards for delegate selection.

As with other state-city relationships, it is impossible to predict whether Chicago's relationship with the state judiciary will change significantly. It is possible, but unlikely, that the organization will change its opposition to merit selection of judges. It is more likely that the organization will continue to try to nominate and elect its candidates for the important supreme court vacancies, hoping for more success than it had in 1976. The political cases that arise will still be decided on the merits of the case, the whims of the judges, political considerations, or a combination of these. There seems no reason to expect a series of decisions for or against the Chicago organization.

So far our discussion has focused on the mayor's relations with elected government officials. Equally important is the relationship with the system and process that put these officials in office: politics.

STATEWIDE POLITICS

Daley was unquestionably the leader of the Democratic party in Illinois, even though he held no state office. His candidates were usually nominated in Democratic primaries, and he usually delivered the Chicago vote for statewide candidates. This depended in part on national trends,[7] and the candidates were not always successful on a statewide basis. He also played a visible role in the largely ceremonial state Democratic conventions. Under a weighted voting system provided by law, his representatives dominated the Democratic state central committee.

Since his death, no state party leader has stepped forward. Bilandic was unable to claim the title. The Cook County Board president and new county party chairman, George Dunne, has no statewide visibility. He did not even make the AP's list of ten most powerful persons in Illinois. Some downstate politicians are saying that Secretary of State Alan Dixon has earned the position of party leader. In November 1976 he gained a plurality of 1.3 million, which nearly matched Thompson's; in November 1978 he raised the plurality to 1.5 million, topping Thompson's 0.6 million plurality. But Dixon has no direct ties to the Chicago organization. He finished seventh in the AP power survey, behind Bilandic and Thompson, and his refusal to run for governor in 1978 reduced his stature, as did his handling of slatemaking responsibilities in the same year. Nonetheless, in a contested primary in spring 1980, Dixon won the U.S. Senate nomination to fill the seat of retiring Senator Adlai E. Stevenson. He then went on to win the Senate seat in the November general election.

In any case, as the 1980s began, the state Democratic party appeared to be without leadership, except for the minimal direction that comes from the state central committee. The long-run picture is unclear. One question a potential leader might well ask is: How did Daley do it?

PARTY ORGANIZATION

The state central committee of each party, created by statute, is composed of one member elected in the primary from each congressional district; the law also provides for weighted voting, based on the primary vote in the district. This means that the Chicago Democrats dominate the Democratic state committee because of their ability to turn out the primary vote. The present chairman, who is selected by the other members, is John P. Touhy, a well-respected former speaker of the House of Representatives and a former member of the Cook County Board. He was politically close to Daley.

Although the committee is created by statute, its powers are open ended. The committee has never been aggressive, and the state party has never played the positive role of its counterparts in other states. It has, for example, no significant role in handling campaign finances. This is due in part to the fact that Illinois is such a sharply divided state. Many downstaters do not want a Chicago-dominated committee interfering in their affairs.

With the clear majority of the votes, the Chicago members, including the chairman, have the votes to dominate the proceedings and to ensure—if they wish—that the committee continues in its passive role. After Daley's death some non-Chicago members felt that the chairman became more open to reason and that suburban and downstate members were listened to more than in the past. These members hope that the state central committee, rather than the Cook County central committee, will play the dominant role in future slating for state offices. Since this did occur in the 1977 slating for the 1978 primary, these members feel a change may be taking place.

Suggestions for other changes have been heard in the post-Daley period. Congressman Paul Simon has said that the Illinois Democratic party should make greater use of the state party central committee and that the party should acquire a professional staff and use extensive computerized voter lists and studies. Others have called for opening up the state committee to give a larger role to women, ethnics, racial minorities, downstaters, and suburbanites. A bill in the 1977 legislative session provided for the committee to be enlarged to fifty-nine members by using legislative (rather than congressional) districts as the arena for representation. This proposal was supported by Comptroller Michael Bakalis, but is was not voted out of the legislative committee to which it had been assigned.

Changes in powers, procedures, and composition of the state central committee may take place in the coming years. But because of the divisions in the state, unless the slatemaking is regularly turned over to the state committee (and the committee acts responsibly from a statewide perspective), there will probably not be any significant change in the committee's role.

THE SLATEMAKING PROCESS

Until 1972 slatemaking had been the established method used by the Democratic party for endorsing candidates in the primary, even though there was no statutory basis for slatemaking and the slated candidate was not designated on the ballot. Usually both the state and Cook County central committees held sessions at which those seeking endorsement presented their cases. Frequently in the past, however, such sessions were a facade. Daley had decided whom to slate before the sessions began; other party leaders went along when they had gotten "the word." If confronted, the leaders argued that the system was really open and cited the case of Bakalis, an unknown who received the endorsement for superintendent of public instruction in 1970.

After the slatemaking process, Democratic workers delivered the votes in the primary for slated candidates. The process followed the doctrine of party responsibility and was accepted by most concerned.

In 1972 Dan Walker, who did not participate in the slating process, successfully defeated the slated candidate for governor, Paul Simon.[8] Walker went on to defeat incumbent Republican Richard B. Ogilvie. The new governor, a maverick in many ways, was a thorn in the side of the organization. In 1976 it retaliated by slating Secretary of State Michael Howlett against the governor, who again did not appear before the slatemakers.[9] Howlett defeated Walker by over 100,000 votes. Howlett, in turn, was defeated by Thompson by the greatest margin in the state's history.

The Future of Slatemaking

The slatemaking process has been criticized by the "outs," who have not been able to crack the system. The Democratic National Committee has also criticized the system as it applied to candidates for delegates to the 1972 national convention, considering the system counter to party rules (*Cousins* v. *Wigoda*). Others have said that the system is not in accord with national political trends, which emphasize such procedures as open primaries. And downstaters criticize the system because Chicago dominates the process. Michael Howlett, after the 1976 elections, was also critical. He was quoted in a political column by Basil Talbot, Jr., as saying: "We must bring the party up to date and do away with slating as it was. Chicago has lost its domination over state politics. A new way must be found to choose Democratic candidates for state office. It has nothing to do with whether Daley is around . . . times have changed" (*Chicago Sun-Times,* Apr. 10, 1977). The same column said that Dixon prefers to do away with slating, but would settle for a radical revision. Bakalis wants to keep slating, but to take the Chicago stigma out of it.

Such pressures did bring changes in the slatemaking process for the 1978 election, but the changes nearly resulted in political disaster for the party. In contrast to earlier times, the slatemaking was conducted by the state central committee, not the Cook County central committee. Cook County and other party representatives were, however, given the opportunity to hear potential candidates before the meeting. In the absence of Daley, state Democratic Chairman Touhy, George Dunne, Alan Dixon, and Michael Bakalis came up with a premeeting slate, but this group's slate was upset by the full state committee. Weighted voting was important in determining the outcome. The final slate provided balance for Chicago, but it had no women, and many felt it shortchanged downstate. No candidate was slated for lieutenant governor; Bakalis chose his own running mate.

Party observers were very pessimistic about the results—results unlike any of the slates developed in the Daley years. Two of the slated candidates had significant opposition, an unheard of occurrence in recent Illinois Democratic politics, except for the successful challenge by Walker in 1972. With the strong help of Chicago and Cook County voters, both of the challenged candidates won nomination handily.

Slatemaking in Illinois is on very rocky ground and, as now practiced, may end. This could have a significant effect on state politics, for the Democratic party could become open to nonorganization candidates. It is difficult to say with any certainty whether such a change in slatemaking would come because Daley died or because the time had come for its end. Probably Daley's death speeded up whatever changes will occur.

GENERAL ELECTIONS

In general statewide elections during the Daley period, the organization met with mixed success. Sometimes circumstances (for example, a strong Republican presidential candidate) were beyond the mayor's control. At other times the organization made the mistake of endorsing weak and inept candidates.

In the future, especially with the split-ticket practices that have developed, the mixed record will doubtless continue. Democratic candidates for state office will probably be able to count on the basic organization vote in Chicago, but their success will depend on their campaign style, finances, and qualifications. All candidates for state office will be less affected in the future by national trends because, since 1978, state elections are held in nonpresidential years. This change, however, has nothing to do with Daley's death; it was a result of the new state constitution.

As in most other areas, Byrne's impact on statewide elections is as yet unclear.

CONCLUSION

It is too early to speculate on the extent of change that will occur in the post-Daley era in the relationship between Chicago and the Chicago political organization, on the one hand, and state governmental and political organizations, on the other. There will be isolated events, such as the drawn-out election of the state Senate president or the 1977 slatemaking process, where observers will comment that this or that would not have happened if Daley were still alive. It is possible that there will be less cohesion in the legislative delegation to Springfield. Slatemaking on the state level may break down completely. Efforts to strengthen the state Democratic party, however, may be increased and may ultimately be successful.

The election of Byrne may well bring about a major upheaval of the political order in Chicago. Her style is so different from what the Chicago politicians know that it is difficult for them to cope. She obviously is trying to strengthen her political power, but whether she will succeed remains to be seen. Her first real test at the March 1980 primaries did not go well. Richard M. Daley's victory in the state's attorney race in November 1980 may well be interpreted as an important defeat for the mayor.

The other question asked at the beginning of this paper—was Daley's external power personal or organizational?—also presents difficulties. In many ways his power was definitely personal, built up during his long service as a party leader. But the organization's ability to deliver the vote is also important. It is the latter phenomenon that will ensure that changes in external power relationships will not be rapid or dramatic. But whether the organization can continue to deliver the vote remains to be seen.

NOTES

1. Since 1972 his son, Richard M. Daley, has served in the Illinois Senate. His successor, Michael Bilandic, had no experience in Springfield; nor did Jane Byrne.

2. The 1979 organization candidate for president, Senator Philip Rock, a Chicago organization Democrat, was elected on the first ballot.

3. Thompson won reelection in 1978, but his plurality over Democrat Michael Bakalis was only 0.6 million.

4. The balloting lasted off and on for a month and a half, ending on February 16. Under the state constitution, the governor presides until the Senate elects its president.

5. Speaker Redmond was reelected in 1977 and 1979 without controversy. He selected Chicago organization man Michael Madigan as floor leader.

6. For a more detailed discussion of this issue, see Chapter 3 herein.

7. Most state offices had been contested in presidential elections. Under a provision of the new state constitution, in 1978 state officers were elected in an off-year election for the first time.

8. The last time a slated candidate for governor was defeated was in 1936, when the organization tried to unseat Governor Henry Horner.

9. Walker had his own slate, which contested the organization candidates for the other state offices. His entire slate was defeated.

REFERENCES

Chicago Sun-Times
Cousins v. Wigoda, 419 U.S. 477 (1975).
Steiner, Gilbert Y., and Samuel K. Gove. 1960. *Legislative Politics in Illinois.* Urbana: University of Illinois Press.
Touhy v. State Board of Elections, 62 Ill. 2d 203 (1976).

MILTON RAKOVE

Jane Byrne and the New Chicago Politics

ANY ANALYSIS OF THE POLITICS of the post-Daley era in the city of
Chicago must be rooted in the context of the long-time and still extant
political machine that has dominated Chicago politics since it gained
control of the city government in 1931. For the past quarter of a century,
political analysts and observers have referred to the machine as the
"Daley Machine." But the machine preceded Richard J. Daley's rise to
power, and, while it reached its apex as a functioning political organization under his leadership, it has survived his passing and will probably
dominate the city's politics for some time to come.

The twin pillars on which the Chicago machine built its long-term political dominance of the city were an unwavering commitment to a particular brand of politics—machine politics—and an ability to adapt to a
changing environment in the city and within the machine.

From the machine's inception a half century ago, its power rested on a
base of three major interlocking entities within the city's body politic—
the ward organizations, the governmental apparatus of the city of
Chicago and the county of Cook, and powerful private interest groups
and constituencies in the community, which had to be dealt with and pacified. In other words, the Chicago Democratic machine has always been
more than a purely political organization. It has been a political/govern-
mental/private interest group coalition, whose elements had a common
objective, the advancement of their private interests at the expense of
some vague generality called the public interest.

The leadership of each of these three constituencies, the people who
spoke for and represented their memberships in the interrelationships
within the machine, were the ward committeemen who controlled the
ward organizations; key bureaucrats who ruled major city and county offices and departments; and bankers, businessmen, and labor leaders.

Before Richard J. Daley came to power as mayor of Chicago in 1955,
the political machine was not controlled by a single dominant figure. It
was, rather, a feudal structure, led by a coalition of powerful ward committeemen who ruled their wards like ancient satraps and who divided up

and parcelled out among themselves the rewards of politics—jobs, money, influence, and status. Collectively, they decided who would run for public office in the city and county. In return for their support, they demanded and received from elected public officials the emoluments they considered to be the quid pro quo for their political support.

The perquisites and jobs that accrued to public officials elected under the aegis of the Democratic machine belonged, not to the elected public officials, but to the political organization. The organization was more important than the government, and public officials and public policies were subordinated to party politicians and party needs. To a considerable extent, the relationship between the Democratic machine in Chicago and the city government was analogous to the relationship between the Communist party and the Soviet government in the Soviet Union or in other such one-party political systems. In other words, in Chicago, before Daley became mayor, politics took precedence over public policy, and politicians were more important than elected or appointed public officials. And the private interest groups in the community at large had to deal primarily with politicians, rather than public officials, if they wanted to influence public policy in the city.

THE DALEY YEARS

Daley significantly altered both the inner dynamics of the political machine and the relationships between the machine's three major constituent elements. Daley understood the need to bring the feudal warlords—the ward committeemen—under his control and to take the control of the city government and public policies away from those politicians.

Daley took the first step toward accomplishing the first objective when he was elected chairman of the Cook County Democratic central committee in 1953. He was, at that time, one of a number of powerful ward committeemen of approximately equal status with approximately commensurate power.

In 1955, when the machine decided to dump the incumbent reform mayor, Martin Kennelly, Daley sought and gained the approval of most of his powerful cohorts to be their candidate to regain control of the mayor's office. In return for the support of the other warlords, Daley promised to relinquish the party chairmanship if he were to be elected mayor. They did not want him to hold both offices, because they did not want anyone to have that kind of power. Moreover, they wanted to be sure that Daley, as mayor, would still be controlled by the party machine.

But it was not to be that way. The future relationship of the ward committeemen to the city government under the newly elected mayor was prophesied by one of the most colorful of them all, Alderman Mathias (Paddy) Bauler of the Forty-third Ward, a German saloonkeeper who knew them all well, but who understood Daley better than they did. "Keane and them fellas—Jack Arvey, Joe Gill—they think they are gonna run things," Bauler proclaimed at a victory party in his saloon at 403 North Avenue on that election night in 1955. "They ain't found it out yet, but Daley's the dog with the big nuts, now that we got him elected. You wait and see, that's how it is going to be."

After Daley was elected mayor of Chicago, he refused to resign the party chairmanship, knowing that if he did, the ward committeemen could do to him what he had just done to the incumbent mayor. But there was a deeper reason behind Daley's refusal to resign the party chairmanship. Daley wanted to be a great mayor, and he knew that would be impossible if the traditional machine domination of the city government was left unchanged.

Before Daley became mayor, an elite group of powerful ward committeemen, who also served as aldermen, controlled the city government and city public policies through their control of the city council. Known as "the grey wolves" during the Kennelly mayoralty, they made up the budget, divided the spoils among themselves, distributed patronage, rode roughshod over the bureaucracy, and subordinated public policies to their private needs. In other words, politics dominated public policy, and politicians ruled the roost in Chicago.

Daley altered that relationship significantly. He used his power as mayor to strengthen his role as party chairman, and he used his power as party chairman to strengthen his role as mayor.

Daley had two tasks he had to perform well if he was to be a successful party chairman and a good mayor. As party chairman he had to win elections for the machine. As mayor he had to govern the city effectively and efficiently.

How could Daley win elections for the machine? Daley had a simple answer: Get more votes for the machine's candidates than the opposition could garner. As Daley always put it when asked why a candidate had lost an election, "He didn't get enough votes!"

How could Daley and the machine produce more votes than the opposition? According to some politicians and campaign strategists, elections are won by presenting the electorate with highly qualified candidates, debating the issues, distributing literature, and then relying on the voters to choose the best candidate for public office on the basis of their qualifications, public records, and concern for the commonweal of the community.

Daley did not believe that. He always paid lip service to those shibboleths, but he practiced a different brand of electoral politics, based on a more pragmatic assessment of the voters' motivation in an election. Daley believed that if you did three things well, the voters would support your ticket. First, pick a slate of candidates who represent the racial, cultural, religious, and social biases of the polyglot constituencies that make up the city's body politic. Second, take care of the basic private needs of the voters. Third, get the voters you represent out on election day. If you did those three things well, elections would be won, not on the basis of the candidates' qualifications or stands on issues, but rather on a quid pro quo relationship of votes in return for emotions appeased, services rendered, and a disciplined organization maintained.

The prime requisite for keeping the voters quiescent and satisfied was to use government services to minister to their personal needs and to see that their passions were not aroused by the failure of government to do so. The precinct captain, Daley told a ward rally on March 29, 1975,

> is a better neighbor than most of us, for partisan reasons. He has solicitude for the welfare of the family in his block, especially if they are a large family with dependable political loyalties. He gets your broken-down uncle into the county hospital, if he lives in the slums. He's always available when you're in trouble. He's the salt of this democratic-small "d" earth. . . . You have provided the service that makes life worth living. . . . You have been available to the young and to the old; you've sponsored . . . softball and basketball teams and baseball teams for the young of our community. You've consoled and helped the widow when she was in trouble and she lost her husband. You've taken unto yourself guidance for the young that were many times fatherless. This is the real strength of our party and they'll never take it away from us. As long as we have the kind of an organization we have in the City of Chicago, we will time and again be victorious.

If the city government was to provide a high level of public services, Daley believed, it had to be taken out of the hands of ward politicians and put under the control of a professional bureaucracy. And that is what Daley did when he became mayor of Chicago. He took control of the budget away from "the grey wolves" in the city council by getting a law passed in the state legislature that placed the formulation of the budget in the office of the mayor. The budget was then sent to the city council for approval under conditions that made it virtually impossible for the aldermen to tamper with the document. That gave Daley control of the two things that count in politics for politicians: money and jobs. The council, which had been controlled by "the grey wolves" in the Kennelly era, came under the strict control of Daley and his Finance Committee chairman, Alderman Thomas Keane, a redoubtable, brilliant politician, lawyer, and parliamentarian.

Daley also took control of the city's administrative bureaucracy and recruited a group of first-rate professional administrators to run the city departments that deal with basic public services. They were hired by Daley and were responsible to him. In this way he wrested the functioning city government from the control of the politicians. This is not to say that ward committeemen had no influence on the bureaucracy. They did. But they did not control the administrators who ran the departments. The administrators, on their side, were expected to recognize the realities of politics in Chicago and to be sensitive to the built-in relationships among the city government, the ward organizations, and the voters whom the city government and the ward organizations had to service together. Daley thus provided the voters with high-quality public services and gave the ward committeemen the wherewithal to keep their constituents moderately satisfied a.id quiescent.

The control of city and county governments also gave Daley and the political machine the resources for carrying out the second essential ingredient of a winning electoral strategy—an army of precinct workers who could mobilize the satisfied and quiescent voters and get them to register and vote right on election day. Control of the city and county offices gave Daley and the machine access to jobs that were distributed to the ward committeemen, to be distributed by them to the minions who labored in the vineyards of the precincts without monetary compensation. The compensation for their efforts in the precincts was provided for by their salaries as city or county workers, and their worth as public employees was measured, not only by their performance on their public jobs, but also by the efficiency with which they serviced their constituents in the precincts and delivered the vote on election day.

By hiring professional administrators to run the departments, Daley ensured a high level of public services and, at the same time, left room in the lower echelons of the bureaucracy for the ward committeemen and precinct workers. Ward committeemen were slated for major elective office with adequate compensation or were appointed to high-level positions in the bureaucracy, not as department heads, but at slightly lower levels, which still provided adequate compensation and public status. And a primary qualification for city and county employment for precinct workers was a willingness and demonstrated ability to help deliver the vote on election day.

The provision of good city services and patronage jobs for precinct workers also gave Daley a tool for disciplining the ward committeemen and holding them to account for carrying their wards. If good city services and jobs for workers were the basic ingredients for electoral success, no ward committeeman could justify his failure to carry his ward in an election on any basis other than his own incompetency or his failure to avail himself of what the city government was providing to ensure success on election day.

In return for good public services for their wards, jobs for their workers, and positions of importance and good salaries for themselves, the ward committeemen turned over to Daley complete control of the city council and of public policy matters in the city. As ward politicians, they had little interest in such matters, since these were the province of the mayor and the bureaucracy.

As for the third element in the success of the machine—the powerful private economic interest groups in the community at large—Daley practiced interest group politics with them. He gave the bankers, the businessmen, and the labor leaders what they wanted for themselves and their constituencies. In return, like the ward committeemen, they gave him what he needed for his city.

In sum then, Daley significantly altered the Chicago political machine and the government of the city. First, the power balance within the machine was changed. Daley strengthened the role of the mayor, improved the quality of the bureaucracy and city services, took control of the city council and public policy away from the ward committeemen, and worked out a partnership built on mutual self-interest with the powerful business and labor elites who provided the major economic underpinnings of the city. He created in Chicago a sophisticated political/governmental/private interest group system of relationships and collaboration based on a pragmatic assessment of the realities of power in a body politic. And he used that system to further what he considered to be the public interest of his city. He was not always right in what he did, and he was sometimes out of touch with the changes taking place in his city. He was, however, a master politician and superb administrator who managed his city well and controlled his political machine for a quarter of a century during a time when most other major cities became unmanageable and their political systems broke down. Breakdowns did not occur in Chicago during the Daley years, and when he died suddenly on December 20, 1976, his true legacy was a city that had worked well under his leadership.

THE BILANDIC INTERREGNUM

Daley's sudden death left the city government, the political machine, and the powerful private interest groups in Chicago in a state, not of shock, but of uncertainty. How would the system he had created survive his passing?

Daley had left no heir apparent, either as mayor or as party chairman. He was faulted by some for what they considered to be crass irresponsibility in failing to provide for the future after his death. But they did not understand three things that were essential to his thinking. One, he would not provide for an heir because he understood his personal situation in the machine. Two, he could not provide an heir, even if he wanted to, given the realities of politics and power in Chicago. And, three, he had provided his successors, whoever they might be, with what they would need to govern effectively, if they used what he had left wisely and well.

First, while it was true that Daley stood head and shoulders above the other powerful ward committeemen in the machine, he was never a dictator. He was, rather, a combination constitutional monarch and benevolent despot who ruled only so long as he delivered for the machine in elections, governed the city well, pacified the other warlords with perquisites, and headed off any possible incipient revolt by other ambitious politicians. Daley was, as it was once said of the British prime minister, first among equals in his entourage, but more equal than the others. He knew what had happened to Mayor Edward J. Kelly, who was dumped by the machine in 1947 after fourteen years as mayor. He must have known, for example, that after he was elected to his second term, Congressman William L. Dawson, the head of the black submachine within the machine, had gone to a leading Polish politician in Chicago and proposed a black/Polish alliance to take the city and the machine away from Daley and Irish politicians. So Daley took care to make sure that no other politician came too close to him or gained enough power to challenge him, not even Alderman Keane, who was number two in the hierarchy. Daley knew that if he designated an heir-apparent, that person's ambitions, and the ambitions of other power seekers, might coalesce in an effort to remove him from office.

Second, Daley knew that he could not designate an heir to succeed him after his death, for he knew that once he was gone all bets were off, all obligations canceled, and all arrangements subject to change. He knew what had happened in a somewhat comparable situation in Soviet Russia after Stalin's death in 1953. The supposedly designated heir-apparent, Georgi Malenkov, ended up running a power station in Siberia; Secret Police Chief Beria was shot; Foreign Minister Molotov was exiled to Mongolia; and Nikita Khrushchev, whom no outside expert had seriously considered as a potential successor, was made the new leader. Daley knew that in Chicago, as in Communist Russia, whoever got the power would have to fight for it and get it on his own, not receive it as a dead man's bequest.

Third, Daley knew that he had created a sophisticated, effectively functioning political/governmental/private interest group system that could survive him and be his true legacy after he left the scene, provided his heirs held the system together. "You guys had better hang together after I'm gone," he had told one of the key leaders, Alderman Edward Vrdolyak, "or you'll hang separately."

Daley's admonition to his successors, like George Washington's fare-well address to his country, was followed in the aftermath of his passing. Representatives of the three major factions in the overall machine—ward committeemen, bureaucrats from the city government, and business and labor leaders—coalesced to hold the machine together. They decided to hang together since they did not want to hang separately.

There were, in the initial stages of negotiations, some discordant notes. Several people aspired to succeed Daley as party chairman. And there was some question as to whether Cook County Board President Dunne would be mayor, party chairman, or possibly both. But the real problem, the one that had to be dealt with expeditiously and without tearing the city apart, was how to appease the blacks without giving them control of the city government.

The Reverend Jesse Jackson, a black civil rights activist who was ever alert to new power opportunities, had immediately proclaimed, on hearing of Daley's death, that the only proper choice for acting mayor was black Alderman Wilson Frost, president pro tem of the city council. Frost, an able, intelligent lawyer and ward committeeman, initially gave credence to Jackson's argument. But, after assessing the realities of the situation, he backed away from Jackson and joined the coalition.

The national media, seldom aware of the realities of Chicago politics and always hoping for the demise of the machine, either predicted chaos or misread the unfolding scenario. Local television commentators con-fused the public even more than usual by consistently raising the irrele-vent question of who was going to be the next Daley, the new boss of the machine. They did not understand that there was not going to be another Daley in Chicago; that Daley had created and ruled a system that re-flected and represented his own considerable talent as a politician and administrator; that it was unlikely that anyone else could do the same thing; and that the machine after Daley would be different from the ma-chine under Daley, just as the machine under Daley had been different from the machine before Daley.

In fact, the reality of the situation after Daley's demise was that the ward committeemen did not want another Daley. He had been too strong, and, while he had understood their needs and distributed their perquisites, he had kept them all under his control, had strengthened the city government and the bureaucracy at their expense, and had forced them to bow to his concept of the public interest and the good of the city. They wanted a milieu in which they would have more power, free from the centralized control Daley had exercised. In other words, they wanted to return to a pre-Daley era in which the political machine was strength-ened vis-à-vis the city government and bureaucracy and in which they could more easily pursue their private interests. But they understood the need to maintain the framework of the structure Daley had built.

Since they did not want another Daley, they were determined that no one would do to them what Daley had done to their predecessors in 1955—hold both the mayoralty of the city and the chairmanship of the party. Whoever would be selected as party chairman would not be mayor, and they would choose as mayor someone who could not be party chairman. But their choices for both offices should be able to keep the Daley system going, so that those elements in the body politic outside of the machine—black activists and white liberal reformers—who would really upset the system if they roused the electorate and gained power could be kept ostracized.

The new coalition decided on Alderman Michael Bilandic as Daley's successor as mayor of Chicago and Cook County Board President George Dunne as the new chairman of the Cook County Democratic central committee. They were both logical choices for their respective positions, given their backgrounds and abilities and the need to govern the city effectively while freeing the ward committeemen from the heavy hand Daley had laid on them.

Bilandic was a life-long resident of Daley's neighborhood, Bridgeport, and the Eleventh Ward. He had been a successful lawyer who had also been active in the politics of the ward. Bilandic had been drafted by Daley to run for alderman, although he was loathe to run for public office, since he was not really a politician. "He wanted to bring me into government," Bilandic told an audience at the Chicago Historical Society on October 14, 1977, reminiscing about his relationship with Daley. "I kept saying no. . . . In 1969, I ran out of excuses. He finally got me to be the candidate for alderman. We talked about it on three separate occasions. . . . I knew I either had to say yes or leave town. I decided to stay in Chicago."

In the council Daley had come to rely on Bilandic as a key person to assist in the development of public policy issues. And when Finance Committee Chairman Keane was convicted of mail fraud in a federal court, Daley asked Bilandic to take over the chairmanship of the committee and assume Keane's role in the council as floor leader. Bilandic was in his element as Finance Committee chairman. A skilled lawyer with an orderly mind, a fascination for figures, and an ability to understand and work with the nuances of the budget, he developed a sound grasp of the city's finances and of the problems of attempting to formulate public policies in a city like Chicago. He knew the key bureaucrats, had worked with bankers, businessmen, and labor leaders, and understood the relationship between the city government and the powerful private interest groups in the city. He could be relied upon to continue Daley's policies and programs and would not precipitously rock the boat in the immediate post-Daley era. Moreover, he was not a ward committeeman and was unlikely to become one, since the Eleventh Ward precinct captains had

elected Daley's son, state Senator Richard M. Daley, to that post upon
the mayor's death. So it was extremely unlikely that Bilandic could be or
would ever want to be chairman of the Cook County Democratic central
committee. The two posts could be kept separate, thus denying Bilandic
the possibility of gaining both offices in the unlikely event that he would
attempt to copy Daley's feat. And since he was not a charismatic politician, but rather a sound, capable administrator, it would be difficult for
him to build an independent power base with the voters outside the structure of the machine. His continuance in office would thus depend on two
factors—his ability to manage the city efficiently and the machine's ability, through the now more independent ward committeemen, to turn out
the vote. That would require a quid pro quo relationship between Bilandic and the ward committeemen in which he would need them to win reelection, and they would have to rely on him to maintain the basis of
their strength in their wards, good city services and patronage jobs for
their workers.

County Board President Dunne was also a logical choice as party
chairman. He had been a member of the Democratic organization for almost a half century, had been a precinct captain, ward committeeman,
state representative, park district employee, and Cook County commissioner. As president, he had established a reputation as an able administrator and public servant. He was well liked and respected by most of the
committeemen, including the suburban township committeemen, with
whom he had established a good rapport since taking office. He was on
good terms with the media, and no breath of scandal had touched him
during a long career in politics and government. He had never actively
sought higher office but had almost always been drafted by the party and
agreed to serve as a matter of party loyalty and public responsibility.
And, what was important to the other committeemen, he was in his middle sixties when Daley died. It was not an age at which a man sets out to
create a new career as a party boss, but rather a time at which most men
begin to wind down their careers and reduce their responsibilities.

So, the power and the responsibilities in Chicago were divided after
Daley's death between a lawyer/alderman/administrator as mayor and a
capable, long-time ward committeeman and public administrator as party chairman. Both men were acceptable to the three major parts of the
machine—the bureaucracy, the ward organizations, and the powerful
economic interest groups in the city.

The ambitions of the Young Turks who wanted more power was
worked out, too. Alderman Vrdolyak was made president pro tem of the
city council and chairman of the powerful Committee on Building and
Zoning. Alderman Edward Burke was given an enhanced leadership role
in the council and made chairman of the important Police, Fire, and Ed-

ucation Committee. Alderman Frost was given the position Bilandic vacated and that Keane had also held, the second most important position
in the city government, chairman of the council Finance Committee and
floor leader, a position from which he could significantly benefit the
black community. Forty-seventh Ward Committeeman Edmund Kelly,
who failed in his bid for the party chairmanship, still had his position as
superindendent of the Chicago Park District, with its attendant patronage and power. All of these Young Turks could afford to wait, knowing
that the new coalition was an interregnum, that their power was enhanced, that their wards would be taken care of, and that those among
them who were lawyers would see their law businesses prosper. At the
same time, the Old Guard committeemen, Alderman Vito Marzullo,
County Commissioner Matthew Biesczatt, Sewer Commissioner Edward
Quigley, and the First Ward's John D'Arco were also satisfied, assured
of what they were interested in—continued patronage, status, and ready
access to the new power structure.

In the city bureaucracy, the status was also quo. Bilandic made a few
minor changes but retained most of the department heads he had inherited from Daley. Indeed, as Bilandic's mayoral term evolved, the power
of the key bureaucrats was enhanced, since control over city patronage
was retained by Bilandic and his administrative assistant, Tom Donovan.
The city bureaucracy remained a highly centralized structure under Bilandic's and Donovan's leadership. But the party organization, under
Dunne, became a much more decentralized structure, with power devolv-
ing to the individual ward committeeman to a degree unknown during
the Daley years. There thus began a gradual shift of power within the
machine from the party organization to the city government, as Donovan
became the man to see about patronage and prerogatives for the ward
committeemen.

As for the third component of the machine, the banking/business/la-
bor constituencies, they, too were satisfied with the new regime. The
relationships with the Daley bureaucracy were retained; the old under-
standings were kept in place. They were as close to the new mayor as they
had been to the old one, and the watchwords were stability, continuity,
and common interests.

What kind of a record did the Bilandic administration write between
January 1977 and January 1979?

On the whole, Bilandic had a sound record of accomplishment, continuity, and some forward motion. The budget was balanced, municipal
bond issues sold at a high rating, labor peace in the city was maintained,
the racial and ethnic strife that had been predicted by some of the media
did not materialize, and the city's public services were maintained at a
high level. The coalition that had constituted the machine under Daley

remained intact, albeit somewhat altered in its internal relationships. The city bureaucrats, the ward committeemen, and the banker/business/labor leadership were content, thankful that the predicted breakdown had not occurred, satisfied with their continued status and power, and tolerant of whatever minor difficulties the new regime had with the media and the public. As for the public at large, while it did not regard Bilandic as a charismatic figure, it, too, accepted the new order in Chicago, since it combined enough of the stability of the old order with some movement on new public policies to satisfy the citizens' needs.

In the winter of 1978, one year into Bilandic's mayoralty, there was, however, a minor upheaval of some consequence. Jane Byrne, who was commissioner of Consumer Sales, Weights and Measures, a small city department, accused Bilandic in the media of "greasing" the city's taxicab companies with regard to a projected fare increase. After a short brouhaha in the press between Byrne and Bilandic, the mayor fired the commissioner. She, in turn, took her allegations to the Cook County state's attorney and the U.S. attorney for northern Illinois. Both of those officials, after investigating Byrne's charges and at the conclusion of the grand jury proceedings, decided that there were no grounds for attempting prosecution and that Byrne's allegations had no merit as far as their offices were concerned.

Byrne had had some political connection to Daley. He had appointed her as cochairman of the local Democratic party's Cook County central committee (an honorary post with no legal status or political power) as a means for dealing with the burgeoning women's political consciousness in the city and suburban areas. She had been removed from that post by Dunne when he assumed that office.

In the summer of 1978, Bilandic and the machine began to prepare his reelection campaign for a full four-year mayoral term. The primary election was scheduled for February 1979, with the mayoral election to follow six weeks later. It was to be a well-planned, carefully orchestrated campaign, stressing the solid accomplishments of the Bilandic mayoralty. There was no serious opposition contemplated, although political analysts of the evolving Chicago political scene had discerned a significant development in the machine's ability to deliver the vote in a contested mayoral primary.

In 1975, when Mayor Richard J. Daley was challenged by a white reform alderman, William Singer, and a black independent Democrat, state Senator Richard Newhouse, Daley had received about 50 percent of the total vote in the primary, but had won easily, since the opposition candidates split the other 50 percent of the vote. And the same thing had happened in the 1977 mayoral primary, when Bilandic was challenged by three opponents—Alderman Roman Pucinski; a black candidate, state

Senator Harold Washington; and former State's Attorney Edward Hanrahan. In that primary election, Bilandic also received 50 percent of the total vote, while his three opponents split the other 50 percent. Clearly, there was a solid anti-machine vote in the city that had to be either contained or divided. If blacks, lakefront liberals, dissatisfied white ethnics, and crossover Republican voters coalesced around a single candidate, the machine's half-century stranglehold on the city's mayoralty could be broken. In the summer and fall of 1978 that possibility seemed farfetched. No black candidate entered the lists; and the lakefront liberals were dormant, discouraged by the failure of their candidate, Alderman Singer, in 1975 and Bilandic's solid record in office.

There was, however, a small cloud in an otherwise clear and sunny machine sky. Former Consumer Sales Commissioner Byrne, aggrieved by her sudden dismissal, convinced that the new regime headed by Bilandic constituted "an evil cabal" that had corrupted the political organization and city government built by her mentor, Richard J. Daley, and bent on revenge for the wrongs done to her and Daley, announced that she would run for mayor against Bilandic in the February 1979 primary.

It was not a candidacy to be taken seriously. Byrne had no money, no precinct workers, no programs of any note, and no support from any of the elements of the power structure of the still extant machine—the ward committeemen, the bureaucrats and public officials, and the business/banking/labor elites. She was unknown in the black community, unwanted by the white-ethnic constituencies, and unpopular with the lakefront liberals who had known her to be a part of the machine during the Daley era. And she was a woman in a city and political system where no woman had ever achieved major public office.

Byrne had some assets as a candidate. She had a sharp intellect, good "gut" political instincts, a long-time familiarity with the political workings of city hall and the ward organizations, an ability to communicate effectively at street level with the voters, and a demonstrated knowledge of how to use the media effectively, a talent she had acquired as commissioner of Consumer Sales. But neither Bilandic nor the machine took her candidacy seriously. Given the odds against her, they ignored the portent of the vote percentages in the last two mayoral primaries, did not subsidize or recruit a black candidate, and did not encourage a liberal candidate to enter the race as insurance against the development of a possible anti-machine coalition that could coalesce around the Byrne candidacy.

Under normal circumstances, Bilandic and the machine would not have suffered from their political mistake. But the winter of 1978–79 was not normal. The worst snowstorm in the city's history paralyzed the city and aroused the citizenry. The city government's inability to clear the snow away, the breakdown of public transportation and garbage collection, the anti–city hall posture of some key media figures, and Bilandic's handling of the public all combined to encourage a massive anti-machine turnout on primary day. Byrne received all of the normal anti-machine vote in the city plus an outpouring of normally lethargic nonvoters who trooped to the polls to register their anger and vent their frustration on the machine's candidate, Mayor Bilandic. Byrne won the primary by 15,000 votes. Six weeks later, with the assistance of the machine she had defeated in the primary, she also won the mayoralty with 82 percent of the vote, a higher percentage than even Daley had received in any of his six mayoral victories.

Byrne's crucial victory, of course, was in the primary, not in the general election. It was in the primary that a new coalition was forged—a coalition of angry blacks, lakefront liberals, and dissident white ethnics, a coalition that overpowered the basic and traditional machine vote in the city. Mayor Bilandic did get the machine vote. Indeed, he got approximately the same vote he had in the 1977 mayoral primary.

THE BYRNE MAYORALTY

Byrne's victory over the machine aroused high hopes among the constituencies of the new coalition. A new day was dawning in Chicago politics, the days of the old machine were numbered, and a reformed, open government, with a new politics would characterize the Byrne era.

Those hopes and expectations were, of course, doomed. The coalition that had helped Byrne defeat the machine in the primary was a temporary alliance among three constituencies that had little in common in terms of their long-range interests. It was a coalition that could only come together for winning an election or, rather, defeating an incumbent. It was not a coalition with which Byrne (or anyone else) could govern the city, unless she was prepared to undertake drastic changes in the thrust of public policies. And if she did that, she would immediately alienate segments of the coalition, since they had contradictory ideas of what should be done and inherently conflicting interests. To give the blacks what they wanted would alienate the white ethnics. To give the white ethnics what they wanted would alienate the blacks and the lakefront liberals. To give the liberals what they wanted would alienate the white ethnics and many of the blacks. Above all, to change the thrust of public policies in the city radically would alienate the real power structure of the city, the three major constituent elements of the machine—the ward committeemen, the bureaucracy, and the business/banking/labor communities. Without their support the city could not be governed effectively. And what they wanted was not radical change, but continued or increased influence and power.

Faced with the reality of the power structure in Chicago, and probably aware of the tenuous character of the coalition that had elected her, Byrne moved, not in any new directions, but rather toward the old, solid ground she was familiar with as a city hall politician and bureaucrat. Taking a leaf from the policies of her mentor, she set about to improve the quality of public services in the city—street cleaning, garbage collection, snow removal for the coming winter, better public transportation, and the other basic functions of city government that were the warp and woof of Daley's long tenure in office. Had it not been the breakdown of those services that had brought about Bilandic's downfall? So she turned on the bureaucracy to shore up her incoming administration.

At the same time, fearful of the powerful ward politicians who had supported Bilandic in the primary, Byrne publicly attacked them in the media as a cabal of evil men who had no concern for the public interest of the city she now had to govern as mayor and sought to bring them to heel by threatening their patronage, prerogatives, and power.

This two-pronged attack at first paid off in Byrne's standing with the media and the coalition that had elected her, both hoping for a new day in Chicago. Since she made headlines every day, the media gave her massive exposure, and the public was impressed with the appearance of movement and radically changed direction of the city's public policies.

Indeed, there was a radical change taking place within the city government, but it was not one of new public policies and new directions. Byrne was operating on two levels simultaneously—a public attack on the politicians and the old policies and, at the same time, a massive and continuing shake-up of the bureaucracy that had served Bilandic and Daley. Those bureaucrats, not the politicians, were the people she was really most uncomfortable with and fearful of. They had worked for and with Bilandic and were probably still his allies and friends, she felt, and thus could not be trusted. Within a year after assuming office, Byrne had removed almost every major department head and replaced each one with her own appointee. She had the right to do that, she argued publicly, as a new chief executive. The president of the United States, Byrne said, appointed his own cabinet when he assumed office, and she should have the same prerogative.

There were two problems, however, with the Byrne approach to the position to which she had been elected. First, while it was true that Byrne had the legal right to recruit her own cabinet, there was a significant difference between the situation in Chicago and that in Washington, D.C. In Washington an incoming American president usually appoints most of his cabinet officers, not so much for their demonstrated administrative abilities, but rather for political reasons of interest group politics—the Treasury Department to someone acceptable to and representative of the banking community; a secretary of labor who represents labor's interests; a staunch supporter of farm price supports for the Department of Agriculture, and so on. Only in the departments of state and defense, which are crucial to national security, and where domestic politics have to be subordinated to the exigencies of national survival in a hostile world, are professional, trained expert administrators needed. And it is generally safe to make political appointments to most cabinet posts, since the professional bureaucracy, which is permanent, keeps the ship of state afloat and carries on public policies and public services.

In Chicago, however, the situation is different. Daley had recruited, and Bilandic had retained, on the whole, first-rate professional bureaucrats to run the city departments. The politicians—the ward committeemen—were put at the second and third levels of the bureaucracy, not where they could control public policies and public services, but at a level that afforded some status and where they could be decently rewarded financially. They did not have major responsibility for running the city. The efficiency of the bureaucracy was buttressed by the machine's policy of giving the best positions in the lower levels of the bureaucracy to the best precinct captains. As Alderman Marzullo, a long-time machine stalwart, once put it, "The qualities that make a man a good precinct captain make him a good worker."

When Byrne cleaned out the top level of the city bureaucracy, many of the city departments were left in the hands of appointees who were unfamiliar with the dynamics, informal relationships, and policies of the system that Daley had created and Bilandic had retained. In other words, what Byrne did was to bring down and disrupt the political/governmental/private interest group system that Daley had created in Chicago.

The question then became, "What would Mayor Byrne put in the place of that system?"

It became clear, fairly quickly, that there was no overall comprehensive plan for doing anything. There was instead a sort of piecemeal, day-to-day movement of the key cogs in the bureaucracy. People were moved around, many were replaced. This is not to say that none of the Daley/Bilandic appointees should have been replaced, or that all of Byrne's appointees were not competent. There were some who could and should have been replaced; there were also some good new Byrne appointees. But there was no well thought-out plan for tearing down an existing structure and building a new one.

The major problem was not so much the individual appointments, but rather a weakness in the policy-formulating and decision-making apparatus at the top of the city government, in the office of the mayor. In Byrne's first year in office, she appointed and replaced two young ex-newspapermen with no administrative background as deputy mayors;

hired and fired a budget director; lost a comptroller through resignation and removed her own appointee to that office; and had a succession of three press secretaries, ending up with her husband, another ex-newspaperman with no administrative experience, who seemed to emerge then as her key adviser and spokesman.

This administrative turnover in the bureaucracy and the lack of centralized planning and direction in the office of the mayor had two major consequences. The lower levels of the bureaucracy, fearful of the thrust of the new regime, somewhat demoralized by the continuing turnover at the top, and concerned about their own survival, gradually retreated into the hoped for safety of anonymity, inertia, and caution. City services were still carried on, but new directions were avoided, criticism of policies muted, and the normal bureaucratic tendencies toward faceless survival strengthened.

The second major consequence of the disruption of the old order, without the creation of a viable new one, was the breakdown of the ties to the business/banking/labor constituencies. Unsure of the direction the new Byrne administration would go, unfamiliar with the bevy of new faces at the top of the bureaucracy, and uncertain of their status in any new order, those constituencies, too, assumed a stance of watchful waiting in their dealing with the new administration.

As for the third component of the old machine, the politicians, they gradually moved into a satisfactory quid pro quo relationship with Byrne and her key advisers. The Old Guard ward committeemen were pacified by recognized continued status, patronage, and clout. The powerful Young Turks, who had been Bryne's original enemies, the "cabal of evil men," became her closest allies in the city council, providing support and leadership for her policies. The bulk of the other ward commiteemen, who were neither Old Guard powerhouses nor Young Turk rising stars, were content as always to go along, following the leaders and grateful for whatever crumbs they garnered from the table of plenty at the top.

It was to the politicians that Byrne turned for help, after her initial attack on them. They were the people she was most familiar with from her years in city hall and her relationship with Daley. In the Daley years Byrne had been, after all, a city hall politician first and a bureaucrat second. Whatever power she had had at that time stemmed, not from her rise in the administrative bureaucracy in city hall, but from a political relationship with Daley. Daley had not consulted with her on major matters of public policy, or on the budget, or even on important administrative problems. He had, rather, used her as a political aide, assigning to her tasks appropriate for a woman in the political organization. So Byrne was essentially a city hall politician who had been elected to a major administrative office without much background and training for that job.

Her demonstrated skills were political, not administrative, and it was
those skills she relied on as mayor. Thus, in her efforts to govern the city,
she turned to the politicians with whom she was familiar and to the
political folkways of city hall with which she was most experienced. In
the early months of the Byrne mayoralty that meant a decline in the
power of the bureaucracy, the alienation of some of the business/bank-
ing/labor elements, and the slow, steady recrudescence of the power of
the politicians, the ward committeemen who had lost power in the Daley
years.

That had a significant impact on the formulation and execution of
public policy by the city government. Chicago's ward committeemen, by
background and interest, are parochial creatures. They are primarily
concerned with their own private economic and political interests, sec-
ondarily with the requirements and prerogatives of their wards on which
their political power and status are based, and only lastly with the needs
of the city. They subordinate public policies, public needs, and the public
interest to their own and their wards' interests and requirements. When
Byrne turned to them in the city council, and for her own counsel, to deal
with matters of public policy in Chicago, she based her administration's
program on her relationship with politicians with little interest in and
concern for the public interest of the city. The bureaucratic elite under
Daley, who were not politicians but professionals, had to be concerned
primarily with the public needs of the city; the public interest took
precedence over the private interests of the ward committeemen and the
parochial needs of their wards. They had served a mayor, Richard J.
Daley, who, despite his allegiance to the political machine, subordinated
that to his role as mayor of Chicago. Daley had strengthened the bureaucrats in their role as public servants against the influence and control of
the ward bosses. And Bilandic in his two-year term had maintained the
same policy. In fact, he had further strengthened the bureaucracy.

Jane Byrne, in her own way a protégée of Daley, wanted to be a good
mayor, too. But she came to office without a well-formed or well-
thought-out program for providing for the city's needs and the public interest of the citizenry at large. She was also inhibited by her lack of major
administrative experience, her unfamiliarity with the city's public policies and fianances, and her relatively inexperienced administrative staff.
When she cleaned out the experienced and trained bureaucracy Daley
and Bilandic had left her, she stood stripped of the protective armor of
the system that would have insulated her from the politicians. The make-
shift coalition of liberals, blacks, dissident ethnic and anti-machine
voters, and crossover Republicans who had elected her in the crucial primary election was useless in helping her govern the city and using and
controlling its power structure. The concatenation of her own instincts,

talents, and weaknesses; her initial action in shaking up the bureaucracy; and the exigencies of having to govern the city during a time of mounting problems and financial stress drove her into an alliance with those least concerned with the public interest and the requirements of long-range public policies—the ward politicians.

In the process, Byrne lost much of the constituency that had elected her and that had expected major reform. The blacks turned away from her and are looking to one of their own to give them what they want. The lakefront liberals resumed their traditional role as the vocal opposition in the city council and the media. The once dissident ethnics—firemen, policemen, and anti-integration and anti-busing constituencies—turned on her after she showed an unwillingness to give their unions control over their departments and because of the integration fight in the public schools.

In the face of these developments, Byrne went back home to the political machine she had defeated. That organization and its leaders, the most powerful ward committeemen, have become her staunchest allies. But they are also the most unreliable allies, since they are politicians, relatively unconcerned with the public interest that must be served, ready to abandon her if her standing with the public deteriorates, and willing to jump aboard any ship that seems to be better able to remain afloat than hers.

At this writing (August 1980), the prospects for a successful Byrne mayoralty are tenuous. She has done some good, notably in facing publicly some of the problems she inherited. But she has not, for reasons this chapter attempts to spell out, dealt very well with those problems.

Byrne changed the politics of the city with her electoral victory over the machine in the February 1979 primary. But she did not know how to exploit that change and did not adequately use the resources Daley and Bilandic had left her for doing what she had to do as mayor, govern the city effectively. She has thus brought down a functioning sophisticated, political/governmental/private interest group system in Chicago, without, to date, replacing it with one of her own. If she is able to do that, she can still govern the city effectively. If not, the prospects for her, and for the city, are dubious.

Notes on Contributors

JOANNE BELENCHIA is a doctoral candidate in sociology at Northwestern University, Evanston, Illinois. She received her B.A. in community studies and sociology from the University of California at Santa Cruz. Her research interests are community and institutional organizations, political movements, and social welfare policy. In addition to the fellowships she has held from the Center for Urban Affairs and Policy Research at Northwestern, Belenchia has served on the staffs of the Chicago Community Trust and United Charities of Chicago.

SAMUEL K. GOVE is director and professor in the Institute of Government and Public Affairs and professor of political science at the University of Illinois/Urbana-Champaign. His primary areas of research are intergovernmental policy, state and federal politics, and higher education. He is chairman of the board of *Illinois Issues* and has written extensively on state problems. His books include *The Illinois Legislature: Structure and Process* (with R. W. Carlson and R. J. Carlson) and *American State and Local Government* (with C. F. Snider).

WILLIAM J. GRIMSHAW is an assistant professor of political science at Illinois Institute of Technology, Chicago. He is the author of *Union Rule in the Schools: Big-City Politics in Transformation* and *Black Politics in Chicago: The Quest for Leadership, 1939–1979.*

DONALD H. HAIDER is associate professor of management and urban affairs and is the director of the Program of Public and Not-For-Profit Management at Northwestern University, Evanston, Illinois. He was the first budget director in the Byrne administration following an appointment as deputy assistant secretary of the U.S. Department of Treasury for State and Local Finance. Haider is the author of *When Governments Come to Washington* and *Economics, Housing and Condominium Development.*

LAWRENCE N. HANSEN has been involved in government and politics continuously since 1966. Except for the period 1971–74, during which he served as special assistant to State Superintendent of Public Instruction Michael J. Bakalis, Hansen was associated with former State Treasurer and U.S. Senator Adlai E. Stevenson. Between March 1978 and January 1981, he was the senator's administrative assistant in Washington, D.C. He has also played a major role in a number of statewide campaigns in Illinois.

KATHLEEN ANNE KEMP is an assistant professor of government at Florida State University, Tallahassee. Her research specialties are urban politics, the impact of the Supreme Court's abortion decision, and economic regulatory policies at the state and municipal levels. She has published articles in the *Journal of Health Politics, Social Science Quarterly,* and *American Politics Quarterly.*

ROBERT L. LINEBERRY is professor of political science and dean of the College of Liberal Arts and Sciences at the University of Kansas, Lawrence. Before his present position, he was at Northwestern University in Evanston, Illinois. His research interests include urban service delivery, and he is now completing a study, with Herbert Jacob at Northwestern, of politics and crime in ten cities during the postwar period. Among his books are *Urban Politics and Public Policy* (with Ira Sharkansky), *Equality and Urban Policy: The Distribution of Municipal Services,* and *American Public Policy.*

LOUIS H. MASOTTI is professor of political science and urban affairs at Northwestern University, Evanston, Illinois. From 1971–80 he was director of Northwestern's Center for Urban Affairs and Policy Research. Following the nomination of Byrne in 1979, Masotti served as executive director of her transition committee. His thirteen books include *Metropolis in Crisis, Urbanization of the Suburbs, The City in Comparative Perspective, The New Urban Politics,* and *Urban Politics and Public Policy.* From 1974–80 Masotti was editor-in-chief of *Urban Affairs Quarterly.*

KENNETH R. MLADENKA is assistant professor of political science at Texas A. & M. University, College Station. He has also taught at Rice University, the University of Virginia, and Northwestern University. His research on urban politics has appeared in the *American Political Science Review, Journal of Politics, Social Science Quarterly,* and *Urban Affairs Quarterly.*

MICHAEL B. PRESTON is associate professor of political science at the University of Illinois/Urbana-Champaign and holds a joint appointment with the Institute of Government and Public Affairs at this university. Preston received his Ph.D. from the University of California at Berkeley and has done extensive research on CETA, labor, and manpower issues as well as black politics.

MILTON RAKOVE is professor of political science at the University of Illinois/Chicago Circle. He has served as a consultant to the Chicago Better Government Association and as a consultant and speechwriter to U.S. Senator Charles H. Percy. He has also been associated with numerous political campaigns in Chicago. His books include *Don't Make No Waves, Don't Back No Losers* and an oral history of the machine, *We Don't Want Nobody Nobody Sent.* He is a frequent contributor to the *Chicago Sun-Times* and *Chicago Tribune.*

JOSEPH ZIKMUND II is dean, School of Letters and Sciences, Menlo College, Menlo, California. Before his present position, he was chairperson of the social science department at the Illinois Institute of Technology, Chicago. His B.A. is from Beloit College; his M.S. is from the University of Wisconsin; and his Ph.D. is from Duke University. In addition, he has a professional degree in urban planning from Wayne State University. His books include *Suburbia: A Guide to the Literature, The Ecology of American Political Culture,* and *Black Politics in Philadelphia.*

Index

Adamowski, Benjamin, 8, 63, 85; 1955 election results, 32; 1963 election results, 37–40
Adams, Charles, 4
AFL-CIO, 64, 185
AFSCME: and collective bargaining, 80, 83, 86
Aldermen: black, 100–101; independent, 107; on distribution of municipal resources, 147–48
Alinsky, Saul, 122
Allswang, John, 2, 4, 15, 31
Almond, Gabriel, 91
Ammons, J., 4
Arvey, Jack, 219
Associated Press: ten most important people in state, 204–5
Ayers, Thomas G., 110

Back of the Yards: Mexican settlements, 121–22
Bacon, Warren H., 68, 86, 114
Bakalis, Michael: Chicago/suburban vote in 1978 election, 178–79; and central committee, 212; on slatemaking, 214
Banfield, Edward C., xiii, 6, 8, 22, 30, 31, 85, 86, 100, 146
Barnes, Eugene, 208
Barnett, Richard, 107
Bauler, Mathias, 219
Biesczatt, Matthew, 227
Bilandic, Michael, ix, x, 74; 1977 primary, 15–16, 42–46, 50–51; reason for choosing, 19; and ethnic politics, 53; blacks and, 58; Latino voters and, 136–37; as powerful statewide figure, 205, 211; and Thompson, 209; background, 225–26; city government under, 227–28; and 1979 campaign, 228–30
Blacks: and machine, xiv, 7, 13–18, 24, 65–68; and Democratic party, 4, 62–63, 72, 76, 100–105, 113–15, 184; mobilization of *vs.* ethnic cultural dominance,

21; growth in numbers, 27–28, 89; and 1975 primary, 42; and 1977 primary, 43, 45, 50–51, 206; and voter blocs, 46–50; and 1979 primary, 50–51; role in future, 55, 196; under Bilandic, 58; electoral support in 1970–80, 75–79; and independents, 78, 79, 104–5; and Chicago mayoralty, 88; need for leadership, 90; socioeconomic status, 91–94; voting behavior and poverty, 93–94; voting among middle-class and non-middle-class wards, 94–100, 107; coalition with Latinos, 114–15; contrasted with Latinos, 132–34, 142–43; availability of parks in black wards, 148–50; and distribution of fire protection resources, 150; and distribution of refuse collection services, 153–54. *See also* Minority population
Brady, Michael, 208
Bridgeport, x, 2, 12
Brooks, Steve, 157
Brown, Reginald, 112
Brzeczek, Richard J., 110
Bureaucracy: Daley and, 220–21, 232
Burgess, Ernest W., 128
Burke, Edward, xii, 111–12, 208, 226; Latino votes in 1980 primary, 141–42
Burnham, Daniel, 161
Burris, Roland W., 114
Byrd, Manford, 110
Byrne, Jane: options and early record, x–xii, 231; and state's attorney race, xii, 111, 208; victory and machine's gatekeeping function, 24; 1977 primary, 50–51; 1979 primary, 50–51, 229; and labor, 58–59, 84–85; election, 74; black voters and, 77, 105–9; on collective bargaining, 80, 208; and transit workers, 82; on fire fighters and collective bargaining, 83–84; black disenchantment with, 109–13; Latinos and, 140–41; election as portent of future,

196; and Thompson transportation package, 209–10; background, 215, 228, 229; commissioner of Consumer Sales, Weights and Measures, 228, 229; coalition behind, 230; disruption of Daley system, 232–34; and machine politicians, 231, 233, 235; loss of constituency, 235

Campbell, A., 91
Capital budget: need for, 160, 171–73
Capital improvement program, 162
Capital maintenance: constraints on, 162–64
Capital stock: inventory, 167
Carter, Jimmy, 111, 186; Chicago vote for, 75; Illinois campaign strategy, 190
Caruso, Angeline, 110
Castro, Ray, 112, 144
Catholics: and Chicago Democratic party, 184–85; ticket-splitters, 194
Cayton, Horace, 4
Cermak, Anton J., x, 31, 32, 52
Chew, Charles, 66
Chicago: population trends, 3, 93–94; general financial situation, 169, 170
Chicago Federation of Labor, 64, 68
Chicago machine: turnout and support, 16–17; future, 23–24; shift to Democratic party in 1930s, 31; and coalition of voter blocs, 46–50; 1955–65, 59–65; 1966–69, 65–71; transformation, 71–72; role in distribution of municipal services, 146–47; attempts to replicate in suburbs, 197; before 1955, 217; under Daley, 217–18. *See also* Democratic party
Chicago Plan Commission, 161
Chicago Teachers Union: bargaining issue, 69–71; effect of militancy, 80–81
Choate, Clyde, 206
Cincinnati: capital maintenance, 160
Clark, Terry, 4
Cleveland: financial crisis, 159–60
Collective bargaining, 207–8; Byrne and city employees, 80; and fire fighters, 82
Columbus Drive Bridge, 168
Committeemen: 1980 primary, 112–13
Community Development Block Grants, 166
Controllability: importance to machine, 2, 8–12; of Latino wards, 138–39
Cook County: political domination by Chicago, 180–83; future control of, 196; governance, 198–99; Democratic central committee, 212, 218, 226
Cose, E., 104, 105

Crosstown Expressway, 207, 209
CTA, 110, 207, 208, 209
Cubans, 127–28
Cultural dominance: *vs.* black mobilization, 20–22

Dahl, Robert A., 89; on ethnic politics, 54
Daley, Richard J.: rise to power, ix; margin in first election, 8, 15; location of support, 34; and C.T.U., 81; Latino voters and, 136–37; and changes in suburbs, 195; and "one-city party," 195; impact on state government, 203; Springfield experience, 205; on income tax, 206–7; and state executive, 208–10; and the judiciary, 210–11; as statewide party leader, 211–12; takes control of machine, 218–19; as mayor and party chairman, 219; election strategy, 219; issue of successor, 222–23
Daley, Richard M.: state's attorney race xii, 111, 208; as mayoral candidate, 115; Latino votes in 1980 primary, 141–42
Dallas: financial position, 160
D'Arco, John, 227
Davis, Danny, 107
Dawson, "Boss" William L., 15, 65, 223
Deliverability: importance to machine, 2, 8–12; of Latino wards, 138–39
Democratic Central Committee, 212–13
Democratic National Committee: on Illinois slatemaking, 213
Democratic party: 1955–65, 59–62; and black voters, 62–63, 113–15; 1966–69, 65; 1970–80, 71–85; and Latinos, 131–37; Chicago *vs.* suburbs and downstate, 177; in suburbs, 183–85, 190–92; and emerging power of suburbs, 195; strategic options, 197–98. *See also* Chicago machine; Machine
Demography: population growth of Chicago, 3, 93–94, 204; and purpose of tax-exempt borrowing, 165; and Chicago's capital budget problems, 170; of suburbs, 180–83; stabilization of Chicago area population, 195
Department of Planning, City and Community Development, 161
DeVise, Pierre, 185
Dixon, Alan: and suburban votes, 178, 188, 189; 1974 election, 188; 1976 election, 188, 189; 1978 election, 188, 189; and ticket-splitters, 193; as powerful statewide figure, 205; as party leader, 211; on slatemaking, 214
Donovan, Tom, 227

Downs, Anthony, 18, 20
Drake, St. Clair, 4
Dunne, George, x, 211, 214, 224; on election of commissioners, 199; as party chairman, 225-26
Dye, T. R., 4

Economy: and Chicago's capital budgeting problems, 170
Elections: low-turnout strategy, 112-13; suburbs and, 186, 189-90; Daley influence on, 214-15
—mayoral: voting blocs, 46-50; and distribution of parks, 149-50; and fire protection distribution, 151; need to split opposition, 229
1931: 31
1955: 8, 16, 17, 32, 34, 35, 74, 78, 106
1959: 16, 17, 36, 63, 68, 74, 78
1963: 16, 17, 37, 38, 40, 74, 78
1967: 16, 17, 36, 65, 68, 74, 78
1971: 16, 17, 36, 74, 78, 97
1975: 16, 17, 36, 74, 78, 97, 106, 229
1977: 16, 17, 74, 78, 97, 106, 229
—presidential: black vote for Democratic party, 62-63
1956-72: 75
1972: 97-98
1976: 97-98
—statewide: 1978, 178. See also Primaries
Eleventh Ward, 53, 55; importance to machine, 12. See also Bridgeport
Elrod, Richard, 199-200
Employment: black, 91-93
Ethnicity: vs. race, 54-55
Ethnics: demands, 18; deliverability and controllability, 19-20; changes in number of, 27-28; spatial distribution of, 29-30; in 1931 election, 31; three dimensions of ethnic politics, 52-54

Federal aid: to cities, 161; capital infrastructure and, 164-66
Finney, Leon, 105
Fire fighters: unionization, 80; and collective bargaining, 83-84; strike by, 110
Fire protection resources: distribution of, 150-52
Ford, Jerry, 190
France, Erwin A., 106
Friedman, Richard, 40-42
Frost, Wilson, x, 19, 101, 106, 114, 224

General Assembly: Daley and, 205-8
Gill, Joe, 219
Gonzales, Jose, 141
Gonzales, Mary, 140

Gosnell, Harold F., xiii, 30, 85, 86, 100, 146
Gottfried, Alex, 30
Governors: Daley and, 208-10
Greenstein, Fred I., 18
Greenstone, J. David, 60, 64, 86
Grossman, David, 159
Guterbock, Thomas M., xiii

Hampton, Fred, 106
Hannon, Joseph, 23
Hanrahan, Edward V., 40-42, 229
Hauser, Philip M., 196
Hays, Samuel, 25
Healy, Robert, 81
Hill, Kim Q., 146, 156
Holden, Matthew, 100
Horner, Henry, 216
Howlett, Michael: 1968 election, 188; 1976 election, 213; on slatemaking, 214
Huel, Patrick, 103
Humes, Marian, 103
Humphrey, Hubert, 68
Hunter, Albert J., 128
Hynes, Thomas, 206

Immigrants, 25; and the machine, 18-22. See also Ethnics
Immigration and Naturalization Service (INS), 123, 124, 127
Income tax: Chicago and, 206-7
Independents: black support for, 78, 79; black voters as, 113-14; in suburbs, 192-95
Irish, 3, 12, 28, 29, 53; and mayoralty, 4, 19, 32, 52-53. See also Ethnics
Italians: population figures, 28; politics of near West Side, 129

Jackson, Jesse, 110, 111, 224
Jarrett, Vernon, 104, 107
Jews: and Chicago Democratic party, 183-84
Johnson, Lyndon, 62
Jones, A. E., 120-21
Jones, Bryan D., 146
Judges: selection, 210
Judiciary: Daley and, 210-11

Kantowicz, Edward R., 34, 55
Katznelson, Ira, 132
Kaufman, H., 169
Keane, Thomas, 63, 220, 223, 225, 227
Kelley, Clifford, 101
Kelly, Edmund, 227
Kelly, Edward J., x, 32, 223
Kemp, Kathleen, 112, 139

Kennedy, Edward, 111
Kennedy, Eugene, xvii, 25, 31
Kennedy, John F., 62
Kennelly, Martin H., x, 8, 59, 63, 218,
    220; 1955 election results, 32
Kerner, Otto: votes, 188, 189–91; Daley
    and, 209
Kerr, Louise A., 121
Kogan, H., 30
Kornblum, William, 121, 128
Kusper, Stanley, 199–200

Labor: political role, xv; under Byrne,
    58–59; alliance with Democratic party,
    84
Ladd, E., Jr., 100
Latinos: and machine, xiv, 139; coalition
    with blacks, 114–15; population figures,
    118, 139; nationalities comprising,
    118–20; community areas, 119, 125–27,
    128–30; political representation, 130–37;
    vs. black political development, 132–34,
    142–43; political behavior, 135–37;
    community organizations, 137–39;
    deliverability and controllability,
    138–39; and Byrne election, 140–41;
    1980 presidential primary, 141; and
    Poles, 142; future prospects, 142–44;
    problem of minority label, 142–43. See
    also Mexicans; Puerto Ricans
Leadership: black, 100–105
Lee, Bill, 68, 82
Levy, Frank S., 146
Lineberry, Robert, 112, 139, 146, 155
Lipsky, Michael, 156
Lorenz, Francis, 210
Lorinskas, R., 3
Lowi, Theodore, xiii, 57, 86

McCormick Place, 209
McFolling, Tyrone L., 112
McGillwray, A. V. M., 115
Machine: model by Gosnell, xiii; defini-
    tions of, xiv, 59, 146; and ethnics, 1, 2;
    and non-zero sum politics, 2, 22–23;
    and deliverability and controllability, 2,
    8–12; balance between ethnics and
    blacks, 6–7; image vs. real control, 7–8;
    need for split in opposition, 24, 48, 50.
    See also Chicago machine; Democratic
    party
Madigan, Michael, 209
Martinez, Elena, 140–41
Marzullo, Vito, 204, 227, 232
Matthews, D. R., 91
Mayder, Thomas, 84
Merriam, Robert E., 32, 59, 63

Merton, Robert K., 6, 25, 30
Metcalfe, Ralph, Jr., 104, 112
Mexicans: population figures, 28; settle-
    ments in Chicago, 120–24; legal prob-
    lems, 122–24; and Democratic organiza-
    tion, 124
Meyerson, Martin, 30, 146
Middle-class voters: and machine, 59, 66;
    black, 94–97, 107
Migration: waves of, 3–4. See also Ethnics
Mikva, Abner, 66
Minority population: misuse of term, 142–
    43; and distribution of urban resources,
    146–57. See also Blacks; Latinos
Mobilization: thesis, 19, 25; of ethnics,
    19; vs. cultural dominance, 21
Morris, M., 90
Muriel, Hugo H., 130, 141
Murphy, Morgan, 112
Muscare, Frank, 80, 83

Nash, Pat, 32
Nathan, Richard, 4
Neistein, Bernie, 68, 86
Neuman, D., 129
New City. See Back of the Yards
Newhouse, Richard H., 15, 40–42, 104,
    114, 228
New York City: financial crisis, 159
Nie, Norman, 90
Nivola, Pietro, 155
Nolan, Sam, 109

O'Connor, Len, xvii, 25, 31
Ogilvie, Richard, 200, 213; and income
    tax, 207; Daley and, 209
O'Hare development, 168

Pace, I. M., 92
Padilla, E., 125
Palmer, Lu, 101, 103
Parenti, Michael, 25
Parks: distribution of, 148–50
Partee, Cecil A., 114, 206
Patronage: and collective bargaining issue,
    69–70; and blacks, 92–93; Daley's use
    of, 221
Patterson, E., 100
Peick, Louis, 80
Percy, Charles, 178, 191
Peterson, George, 160, 182
Peterson, P., 23
Peterson, Paul E., 60
Pilsen: first Mexican settlement, 120–21
Poles: and machine, xv, 19; arrival in
    Chicago, 3, 25; and 1977 primary, 12,
    43, 45, 50–51; voting behavior, 12,

31–32; after Daley's death, 19; as renegades, 19–20; population figures, 28, 29; and mayoral elections, 34, 36, 37, 39, 40; population distribution, 39; and voter blocs, 46–50; 1979 primary, 50–51; and Latinos, 142. *See also* Ethnics
Police: unionization, 80; appointment of superintendent, 109–10
Politics: and Chicago's capital budgeting problems, 171. *See also* Elections; Primaries
Population: of Chicago, 3, 93–94, 204. *See also* Demography
Poverty: among blacks, 91; and black voting behavior, 93–94
Power, Joseph, 210
Primaries: significance for classic political machine, 59; changes in from 1966 to 1969, 66, 67; loss of Democratic control over, 72, 73; suburban turnout, 187; legislation to constrain independents, 197
—mayoral:
1955: 16, 17, 20, 32, 33, 34
1957: 17
1959: 16
1963: 16, 17
1967: 16, 17
1971: 16, 17
1975: 9–10, 12, 16, 17, 40–42, 46, 49, 96–97, 137, 138
1977: 8, 11–12, 16, 17, 20, 43–46, 49, 51, 95–97, 137, 138
1979: 50–52, 74, 78, 106–9, 140, 228–30
—presidential:
1980: 109, 111. *See also* Elections
Prothro, J., 91
Przeworski, A., 25
Public Building Commission, 164, 165
Pucinski, Roman, 8, 228; 1977 primary, 15, 20, 43–46; and collective bargaining issue, 83; Latino voters and, 136–37
Puerto Ricans: population growth, 124–25

Quigley, Edward, 227

Race: and collective bargaining issue, 68–69
Rakove, Milton, 8, 12, 30, 31, 37, 52, 85, 100, 146
Ray, Eugene, 101
Redmond, William, 191, 206
Reformers: and classic political machine, 60
Refuse collection services: distribution of, 153–54, 156
Reid, Ellis, 104

Renegades: problem for machine, 9–10; Polish, 19–20
Republican party: support, 65; coalition with independents, 115; in suburbs, 175; successes in Democratic areas, 191; Cook County and, 199–201
Resource distribution: machine and, 146–47
Robinson, Renault, 104, 109
Rock, Philip, 216
Roosevelt, Franklin D., 183, 194–95
Ropa, Matt, 204
Rose, Don, 101, 103, 109, 111
Royko, Mike, xvii, 31, 100, 111
RTA, 207, 209

Sacks, Paul M., 25
Salces, Luis, 118, 125, 127, 128, 131, 134, 135–36, 137
Savage, Gus, 79, 112
Sayre, W. S., 169
Scammon, Richard M., 115, 179, 180, 181, 182, 193
Schools: desegregation and politics of coalition maintenance, 23; racial strife and city politics, 69; school board, 110; distribution, 152–53; and capital needs of Chicago, 171–73
Scott, William, 178–79, 191
Sewers: cost of replacing, 168
Shapiro, Samuel: Daley and, 209
Shaw, Robert, 107, 112
Shea, Gerald, 206
Sherman, Niles, 107, 112
Simon, Paul, 212
Simon, Seymour, 210
Sinclair, Upton, 121
Singer, William, 15, 60, 228; 1975 primary, 40–42; Latino voters and, 136–37
Skogan, Wesley, 25
Slatemaking, 213–14
Smith, Kenneth B., 110
Sorenson, A., 14
South Chicago: Mexican neighborhood, 121
Soviet Union: Communist party compared to Chicago machine, 218, 223
Speer, Allan H., 132
Sprague, J., 25
State's attorney: 1980 race, 111–12
Steiner, Gilbert Y., 204
Stevenson, Adlai, 186, 205
Stevenson, Adlai III, 192, 193; suburban votes for, 188, 189
Stewart, Bennett, 103, 112
Stratton, William G.: Daley and, 208–9
Suburbs: political importance of, 175; in-

dependence of voters, 178; political characteristics, 179; growth of, 180–83; Democratic party in, 190–92; independents in, 192–95; ticket-splitters, 194; attempts to move machine to, 197; changing population, 201
Sunbelt-Frostbelt dichotomy: Chicago and, 4
Supreme Court: state, 210
Suttles, Gerald D., 129

Taeuber, Karl, 13, 14
Talbot, Basil, Jr., 111, 213–14
Taylor, Paul S., 120, 123
Teachers: strike, 110
Teeter, R., 193, 194
Thompson, "Big Bill," ix, x, 31
Thompson, Daniel, 100
Thompson, James, 110, 191, 207; Chicago/suburban vote in 1978, 178–79; as powerful statewide figure, 205; and Bilandic, 209; 1976 election, 213
Ticket-splitters: suburban, 178–79, 193
Touhy, John P., 212, 214
Transit workers: under Byrne, 82–83; strike, 110
Troy, Richard, 178–79
Tucker, Robert, 104
Turnout: importance to machine, 16–17

UAW, 185
Unions: public employee, 63–65; collective

bargaining agreement of 1966, 68; growing dissatisfaction with Democrats, 80; and population shift to suburbs, 185; ticket-splitters, 194
Urban Development Action Grants, 166

Velasquez, Carmen, 141
Verba, Sidney, 90, 91
Voters: loss of in Chicago, 177–78
Vrdolyak, Edward, 223, 226

Wade, Richard, 25
Walker, Daniel, 207; 1972 election, 188; Daley and, 209; and slatemaking, 213
Walton, H. W., Jr., 92
Walton, John, 118, 125, 127, 128, 131, 137
Washington, Harold, 15, 79, 89, 104, 112, 114, 206, 229; 1977 primary, 43–46
Wattenberg, Ben, 179, 180, 181, 182, 193
Wendt, Lloyd, 30
White, Michael, 167
Whitehead, Ralph, 184
Williams, O. P., 20
Wilson, James Q., 6, 8, 15, 19, 22, 86, 91, 92, 100, 146, 155
Wilson, Paula, 101, 102, 103, 104
Wilson, Peter, 160
Wolfinger, Raymond, 25, 134

Zikmund, Joseph II, 139
Zorbaugh, Harvey W., 129